LOUISIANA STATE UNIVERSITY STUDIES
Max Goodrich, General Editor

Social Science Series
Walter C. Richardson, Editor

Number Fifteen
The Louisiana Economy

The
Louisiana
Economy

Edited by Thomas R. Beard

Louisiana State University Press
BATON ROUGE

PREFACE

Little in the way of a broad and comprehensive analysis of the Louisiana economy now exists. The present volume arose out of a desire to fill, at least partially, this lacuna. This writer's contribution to the book—as editor and author—was made possible by a grant from the LSU Foundation. While the coverage of the book is admittedly far from complete, the essays do provide a reasonably broad coverage of some of the more significant aspects of the state's economy. Nevertheless, this book must be viewed as only a beginning; it merely scratches the surface of what needs to be done in the way of describing and analyzing Louisiana's complex economy.

The eight essays contained in this study were completed over roughly a two-year period. In those cases where statistical data were utilized, the terminal dates generally range from 1963 to 1966. Thus, the overall picture of the state's economy that emerges reflects the economic conditions of the mid-1960's.

Each author was given a wide latitude in his particular subject area, and editorial changes have been held to a minimum. As a result, each contributor bears the major responsibility for the contents of his study. Little uniformity has been forced upon him. Virtually the only prior suggestion made as to content was that he attempt to blend description and analysis in such a way as to make his essay interesting not only to his fellow economists but to college students and educated laymen as well. In addition to its potential use in the classroom and as a reference source, it is hoped that this

book will find its way to the shelves of businessmen, government officials, legislators, and others interested in the economic welfare
of Louisiana citizens.

Thomas R. Beard

February, 1969

CONTENTS

The Louisiana Economy

INTRODUCTION

An Overview of the Louisiana Economy
Thomas R. Beard

In recent years a great deal has been written about the South as an economic region.[1] While "the South's" geographical boundaries are not entirely clear, it is customary to include Louisiana as an integral part of this region. What is characteristic of the South in general is often (but not always) true of Louisiana as well.

It is a widely known fact that the South has suffered from economic underdevelopment relative to the rest of the nation. For more than a century it has lagged behind other regions in its level of economic well-being, whether measured in per capita income, wealth, or similar terms. The reasons for this gap are many and varied.

J. J. Spengler has suggested that the relatively low level of southern incomes had its origin in the region's economic and cultural history, with several types of factors acting in combination to retard the expansion in income. Spengler groups these factors under five headings.[2] First, certain demographic characteristics result in a lower ratio of the labor force to total population in the South than in the nation generally; second, owing to the relatively slow rate of growth in

---

[1] See William H. Nicholls, *Southern Tradition and Regional Progress* (Chapel Hill, 1960); Edgar S. Dunn, Jr., *Recent Southern Economic Development* (Gainesville, 1962); M. L. Greenhut and T. Whitman (eds.), *Essays in Southern Economic Development* (Chapel Hill, 1964). An earlier and highly important study was C. B. Hoover and B. U. Ratchford, *Economic Resources and Policies for the South* (New York, 1951).

[2] J. J. Spengler, "Southern Economic Trends and Prospects," in John C. McKinney and Edgar T. Thompson (eds.), *The South in Continuity and Change* (Durham, 1965), 112–21.

capital per capita, both southern agriculturalists and nonagricul-
turalists are not so well equipped with land and other forms of physical capital. Third, the occupational structure of the labor force is
comparatively unfavorable in the South since it includes relatively
larger numbers of workers in employments where earnings are below
average, e.g., agriculture, household service, and blue-collar categories. Fourth, value added by manufacturing per employee as well
as hourly wage rates of production workers in manufacturing are
lower in the South than elsewhere. Not only are rates generally lower
for the same type of work, but the South has a relatively larger number of low-income industries.

The fifth factor—the quality of the population and the factors
governing quality—is said to be the most crucial. Spengler has noted
that "both average income in the South and capacity to increase it are
depressed more by lack of training in the population than by any
other condition, especially in the rural white population and in the
nonwhite population, rural and urban."[3] It appears that this view has
become widely held in recent years, and economists have increasingly
turned their attention to the regional deficiencies in the quantity and
quality of education.[4]

In considering the role of human inequalities in southern underdevelopment, Mary Jane Bowman concluded that "the data . . . have
demonstrated again and again the concentration of the South's problems in its undereducated of both races and in its racial inequalities."[5]
For southern Negroes, average income is less than that for southern
whites at all educational levels, and it is also less than that for Negroes in the North at all educational levels. But, perhaps surprisingly,
the income levels of whites who have achieved the higher levels of
education in the South are virtually on a par with those of northern
whites. For whites, the differences between the South and the rest of
the nation lie in the greater spread between high and low incomes and
in the greater rate at which incomes fall off with lower levels of educational achievement. Professor Bowman's conclusion is that the
South's problem is not so much a shortage of well-educated persons

    [3] *Ibid.*, 117.
    [4] See, for example, the symposium edited by James W. McKie entitled "Edu-
cation and the Southern Economy," *Southern Economic Journal, Supplement,*
XXXII (July, 1965), 1–128. On various aspects of human capital in the southern economy, see Marshall R. Colberg, *Human Capital in Southern Development,
1939–1963* (Chapel Hill, 1965).
    [5] Mary Jane Bowman, "Human Inequalities and Southern Underdevelop-
ment," in "Education and the Southern Economy," 101.

as a surplus of uneducated ones, and she suggests that the first educational task is to "pull the bottom up toward the middle."[6] Based on her data, the overall picture of the South that emerges is one of a land of contrasts where differences in education and income exceed those in other regions as between races, between urban and rural populations, and even between the highest and lowest brackets within the white urban group.

In analyzing the quality of higher education in the South, Allan Cartter has suggested that while many of its institutions are good, not a single one is truly outstanding on the national scene. Many are poor. In Cartter's view, the South has tended to favor quantity over quality in higher education; many states have scattered their educational dollars haphazardly rather than concentrating on those institutions where significant quality improvement is feasible. Furthermore, the South has traditionally overvalued the social aspects of higher education and undervalued the intellectual and economic benefits. The quality lag is difficult to overcome, for this depends on environmental changes which would render the southern community more appreciative of scholarly and scientific attainment and less distrustful of intellectual pursuits. Cartter warns that this lack of excellence is likely to have an adverse effect on economic development.[7]

The Cartter view of quality versus quantity is not universally accepted. Even a tendency "to convert the former teachers colleges into universities and to begin community colleges in every metropolis" is not wholly without merit. Such a policy greatly expands educational opportunities, even though it diminishes quality at the very top of the education pyramid by spreading available finances too thinly. And then there is the problem of higher education for the Negro in an integrated system. As Howard Schallar has noted, if southern institutions limit numbers by the use of uniform admission standards, this policy will have a differential effect on Negroes and whites since the former have had generally inferior opportunities at the pre-college level. In addition, there will be differential effects within both races because of rural versus urban differences in prior educational opportunities.[8]

[6] *Ibid.*, 102.

[7] Allan M. Cartter, "Qualitative Aspects of Southern University Education," in "Education and the Southern Economy," 39–69.

[8] Howard Schaller, "Comment," in "Education and the Southern Economy," 70–72.

Some students of the South, most notably William H. Nicholls, have stressed the region's tradition-oriented culture as a serious stumbling block to economic advancement. In *Southern Tradition and Regional Progress*, Nicholls argued that in spite of economic advances in recent decades, the South must choose between progress and tradition if it is to achieve the high rate of industrialization necessary to correct the region's excess of rural population. Certain elements in the southern tradition were seen as inhibiting industrial expansion and thus economic progress—the persistence of rural values, the rigidity of the social structure, the undemocratic political structure, the weakness of social responsibility, and the conformity of thought and behavior.

Not all writers have emphasized so strongly the negative aspects of tradition, but the stress on industrialization has been at the heart of academic discussions for decades. In his excellent survey of the literature Clarence Danhof uncovered four basic approaches to the region's problems. One view "looked backward to an organization reaffirming traditional values"; another "concentrated on incremental improvements in the position of farmers." A third view, not incompatible with the first two, held that "disaffected Southerners should migrate out of the region." The fourth view, however, was the most important. It "looked towards industrial development within the region as the solution to its problems."[9]

But is it really meaningful to talk about the South as if it were a single, relatively underdeveloped area? Such an obvious oversimplification can be misleading. There are three Census regions of the South—the South Atlantic region, which includes Delaware, Maryland, West Virginia, Virginia, North Carolina, South Carolina, Georgia, and Florida (and the District of Columbia); the East South Central region, which includes Kentucky, Tennessee, Alabama, and Mississippi; and the West South Central region, which includes Texas, Oklahoma, Arkansas, and Louisiana. Considerable differences exist both among and within these regions—differences which are in many cases at least as great as those between the averages for the South and the rest of the nation. Most writers think of the South as composed of a smaller number of states than the sixteen listed above. Delaware and Maryland (and the District of Columbia) are

[9] Clarence H. Danhof, "Four Decades of Thought on the South's Economic Problems," in Greenhut and Whitman, *Essays in Southern Economic Development*, 12.

customarily omitted; West Virginia and Oklahoma are often excluded.

Although Louisiana is part of the South, it is also different from the "average South" in many important respects. In fact, it is often useful to compare Louisiana with the nation generally rather than with the region. In the essays that follow, the authors have more often than not adopted this procedure. The persistent inclination of many southerners to compare Louisiana only with other southern states—and them with Louisiana—is a self-defeating exercise so far as economic development is concerned. Public policies must be geared to different comparisons if the state and the South generally are to realize their full potential. It seems much more important, for example, to focus on the fact that per capita education expenditures in Louisiana tend to lag behind the national average rather than on the fact that those expenditures are among the highest in the South.

Most observers feel that the trend in per capita personal income is the best single indicator of economic performance. Following the Civil War per capita incomes in the southern states were depressed to low percentages of the national average. In 1880 per capita income in the West South Central states was only 60 percent of the U.S. average, and this figure was only 61 percent in 1900. Under the impact of World War I the percentage increased, becoming 72 percent in 1920, only to decline to 62 percent in 1930. Recovery began in the late 1930's and by 1950 the figure had risen to 81 percent.[10]

It may be noted that per capita income rose appreciably more rapidly in each of twelve southern states than in the nation generally between 1929 and 1966.[11] Income in Louisiana rose from 59 percent of the national average in 1929 to 77 percent in 1966. While this gain is encouraging, it only reduced the relative inferiority of Louisiana income. The relative gain did not close the absolute dollar gap, which in current dollars grew larger and in real terms changed little. Furthermore, per capita incomes rose even faster in almost all of the other southern states.

Although low by national standards, Louisiana ranked well at the

[10] Spengler, "Southern Economic Trends and Prospects," 109.

[11] For purposes of this comparison, the twelve southern states are Alabama, Arkansas, Florida, Georgia, Kentucky, Louisiana, Mississippi, North Carolina, South Carolina, Tennessee, Texas, and Virginia. Subsequent data for 1940 and earlier are taken from U.S. Department of Commerce, *Personal Income by States Since 1929* (Washington, D.C., 1956), 142–43; later data are from *Survey of Current Business*, XLVIII (April, 1968), 14.

top of the "middle five" southern states (including Georgia, North Carolina, Kentucky, and Tennessee) in 1929. As compared to Louisiana's income ratio of 59 percent, the other four states fell in the range of 48 to 54 percent of the national average. Louisiana's figure greatly exceeded that of the "bottom four" states of Alabama, Arkansas, South Carolina, and Mississippi, and approached the 62 percent figure of Virginia, the lowest of the "top three" states of Texas, Florida, and Virginia.

Despite an absolute decrease in per capita income during the Great Depression, Louisiana's relative inferiority to the national average had diminished slightly by 1940. While the state's income had risen to 61 percent of the national average, increases in the relative position of many other southern states were larger, especially in Virginia. Louisiana's figure had risen dramatically to 75 percent by 1950, and in general this period was one of strong advance for the state and region. Despite a roughly similar position nationally, Louisiana's relative superiority over the other southern states in the "middle five" had about disappeared by 1960. In 1962—the relative low point for the state's economy—per capita income in Louisiana was $1,748, or 74 percent of the national average. By comparison, Georgia's figure was $1,775, or 75 percent, and there was little difference among the standings of Louisiana, Kentucky, and North Carolina.

There are encouraging signs for Louisiana in more recent years, however, even if the state's position vis-à-vis the "middle five" has not improved. From 1963 to 1966 the state's per capita personal income rose as a percentage of the national average and stood at $2,277, or 77 percent, by the latter date. Many of the more optimistic of the state's citizens are now hailing the dawn of a new era of industrial expansion and prosperity. To be sure, there appears to be a new awareness of the importance of education; an increasing emphasis on and willingness to accommodate industrial expansion; and in general, a greater inclination to look to the state's future rather than to dwell on its past. But Louisiana still has a long way to go to match even the income levels of Virginia, Texas, and Florida, to say nothing of the U.S. average.

Much can be learned about a state from a study of its employment structure by type of industry. One indication of the urbanization and industrialization that has characterized the state in recent decades is the absolute and relative decline in agricultural employment. According to U.S. Census data for 1940 and 1960, employment in agriculture as a percentage of total employment declined from 32.3 percent to 7.3 percent over this period. For the nation as a whole, the figures were 18.7 percent and 6.6 percent, respectively, thus indicating that the decline in Louisiana was even more pronounced than the national trend. Partly as a consequence of the more rapid decline in agricultural employment, the percentage increases in several other categories exceeded the national advances, e.g., in construction; transportation, communications, and public utilities; wholesale and retail trade; and other service industries. In manufacturing, Louisiana's percentage rose from 12.8 to 15.6 percent over this period, but the U.S. figures increased from 23.7 to 27.1 percent. The percentage of total employment in private households and forestry and fishing declined in both the state and nation.[12]

One of the most interesting changes occurred in mining. While, for the nation as a whole, mining employment declined from 2 percent of total employment in 1940 to 1 percent in 1960, it rose in Louisiana from 1.9 percent to 3.6 percent. It should be noted that mining employment in Louisiana consists almost entirely of oil and gas production; in the rest of the nation it also includes the extraction of various other minerals—mainly coal and metallic ores. Most of the employment in the production of oil and gas is in connection with the drilling and equipping of wells, while the major part of employment in other mineral industries is associated with extraction proper. Based on figures for value added by manufacturing as a percentage of U.S. figures, the principal growth industry in Louisiana in recent decades has been petroleum, with chemicals a distant second.

The following comparisons of nonagricultural employment can be drawn for 1966.[13] Some 5.3 percent of Louisiana's nonagricultural employment was in mining and 9.2 percent in contract construction. Both percentages were well above the comparable national figures of 1 percent and 5.1 percent, respectively. Considering a twelve-state South, Louisiana outranked all other southern states in both of these categories—although West Virginia (9.6 percent) and Oklahoma (6.2 percent) had larger portions of their nonagricultural employment in the mining sector. Louisiana, with 9.3 percent, topped all other

[12] See also the study by Kyou E. Choi for the 1947–64 period. Kyou E. Choi, *Employment Trends in Louisiana, 1947–64*, Research Study No. 3, Division of Business and Economic Research, Louisiana State University in New Orleans (New Orleans, 1966).

[13] Data are from Bureau of Labor Statistics, *Employment and Earnings Statistics for States and Areas, 1939–1966*.

southern states and was above the U.S. average of 6.5 percent in transportation and public utilities. Louisiana's percentages in trade (22.2 percent) and government (18.7 percent) exceeded the national figures of 20.7 and 17 percent. On the other hand, the state's percentages of nonagricultural employment in finance, insurance, and real estate (4.5 percent) and in services (13.3 percent) were below the U.S. figures of 4.8 and 15 percent. It was in manufacturing, however, that Louisiana deviated the most from the national figure. Only 17.3 percent of the state's nonagricultural employment was engaged in manufacturing—a ratio well below the U.S. figure of 29.9 percent and below that of all other southern states except Florida.

A good indicator of a state's manufacturing status is its value added by manufacturing. In terms of value added, the leading categories of manufacturing include chemicals and allied products, food and kindred products, petroleum products, paper and paper products, and primary metals. In addition, lumber and wood products rank high in manufacturing employment. In general the manufacturing categories ranking highest are those directly related to the state's supply of resources and materials—petroleum, timber, and agricultural products. The production of chemicals is closely related to the state's abundant supply of petroleum, and Louisiana ranks second in the nation in petroleum production.

The eight essays that follow are divided into three major categories: Economic Development; Banking, Trade, and Regulation; and The Public Sector. In the first essay of Part I, Lee J. Melton, Jr., surveys the major factors affecting economic development in Louisiana. As he notes, Louisiana must be classified as one of the least developed parts of the most developed nation in the world. At the same time, one must also recognize the striking contrasts which exist within its borders. In certain geographic areas Louisiana has achieved growth rates among the highest in the nation, while in other areas the level and rate of growth is among the lowest.[14]

What are the prospects for narrowing the gap between the average level of well-being in Louisiana and the national average? As Melton

[14] Based on estimated per capita incomes in 1965, twenty-four of Louisiana's sixty-four parishes had incomes less than 75 percent of the state average. Six parishes had incomes of under 60 percent of the state figure. The top four parishes—Orleans, East Baton Rouge, Jefferson, and Caddo—had estimated per capita incomes of more than twice that in the four poorest parishes. *Statistical Abstract of Louisiana* (2nd ed.; New Orleans, 1967), 137–39.

points out, it is certainly *not* inevitable that Louisiana will undergo economic growth at a rate sufficient to overcome the existing differential in per capita income. It is even *possible* that the state could become relatively worse off. (As noted in the McDonald essay, this is precisely what happened in the 1957–62 period.) On the other hand, Louisiana has numerous positive factors in its favor and many observers feel that its chances of at least reducing the income gap are good.

It is convenient to divide the determinants of economic development into two broad categories—the natural and the human or man-controlled. Little can be done to alter the first; fortunately, most observers feel that the state has the natural endowments—land area, soil, climate, mineral and other resources—to support a well-balanced agricultural and industrial economy. In fact, the natural base is thought to be adequate to sustain more rapid growth than has occurred in the past. The man-controlled determinants of growth include such factors as the quantity and quality of the population, technology, the rate of capital accumulation, and the institutional structure. These factors are subject to change. In the past, several of the human factors have served as the chief barriers to faster economic development.

One of these deterrents has been the unfavorable impression created by the state's political climate—in particular, the lack of consistency and stability in governmental policies. The role of government in economic development is obviously crucial; but its role is complex and many-sided, and thus controversial. On the one hand, economic development depends critically on adequate education, highways, and other social goods that only government can provide (at least in sufficient quantities). On the other hand, public expenditures require tax dollars, and the added costs of government, if excessive, can in turn deter industrial expansion within the state.

One negative factor which Melton emphasizes is what he calls a "go-it-alone" delusion on the part of many of the state's citizens. This attitude involves a resentment of "outside" capital, both human and nonhuman, and, in fact, a resentment of outside influences of any type. If Louisiana is to reach its full potential, an excessive regionalism can only be a serious stumbling block.

Certainly, one of the most crucial aspects of economic development in the state is the qualitative characteristics of its population. This involves not only attitudes but also skill levels and general educational attainment. As Melton concludes in his essay, "The principal factor holding back the rate of economic growth in the state of Louisiana is the skill level of its people." This theme appears in other contributions to the book—especially in Roger L. Burford's essay, "Louisiana's Population: Its Growth and Distribution."

Using, primarily, Census data for 1950 and 1960, Burford discusses the demographic characteristics, growth, and geographic distribution of the state's population. Louisiana has an unusually young population, and in 1960 the proportion that was nonwhite was surpassed by only two states—Mississippi and South Carolina. These factors are closely related since birth rates, and consequently the proportion of young people, are substantially higher for nonwhites than for whites. The race factor is also related in part to the state's relatively low educational level, for, on the average, nonwhites have completed fewer years of schooling. Considering both its white and nonwhite population, median school years completed by all adults twenty-five years of age and over in Louisiana was 1.8 years *below* the national average in 1960. Age, race, and education are all interrelated factors; in turn, as Burford stresses, these factors help account for Louisiana's relatively low level of per capita income.

Within the state the distribution and redistribution of population is importantly related to the economic development of particular areas. During the 1950–60 decade the more populous parishes generally gained population by migration while the less populous parishes tended to be the losers. Burford notes that this redistribution resulted largely from the fact that parishes with small populations tend to be more heavily dependent upon agriculture. The most important single explanatory factor with respect to migration is thought to be relative economic opportunities. That is, migratory flows are generally from areas of relatively poor economic opportunities to areas which offer greater opportunities. Thus, the rural to urban movement appears to indicate the poorer opportunities on the farms as compared with nonfarm employment—a conclusion also evidenced by the lower per capita incomes in predominantly rural parishes. Since areas with expanding populations—with their growing markets and labor supplies—are more likely to attract industry than are areas of declining population, the plight of rural areas is heightened.

Although Louisiana is less dependent on farming than are many southern states, a larger proportion of its population is engaged in this endeavor than is the case nationally. Is the outlook for agriculture as bleak as is sometimes imagined? Such is not the case implies Fred H. Wiegmann in his essay, "Agriculture in the Louisiana Economy"; in fact, the picture he paints of the agricultural industry in Louisiana is optimistic in many important respects, both as regards its present status and its future prospects.

As Wiegmann points out, the agricultural industry (considered as a whole) is in many respects still the largest of the state's basic industries. At least this is the case if we think of the agricultural sector in the broadest sense as including not only the farm itself, but the whole complex of closely related and agriculturally-oriented businesses. This nonfarm sector of the agricultural economy includes both those businesses supplying production requirements to the farm and those firms processing and marketing farm products. While the total number of people on farms continues to decrease, those engaged in agriculturally-oriented businesses continues to expand.

In his essay, Wiegmann provides a considerable amount of descriptive and statistical material on such topics as the kind, location, and value of farm production in the state, and the size and location of farms. Several significant trends are strongly emphasized. One is the general increase in yields per acre in recent decades due to rapid improvements in technology and productive practices. Another is the startling decline in tenant and "subsistence" farms, a factor which largely accounts for the decline in total number of farmers. At the same time, there has been a relative stability of numbers and an impressive growth in both size and average dollar value of owner operated family farms.

Although mechanization and technology have created many complex economic and social problems connected with the inevitable disruption of share cropping and tenancy, these factors have also led to predominantly family owned farms which are increasingly efficient, larger, better equipped, better financed, and better managed. Professor Wiegmann suggests that "this kind of change adds strength to any industry."

In the final essay of Part I, Stephen L. McDonald analyzes economic growth and fluctuations in the state's economy in the period 1947–63. Since Louisiana, like any state, is an integral part of the national economy, one expects to find some basic similarity between its growth and fluctuations and those of the national economy. Yet every state specializes to some extent in such goods and services in which it has a comparative advantage. This specialization makes it possible for growth rates to differ and fluctuations to be more or less severe among various states. According to McDonald's view, given the conditions of supply, relative growth and fluctuations depend upon the nationwide demand for those goods in which a state specializes. The fast-growing or cyclically unstable areas, for example, are those which are relatively specialized in fast-growing or cyclically unstable industries. Over time, of course, the pattern of local specialization within the national economy will change as incomes change, resources become exhausted, population shifts, and technological progress takes place.

Based on an empirical study of per capita personal income, total nonagricultural employment, and the narrower aggregates of employment in manufacturing, mining, and contract construction, McDonald finds that Louisiana experienced a long investment boom from 1947 to 1957, followed by a pronounced lull from 1957 to 1962. The state's per capita personal income rose as a percentage of the national average in the earlier period and then declined in the later period. Nearly all of the decline, however, occurred between 1957 and 1960. Since the cutoff date for McDonald's study, this percentage has gradually improved, hopefully signaling the beginning of another long expansionary phase.

In the 1947–57 period during which Louisiana grew more rapidly than the nation as a whole, the state's business recessions were milder than the nation's; in the 1957–62 period the reverse was true. Over the entire 1947–62 time span covered by McDonald's study, Louisiana lagged behind the rest of the country at cyclical turning points— a factor which indicates that the state's economy typically responded to cyclical disturbances originating elsewhere. McDonald further suggests that the state's growth pattern and its lags at cyclical turning points were closely associated with similar developments in the oil and gas industry and in contract construction.

Part II contains essays on three highly important aspects of Louisiana's economy that have received surprisingly little academic attention in recent years—banking, international trade, and public utility regulation. Although each area is crucially related to the state's economic development, the authors have not chosen to investigate their topics solely from this point of view.

Few would deny the crucial role of financial institutions in the modern economy. In the essay "Growth, Structure, and Adequacy of Commercial Banking in Louisiana," Thomas R. Beard and Edward

B. Selby, Jr., investigate that particular type of financial institution which historically has been singled out for the most attention.[15] The authors discuss the structure of commercial banking in Louisiana according to the type of bank charter held, the prevalence of unit or branch banking, membership in the Federal Reserve System and the Federal Deposit Insurance Corporation, and the prevalence of par versus nonpar banking. It is found that Louisiana has a below average ratio of both national- to state-chartered banks and Federal Reserve member to nonmember banks. The relatively low percentages of national and member banks are undoubtedly related to the widespread practice of nonpar banking. In 1964 nearly two out of every three nonmember banks continued to levy an exchange charge on many checks presented for collection by out-of-town banks. The authors consider such a practice to be inequitable and inefficient.

Branch banking is permitted in Louisiana, but generally confined to the parish in which the main office is domiciled. For a state which permits limited branching, Louisiana's experience as to numbers of commercial banks has been quite different from the national trend in recent decades. Consistent increases have been recorded in bank numbers in the state, particularly since the end of the Second World War. At the same time, considerable branch expansion has also occurred; as a result, the population per banking unit has been declining. While still above the U.S. average in people per banking unit, the expansion of Louisiana's bank facilities in the last two decades has proceeded at a rate well in excess of the national average.

Finally, Beard and Selby offer some tentative suggestions on the "adequacy" of bank facilities. In any particular town or parish, the adequacy of existing facilities depends partly on a number of quantitative factors—people per bank and per banking unit, the ratios of bank deposits and bank loans to income, etc.—and partly on certain intangible and nonquantifiable factors. In the final analysis, the problem of determining adequacy is a difficult one, especially in view of the desirability of maintaining vigorous competition in banking markets.

As Robert A. Flammang points out in his essay "Louisiana and

[15] For a study of the growth of savings and loan associations, credit unions, and time and savings deposits in commercial banks, see James R. Bobo, *Savings Media in Louisiana, 1945–1965*, Research Study No. 4, Division of Business and Economic Research, Louisiana State University in New Orleans (New Orleans, 1967).

the World Economy," few states can match Louisiana's involvement in international trade. What is surprising to many people, New Orleans is the country's second-ranked port, and Baton Rouge is in the top ten in terms of waterborne tonnage. In addition, Lake Charles is an important outlet. Clearly, the state's sizeable volume of international trade exerts a significant impact on its personal income, employment, and price level.

In 1963 Louisiana ports handled over 8 percent, by value, of the nation's foreign waterborne commerce, with New Orleans accounting for about four-fifths of the state total. Although this percentage is impressive, the state's share of exports (over 11 percent) is even higher. Thus, Louisiana is somewhat of an "export" state, with the value of all exports about two and one-half times the value of imports. While Louisiana's foreign trade has generally declined somewhat in *relative* importance since the late 1940's, the basic factor has been a lag in import, rather than export, activity. One result has been a growing surplus of exports over imports. Even though such a surplus has certain advantages in view of the nation's balance of payments difficulties, there are also some compelling reasons, as Flammang strongly emphasizes, for adopting measures to expand import activity.

In the final essay of Part II, James P. Payne, Jr., describes and analyzes the "Regulation of Public Utilities in Louisiana." Even in a predominantly private enterprise economy, every type of business is necessarily subject to at least a minimum of government regulation. But because the technical and economic facts of production in certain enterprises require a high degree of concentration and because uncontrolled monopoly is contrary to society's best interests, regulation has traditionally been more comprehensive in the case of those enterprises classified as public utilities. Extensive government regulation is generally imposed in such areas as common carriers by rail, motor, water, and pipeline; communications by telephone, telegraph, and cable; and electric, water, gas, and urban transportation utilities. Coupled with a quasi-monopoly grant by the government is the right to exercise control over entry, rates, and the quantity and quality of service provided by the utilities.

Payne traces in some detail the evolutionary development of the modern concept of regulation and the regulatory commission. Particular attention is then given to the jurisdiction and operations of the Louisiana Public Service Commission. The process of regulation is very complex and intricate, and as the author suggests, it is only through the study of formal commission proceedings that a clear understanding and appreciation of regulation can be obtained. With this in mind, he summarizes the major elements presented in two significant Louisiana cases involving the regulation of telephone rates. Finally, regulatory practice and the regulatory framework in Louisiana are compared briefly with that in the nation generally.

Part III focuses on the public sector of the state's economy. This part contains by far the lengthiest essay in the book, "Government Revenues and Expenditures in Louisiana," by Thomas R. Beard. Comparisons of the state with the nation generally indicate that Louisiana receives an above-average percentage of its revenues from federal grants and in turn displays a high degree of fiscal centralization within the state. Local units raise a below-average proportion of combined state and local revenues, a fact attributable largely to the relative unproductiveness of property taxation.

As in the nation as a whole, the three major functions of state and local government in Louisiana are education, highways, and public welfare. However, the relative emphasis attached to the education and welfare functions in Louisiana is striking. On a per capita basis, support of education is below average, while support of public welfare exceeds that in all but one other state. Considering all types of expenditures, Louisiana provides for its residents an overall level of public services which is about average by U.S. standards. But even this average expenditure level appears to require a considerable revenue effort because of the state's below-average per capita personal income.

Perhaps a partial explanation for Louisiana's surprisingly high overall level of government expenditures lies in the manner in which these expenditures are financed. In addition to receiving above-average amounts of federal grants—a fact which is attributable largely to the public welfare function—the state enjoys significant revenue sources that represent little burden to the typical taxpayer-voter. In particular, the state collects sizeable revenues from royalties and bonuses on public lands, and the severance tax is the major single tax source at the state level. On the other hand, taxes on income and property—which are more likely to encounter voter opposition—are low by comparison with most other states. At the same time license charges and general and selective sales taxes are moderate.

Two important areas of concern in any state are the need for fiscal reform and the ability of state and local government to meet the rising demands for public services. As to the first concern, Louisiana's excessive dedication of revenues is frequently criticized. Most major state taxes are earmarked wholly or partially to specific purposes, thus severely limiting general fund revenues and introducing inflexibility into budget decisions. As to the second area of concern, it is not clear whether Louisiana will be able to meet the rising costs of public services in the next few years without enacting a tax increase. Uncertainties attached to forecasting bonus and royalty income, severance tax collections, and the terms of the eventual tidelands settlement make projections for Louisiana unusually risky. However, since Louisiana has a tax structure that is relatively income inelastic—coupled with the need for considerable expansion in education expenditures if the state is to reach or exceed the national average—it seems likely that Louisiana will be forced to raise its rates on selected taxes in the next few years. Among the prime candidates for a rate increase at the state level are the personal income tax, motor vehicle license fees, and tuition charges in institutions of higher learning; at the local level, much can be done to improve the yield of the property tax.

PART I
ECONOMIC DEVELOPMENT

SOME FACTORS
AFFECTING THE ECONOMIC
DEVELOPMENT OF LOUISIANA
Lee J. Melton, Jr.

The interest in economic development since World War II has been phenomenal. It can only be compared to that displayed in the period of "mercantilism" when the national states of Western Europe were emerging, and for sheer magnitude and intensity it surpasses anything the world has ever seen. Why is this so? In part, it is a matter of contact. Poverty is both absolute and relative. It is possible to be poor in the relative sense and still be content—for what one has never seen, one does not miss. However, in this day of rapid transportation and even more rapid communication, the populace of underdeveloped areas have observed what can be done and are no longer content with their lot.

For that matter, even the advanced areas wish to experience further growth, for human wants are insatiable and higher levels of living create the desire for even higher levels. Every society is beset with demands for goods and services that cannot be fully met, with the result that all demands have to be curtailed in part, or some completely, or both. Economic growth leads to greater area income—a bigger pie, so to speak—and to a degree lessens the problems associated with the recipients of the smaller shares.

This fervor for economic growth is not an unmixed blessing. History indicates that a high order of economic development is the exception, not the rule, and further that it is painful, expensive, and usually slow. To the extent that efforts are expended for increased development and fail, the dissatisfaction and disappointment of the people involved may constitute a barrier to further efforts. This danger notwithstanding, it can for purposes of policy be ignored, for there is no choice but to try.

Developed or advanced areas fall into three classifications: those that are continuing to advance; those barely maintaining their position; and those losing ground. The underdeveloped areas may be grouped under four categories: those not developing and with little or no potential for development; those not developing but apparently possessing great potential for development; those that are developing but with a limited potential; and those developing and possessing great potential for continued growth.

Although we tend to classify a nation, region, or state as a whole, even the best contain all the categories of advancement and underdevelopment. So do the worst. Only the proportions differ.

As a state, Louisiana must be classified as one of the least developed parts of the most developed nation in the world. Yet, in certain of its geographic areas Louisiana has achieved levels of growth that are among the highest, just as in others the level is among the most miserable. There is a tendency on the part of those writing or speaking for public consumption to become extremely optimistic over the possibility of Louisiana quickly closing the gap that now exists between it and national levels of economic achievement. For this reason the folklore persists that the state is something of a Sleeping Beauty, requiring only the kiss of a searching prince to initiate the upward spiral. The princes of the industrial world—these days called locational experts—have been carrying on constant investigation of the economic potential of various areas in the state. Louisiana has not been overlooked; she has been looked over and found wanting.

THEORIES OF ECONOMIC DEVELOPMENT

The interest of the economist in the growth and development of the economy of a nation, state, or region is as old as the discipline itself. Formerly called political economy—still the more descriptive term—the study of economics recognized that the welfare of the group and its continued advancement to a higher order of economic achievement was a public goal. So, from the beginning, there have been attempts to explain the process of economic growth and to formulate a theory of such growth that would possess universality in its applicability. All such attempts have, so far, been unsuccessful, and it is suspected that efforts to develop a general theory of economic development will continue to disappoint the social scientist. Nevertheless, from the centuries of thought and investigation that have gone into these matters, partial theories of economic development have been formulated, and from such theories may be extrapolated certain key elements that have significant bearing on the rate of economic growth, even though the degree of importance may vary from one situation to another.

A natural process?

The fathers of the school of classical economics were deeply interested in the matter of economic growth, but—as a group—they considered it something of a natural process. There were dissenters, of course, and Malthus, for one, pointed out that there was nothing at all natural about it.[1] Certainly, history has not indicated that economic development is simply a process of natural evolution. Further, the gap between the developed countries and the underdeveloped ones is not narrowing, it is widening. It is not inevitable, then, that Louisiana will undergo economic growth at a rate sufficient to overcome the differential in per capita income in this state compared to the national average, much less surpass it. It is conceivable that the differential might even worsen. Unless the climate for economic development is improved and the seeds of its existence sown in greater quantity, Louisiana might well remain at the lower end of the spectrum of per capita income in the United States.

Geographic determinism

Geographic determinism is the limitation placed on economic development by the natural environment. Indeed, it goes beyond this and makes the economy a somewhat hopeless victim of natural physical forces. No competent economist has ever denied that physical environment is a strong conditioning force—exceedingly so—but enough examples abound of nations with few resources and relatively high levels of developmental achievement to justify the hypothesis that the geographic conditioners of an area may impede development but cannot, of themselves, prevent it if other factors are favorable.

[1] T. R. Malthus, *Principles of Political Economy* (Reprints of Economic Classics; New York, 1964), 311–14.

Natural resources and geographic factors have posed no great barriers to economic growth in Louisiana. On the contrary, much— if not most—of the growth to date has been directly related to the exploitation of mineral resources, with the result that the economic complex is perhaps oriented disproportionately toward the processing of raw materials and producers' goods.

Capital formation

The test of essentiality is a rather poor one, and to state that one factor of economic development is more important than another is fraught with peril. Nevertheless, the one factor that is mentioned more than any other—and this has been true throughout the history of economic thought—is that of capital formation. Certainly it is a critical factor. For the underdeveloped country the lack of capital may present an almost insurmountable obstacle. For Louisiana, this is not so. As a part of a well-developed nation possessing the greatest store of capital goods in the world, there are no political barriers to the flow of capital into Louisiana. Only the opportunity for use more profitable than other alternatives outside the state is required. For those with a fetish about locally raised capital, the low per capita income in the state probably precludes significant increases in the rate of local accumulation.

Entrepreneurship

Many have considered the role of the entrepreneur as the critical element in economic growth.[2] This assumes, of course, some sort of free enterprise system which permits this type of individual to function, for the profit motive and the possibility of sufficient returns are the voices calling these unique individuals to the market place. To a considerable degree, entrepreneurship is a function of the social climate; it does not thrive where the attitudes of the populace and the governmental units are hostile. In the past Louisiana has been frequently accused of anti-business bias. Much of this clamor has been simply the effective use of an offensive weapon by the variety of business interests operating in the state. But it is true that much

[2] J. A. Schumpeter, *The Theory of Economic Development* (Cambridge, Mass., 1934), 61–90.

anti-business bias has been prevalent, a not unusual occurrence in an agrarian state with a traditionally rural population.

As in the case of any area whose economic development has failed to keep pace, Louisiana has the advantage of imitating the innovational procedures of its more successful sister states to close the lag in the time gap, and it is possible to import innovators after the gap has been closed. Still the encouragement and development of greater amounts of indigenous entrepreneurship is to be encouraged. A note of caution at this point. A government policy or attitude that is not in keeping with what business would prefer is nearly always considered "anti-business" by the representatives of business interests. The proper role of government is to be neither pro-business nor anti-business, nor pro or con any other segment of the economy for that matter. Its proper role is concern for the interests of the group as a whole, without bias for any segment. However, insofar as the encouragement of any group can be undertaken which promotes the welfare of the larger state family, it should be done.

The causes which enable or compel an individual to act as an entrepreneur are not fully understood, but among them appears to be an intense need for achievement, and there is ample evidence that this motivational factor has been much less plentiful in underdeveloped areas than in the advanced. The inference is that for economic development to proceed at a more rapid pace, the number of individuals with the entrepreneurial complex will have to be greatly increased. What appears to be the origin of such individuals? Probably neither the most depressed economic group nor the highest echelon of the well-to-do will furnish it. It appears to come mostly from the lower-middle-class members wishing to advance. As Louisiana broadens this group, the base for potential entrepreneurs increases proportionately. Certainly, the sociological barriers to growth have constituted a major force in the past, and the impact of these barriers will last well into the future.

Dualism

Frequently in underdeveloped areas there appear to be two distinct sectors of the economy. This is usually the aftermath of the backward area coming into contact with more advanced regions. In the resulting clash of systems the techniques of the advanced group will be grafted on a segment of the less developed economy, but other sectors will remain unaffected, insulated by economic, sociological, psychological, and cultural factors that appear either impervious or highly resistant to change. The consequence is that no one policy of a uniform nature can be adopted to promote growth in such a situation.[3]

Any casual examination of the Louisiana economy reveals a pattern of striking contrasts. Pockets of industrial complexes representative of economic advancement of the highest order are not far removed from areas of abject poverty and the absence of economic growth, or its probability under present conditions. It is not particularly startling that this should be so. The nature of much of the industrialization that has taken place makes it almost axiomatic. While not without some carry-over impact, the influence of the raw materials processing industries appears to have had negligible impact on the indigenous activities. This is the typical response of underdeveloped areas to the extraction and processing of raw materials, even when done by the most advanced techniques. The spill-over effect is sometimes disappointing. The phenomenon is often observed in agriculture, with the most advanced techniques existing side by side with what constitutes subsistence agriculture.

The cleavage between the advanced and less developed sectors of the Louisiana economy has diminished to a considerable degree. Nevertheless, degrees of difference in the levels of, and the rates of, economic development do exist between various parts of the Louisiana economic complex. One does not have to accept the theory of sociological dualism to appreciate the role of cultural, sociological, and psychological factors in economic development. Indeed, the provincial attitude of the Louisiana populace may prove a more formidable barrier to economic advancement than purely economic obstacles.

The big push

Professor Harvey Leibenstein has placed major emphasis on what he termed "the critical minimum effort."[4] Put succinctly, this thesis holds that an underdeveloped area is characterized by a certain de-

[3] J. H. Boeke, *Economics and Economic Policy of Dual Societies* (New York, 1953), 289.

[4] Harvey Leibenstein, *Economic Backwardness and Economic Growth* (New York, 1963), 94–106.

gree of apparent stability. In order to achieve sustained growth, it is necessary that stimulants to development be of a certain minimum size. At any one time there are forces at work in the economy tending to increase per capita income and there are forces at work tending to decrease per capita income. In the former group are increased savings and investment, higher levels of work skills, resource discovery and utilization, increases in entrepreneurial numbers and energy, and economies of scale. The latter includes increases in surplus population, failure of firms and entrepreneurs to realize expectations, institutional rigidities, and resistance to new ideas and change. The critical minimum effort must be of such magnitude as to set off income generating forces that are sufficient to overcome the deterrents and reinforce themselves in succeeding periods.

It behooves planners for economic development not to undertake too much too soon, and to concentrate efforts in carefully selected areas and activities rather than to utilize a shotgun approach to all areas and activities.

Take-off into sustained growth

Walt W. Rostow has traced rather carefully the stages through which a nation passes on its journey to economic development.[5] The Rostow treatment indicates the necessity of separating the stages of economic development and ascertains certain common characteristics of particular stages as they have occurred in different countries. The stages are: (1) the traditional society; (2) preconditions for take-off; (3) take-off; (4) drive to maturity; and (5) age of high mass consumption.

Because the lack of economic development in Louisiana is a relative proposition and we feel impoverished as a state only in relation to states with an even higher degree of economic achievement, Louisiana is already in the fifth stage. After all, a part of a complex cannot long remain isolated from the other parts. Still, it might be conceived that Louisiana is in the take-off period insofar as an era of rapid industrialization is concerned. While it is probable that the preconditions have been met in at least minimal fashion, it is regrettable that an even better educational and institutional base has not been

[5] W. W. Rostow, *The Stages of Economic Growth* (Cambridge, Mass., 1961).

provided. Even so, an adequate base probably exists. It is possible, however, to accelerate economic growth and to extend the ultimate potential for development if increased attention is given to the educational and institutional base.

Backwash effects

Elaborate theses have been developed to indicate that the commercial intercourse between developed and underdeveloped areas (especially as it concerns manufacturing areas and producers of raw materials and primary products) might have certain backwash effects on the underdeveloped member.[6] By backwash is meant that there may be a small multiplier effect from the export industries of the underdeveloped area, that the terms of trade for the raw materials may steadily worsen, and that specialization in the raw materials curtails the promotion of industry that might otherwise occur and the spill-over effects that would accompany such industralization. This argument is usually presented as a case for protectionism by underdeveloped nations to help force economic growth. The state of Louisiana is virtually powerless to impose effective restrictions on imports from and exports to other states in the union, but—insofar as it is within the power of planners to affect the course of private business—emphasis should be put on increasing the value added by Louisiana processors.

Continued development

One problem that is of constant concern to the advanced areas of the world, and of this country, is the matter of maintaining growth. This is perhaps not so acute a problem for Louisiana in the direct sense. In the indirect sense it is very real, however, for it is a problem for the nation as a whole, and the effects must overflow into the state economy. The essence of the problem is that the voluminous amounts of investment needed to keep the advanced economy at a level of full and growing employment will, in turn, bring about tremendous increases in the level of productive capacity, which will call for still more investment.[7] In other words, this ability of the

[6] B. Higgins, *Economic Development* (New York, 1959), 345–53.

[7] E. D. Domar, "Expansion and Employment," *American Economic Review*, XXXVII (March, 1947), 34–55.

advanced economy to produce a market surplus of many goods and services sometimes makes further economic growth difficult in a given period of time. For an underdeveloped area within a national economy of advanced development—and this is Louisiana's position vis-à-vis the United States—this means that surpluses outside its borders diminish the demands for its exports and increase the available supply of goods for import, thus impeding the growth of both its raw materials sector and its finished goods sector. Recessions in the United States' economy can have particularly severe repercussions for Louisiana, as the demands of the nation for the raw materials and semifinished goods produced in this state are reduced, at least in relative terms, and the competitive surplus of such manufactured goods as Louisiana does produce becomes more abundantly available.

SPECIFIC FACTORS IN
LOUISIANA'S ECONOMIC DEVELOPMENT

Introduction

If the discussion is moved from general concepts of economic development to a critical examination of more specific factors, what are the forces currently exerting the greatest influence on the economic development of Louisiana, and how may these forces be marshalled in such a way as to maximize the growth potential of the state and its component parts?

What one might call the ingredients of economic development can be divided into two broad categories: the natural and the human or man-controlled. The natural includes such things as land area and its quality, climate, and resources. The better the natural base, the more favorable the growth potential. It should be stressed that the potential for growth and the rate of growth may be two entirely different things. Examples abound of areas that are "have-nots" and yet have still achieved significant economic development. Nevertheless, the natural base—if inadequate—does serve to severely limit the ultimate level of economic development. At least this has been true in the past. Improved transportation, and therefore, the increased ease and decreased cost with which resources can be moved from one geographic location to another, is lessening the pull of natural resources. The importance of natural ingredients notwithstanding, if such a lack exists, there is little that can be done about it. If the framework of natural resources is inadequate, the role of the man-controlled factors, which is always critical, simply becomes more so.

The man-controlled ingredients, because they are amenable to change, are perhaps of more long-run significance to the area seeking economic development. Unlike the natural ingredients, they can continually be increased and augmented. The man-controlled ingredients include population, both quantity and quality; technology; the rate of capital accumulation; and the institutional structure. All of these are basically functions of the quality of population. If there is any secret to economic development, it surely lies in the qualitative aspects of the population. Low quality of population is a common ingredient binding all underdeveloped areas—whatever else their differences—in a common union.

When comparing one underdeveloped region with another, one subject for examination would be the institutional framework established for the solution of the various economic and social problems. Although the structure of Louisiana is not basically different from that of any other state, the utilization, quality, and attitudes of institutions sometimes differ a great deal.

Natural ingredients

Geographically, Louisiana is located roughly between latitudes 29.5 degrees N and 33 degrees N and from the 94th meridian eastward to the Mississippi River as the northern part of that boundary and to the Pearl River as the southern part. Elevation ranges from sea level in the coastal areas to over 500 feet above sea level in the hills of the northwest.[8] The total area of the state encompasses 48,523 square miles, ranking it thirty-first among the states. This area consists of 45,106 square miles of land and 3,417 of water.[9] Only four other states have a greater area of water within their borders.

Mean annual precipitation ranges from 46 inches in Caddo Parish in the north to 66 inches in parts of the south, with a median of approximately 56 inches. Snow and sleet are of little importance in

[8] U.S. Weather Bureau, *Climates of the States—Louisiana* (Washington, D.C., 1959), 1.
[9] U.S. Bureau of the Census, *Statistical Abstract of the United States* (Washington, D.C., 1964), 169.

Louisiana, rarely reaching damaging proportions although snow does occur more frequently than is generally realized. The average annual temperature varies from 66° F in the northern portions of the state to 69° F in the southern parts. In January the lowest average is 49° F in the northwest and north-central and 57° F in the southeast. The highest July averages extend from 83° F in the north and north-central to 81° F in the east-central. The average number of days with freezing temperature, or lower, ranges from twenty-four at Shreveport to four at New Orleans.[10]

Rains of flood-producing proportions may occur at any time of the year but are most likely to come during late winter and early spring and least likely in the fall. Tropical storms and tornadoes are a threat to life and property in some areas.[11] Water conservation measures, flood control, and accurate weather forecasting, however, have greatly diminished the loss from such forces.

The climate of Louisiana, then, suits the state to a wide variety of agricultural and industrial pursuits.

The commercial requirements of present-day industry and agriculture, added to the private needs of individual citizens, severely tax the water resources of the nation. These demands will obviously become more acute as population grows. Louisiana has been fortunately endowed with ground and surface water resources. However, the popular idea that Louisiana has water to waste is simply not true. Although Louisiana is considered to be a "water-rich" state, there are several areas where little or no fresh ground water is available.[12] Further, the requirements for surface water have increased to the point where improper utilization could severely limit industrial expansion.

The large inland water area of Louisiana and its coastal position are conducive to an extensive harvest of fish and seafood, which in 1962 amounted to 766,540,000 pounds valued at $28,923,000, second highest in the South and Southwest.[13]

The forest land of Louisiana covers 15,990,000 acres. Of the southern states, only North Carolina contains more live saw timber.[14]

[10] U.S. Weather Bureau, *Climates of the States*, 2–3.
[11] *Ibid.*
[12] Department of Conservation, *Ground Water of Louisiana* (Baton Rouge, 1960), 47.
[13] U.S. Bureau of the Census, *Statistical Abstract of the United States*, 696.
[14] *Ibid.*, 681.

The production of lumber, pulp, and forest products ranks as one of the state's major economic activities.

In total mineral production, Louisiana stands second in the nation. Further, Louisiana contains the second largest amount of proven crude oil and natural gas reserves and is the second largest producer of both of these minerals. Louisiana's output of carbon black is exceeded by only one other state. The state is also a major producer of salt and a principal source of sulphur.[15]

Louisiana has sources of clays, stone, lime, shell, and sand and gravel.[16] Deposits of other major minerals such as coal and iron ore are of no commercial significance.

In summary, it may be said that Louisiana is indeed rich in some mineral resources, particularly oil and natural gas, but that it is only adequately endowed with others, and woefully lacking in still others. The fact remains, however, that Louisiana has a natural endowment equal to, and in some cases superior to, many other states that have shown a more rapid rate of growth. A fact to keep constantly in mind about those resources which Louisiana does have in abundance is that while compelling resources will attract, other factors must be given superior weight if alternative sources are available. It should further be recalled that resources are becoming more transportable, so that transformation does not have to occur at source. Nevertheless, we may work under the hypothesis that the natural base of Louisiana is adequate to sustain far more rapid rates of growth than have occurred in the past.

Man-controlled ingredients

While technological progress and capital accumulation are critical factors in economic development, their lack does not have the same implication for a state which is a member of a well-developed national economy that it does for underdeveloped areas that are entities in their own right. Louisiana has available to her the technical and capital resources of the nation in that there are no legal obstacles to their importation. The barriers to capital and technical flows into Louisiana are barriers of opportunity. To the extent which oppor-

---

15 U.S. Bureau of Mines, *Mineral Yearbook* (Washington, D.C., 1962).
16 *Ibid.*

tunity is not blocked by lack of a specific natural resource, the impediments must be sought in the population and in the institutional framework.

a) *Population*

The projected population of Louisiana for 1965 was 3,544,000, consisting of 2,420,000 white and 1,124,000 nonwhite.[17] From an educational standpoint the level is quite low. The Census of 1960 indicated that in excess of 20 percent of those twenty-five years of age or older were classed as functional illiterates (fifth grade education or below), and it is this age group which constitutes the bulk of the labor force.[18] This means that many of those in the unemployed category must actually be considered unemployable, and—unless the skill level of this group is raised—the proportion of those unemployable will increase as the demands of industry for workers with high capacities continue to grow.

Because areas experiencing rapid economic development normally undergo increases in population, population increments frequently come to be regarded as desirable in and of themselves. Each new family is thought of as representing a certain amount of additional purchasing power in the community and as a source of increased demand for goods and services. Overlooked is the fact such population also represents a demand for additional social services. So long as the ability of the increment to produce is equal to or in excess of its consumption, well and good. However, a part of the increased population frequently represents nothing more than an additional drain on the resources of the community. As the shift from rural to urban residence continues, many Louisiana communities will no doubt find their population increasing, but much of it may consist of displaced agricultural labor which will constitute a burden rather than an asset.

It is predicted that by 1970 Louisiana's population will have increased to 3,830,000.[19] As indicated in the previous paragraph, this

[17] A. L Bertrand and J. Wright, Jr., *Louisiana's Human Resources* (Baton Rouge, 1964), Pt. 3, p. 7.
[18] U.S. Bureau of the Census, *1960 Census of Population* (Washington, D.C., 1961), I, Pt. 20, Table 47.
[19] Bertrand and Wright, *Louisiana's Human Resources*, 7.

may prove to be a mixed blessing. The ability of many of these people to consume may not be matched by their ability to produce. Louisiana cannot afford the burden of increased population unless the proportions of high quality-low quality population undergo marked change.

b) *The community*

Some communities have industrialization thrust upon them because of factors beyond their control. Still, the frequency with which industry has some choice of communities—at least within a region—is increasing. It therefore behooves any community to make itself more attractive to those enterprises which might conceivably locate there. For that matter, community improvement is a desirable objective for its own sake. High quality schools, streets, utilities, fire and police protection, drainage and sanitation, medical facilities, public transportation, and recreational areas enhance the productivity of those already living in a community as well as providing the inducement for industry.

Zoning for effective land use can transcend city boundaries and become a parish, as well as a state, matter. Nevertheless, the principles applicable to one governmental subdivision are equally applicable to all. Maximum land-use efficiency requires overall planning and sensible restrictions on use. Failure to act in this respect means a hodge-podge of residential, commercial, and industrial use that detracts from both productivity and beauty. Historically, Louisiana communities have been notoriously lacking in the planning and enforcement of such policies.

Economic development means change, and change is never altogether painless. Older firms in a community become of less significance and import. Because political influence so often flows from economic concentration, the power complex of the community may be altered, or at least such alteration may be threatened. As a consequence, the attitudes toward economic growth will not be uniform. Some will prefer that conditions remain static, for their relative position is strongest when conditions remain just as they are. The significance of these attitudes must never be underestimated, for the controlling complex—through land ownership, political influence, and control of local financial institutions—may possess ample power to thwart the events upon which economic development is predicated.

These impediments are perhaps more critical for small industry than for large. There is no definitive solution to deal with them.

c) *Social-overhead capital*

The provision of social-overhead capital—that is, facilities that must be provided by public authority such as education, highways, and various public works—is a vital ingredient in the process of economic development. Louisiana has poured relatively more of its resources into education and highways than the bulk of the other southern states. In per capita terms, however, state-local expenditures on education rank below the national average, and highway expenditures rank only slightly above average.[20] Instead of holding its own, or advancing, the state has been losing ground.

Although state contributions to education, in relation to ability to support, have been admirable, contributions at the local level have been extremely small. Additional needs will—and now—require that larger contributions come from local sources than has been the case in the past. Since it has been estimated that education expenditures can yield as much as a 30 percent return on investment, any concerted effort to promote economic growth will call for heavy expenditures in this area.[21]

Effective transportation is indispensable to economic development, as all economic, social, and political activities require interaction over distance. While all forms of transportation are important in the economic complex—though the degree of importance of particular types of transportation varies from industry to industry and in the aggregate—private ownership provides the ways utilized by only one mode, the railroad. Highways, waterways, and airways are maintained by government. In the case of the highways, user charges in the form of taxes are utilized to recoup the bulk of the expenditures, although highway studies have consistently indicated that certain categories of highway users do not pay charges consistent with their responsibility for highway costs.[22]

[20] U.S. Bureau of the Census, *Governmental Finances in 1964–65* (Washington, D.C., 1966), 46.

[21] Howard G. Schaller, *Decade of Decision* (New Orleans, 1965).

[22] One example, particularly pertinent, is William D. Ross, *Financing Highway Improvements in Louisiana* (Baton Rouge, 1955).

The upkeep of airways is primarily the responsibility of the federal government, and there has been no reluctance on the part of the central government to appropriate money for such purposes whenever there is the slightest demonstrable need. The primary demand on the state for social-overhead capital in the field of transportation will be highways.

Lack of transportation is not now, nor is it likely to be in the future, a problem of insurmountable magnitude standing in the way of Louisiana's economic development. Although transport facilities may not be as extensive in Louisiana as in some other sections of the country, they are as adequate to meet current needs as one usually finds. The provision of highways, particularly, nearly always runs behind, or at best only slightly ahead, of public desire. When highways are properly priced to include all the social and economic costs involved —which is seldom if ever the case—the effective demand for additional highway improvements may not be so great as ordinarily thought.[23] Even so, when transport demand increases, facilities to provide the wanted services will keep pace.

Although utility services are more often than not provided by privately owned companies operating under public regulation, these services are frequently lumped into the category of social capital because their availability is critical to the well-being of the populace and the functioning of the economy. Many of Louisiana's citizens are as yet without adequate utility service. Some are without a telephone, electricity, convenient fuel, or safe water; others simply lack desired quantities of such services. This inadequacy flows from Louisiana's level of economic development and low-income status, and will be overcome only as the level of development and income rises. Lack of utility service in Louisiana is a function of economic underdevelopment and not a basic causal factor.

d) *Government*

Much has been made of the unfavorable impression created by Louisiana's political climate. Granted, it has not been the best in the eyes of most unbiased observers, and pleas for, and promises of, good government have permeated political campaigns for genera-

---

[23] James M. Buchanan, "The Pricing of Highway Services," *National Tax Journal*, V (June, 1952), 97–106.

tions. A stable political situation is always desirable for economic growth, other things being equal. Without belittling the importance of good government, the factor of stability is perhaps equally important. Industry can, and will, tolerate government that is less than optimum if that government has consistency so that one can adjust to the rules of the game. Even so, good government, like community improvement, is desirable in its own right. The fact that it plays a part in the promotion of economic development is an added benefit.

The aspect of Louisiana government which is most closely related to the attraction of industry is tax structure and policy. One constantly hears tales of the industry that is kept out of Louisiana solely because of high state taxes. In many respects the thesis that Louisiana is a high tax state is a myth. Louisiana, true, did rank ninth among states in per capita tax revenues in 1965.[24] However, in terms of both state and local taxes per capita, Louisiana ranked thirty-sixth, a position more in keeping with its economic status.[25] The difference in the two rankings is to be explained by the role of the state as a centralized collection agency for taxes, a considerable portion of which is remitted to parishes and local governments. Reform of the property tax assessment procedure and equalization of such assessments between parishes is badly needed to end the capriciousness of this levy, but the overall tax picture is not nearly so unfavorable to the attraction and development of industry as is often indicated by those whose primary purpose is to remove or reduce all indirect business taxes. Certainly, the state of Louisiana and its various subdivisions have the obligation to operate those services desired by the citizenry as economically as possible. Obviously, any industry would benefit from a reduction in its tax burden, but the readily discernible needs of the state for social-overhead capital indicate that tax rates will rise rather than fall.

In their eagerness to attract industry from other areas and under the stress of competition—real or imagined—with other potential sites, states and localities are often tempted to offer inducements in the form of tax relief or exemption or through the subscription of funds to construct plants, purchase equipment, and the like. Studies have shown that such concessions are of doubtful significance in the at-

[24] U.S. Bureau of the Census, *Compendium of State Government Finances in 1965* (Washington, D.C., 1966), 11.
[25] U.S. Bureau of the Census, *Governmental Finances in 1964–65*, p. 45.

traction of desirable industry.[26] Certainly, a state should be wary of offering undue tax concessions. A worthwhile enterprise should have a stake in the state and community and be willing to pay its own way. Louisiana currently has enough home-grown poverty. There is no necessity to import more.

e) *Regionalism*

The poor are nearly always sensitive, singly and in the aggregate, and the underdeveloped area is no exception to the rule. This sensitivity often works itself out in the form of isolationism and a strong nationalistic feeling. The South has frequently exhibited this regional antagonism and the more underdeveloped the southern state, the stronger its force. This resentment of outsiders which leads to a "go-it-alone" delusion is one that must be mitigated or eradicated if Louisiana is to realize its full potential in the attraction of the capital and technology necessary to overcome the gap between it and the more developed states.

Market size and quality

One aspect of the Louisiana economy long lamented is that the state's raw materials are processed into producers' or semi-finished consumers' goods and then transported to destinations outside the state for finishing. Louisiana has had considerable success in attracting these extractive and producer goods industries, but the supply of raw materials and semi-finished goods flowing out of the state from these industries is enormous. It would be desirable if more processing took place and, consequently, more value were added within the borders of the state. This unfavorable situation is principally a market phenomenon. Lack of population concentrations and low per capita incomes mean inadequate consumer demand to support such market-oriented production. This type of enterprise will not be attracted in desired quantities until economic development has advanced far enough to raise per capita incomes to more adequate levels.

[26] William D. Ross, *Louisiana Industrial Tax Exemption Program* (Baton Rouge, 1953).

CONCLUSIONS

The principal factor holding back the rate of economic growth in the state of Louisiana is the skill level of its people. Poverty begets poverty. The forces of low income, illiteracy, inadequate nutrition, low standards of sanitation and health care, and the second-rate social institutions by which they are accompanied tend to reinforce themselves through succeeding generations unless a concerted effort is made to end the cycle. Louisiana has made significant efforts, relative to its financial resources, to initiate programs designed to this end. Yet, its position relative to that of the national average has deteriorated in several crucial respects. The malady requires dosages of greater intensity and frequency to maintain even the status quo. To gain, and gain quickly, may require greater amounts of private capital importation and greater expenditures of state and federal funds for social-overhead than has been the case in the past.

The image that Louisiana government has projected to the nation has not been favorable. The criticisms have not been without foundation. Efficient government is the reflection of a demanding electorate. The voters of Louisiana have been subjected to government of about the quality they deserve. It might not be unkind to say that they have received the kind of government they have insisted upon. It is to be hoped that rising standards of education will produce an electorate that will demand more effective administration on the part of elected officials. There is some indication that this may be happening.

One noteworthy feature of government deficiency has been the frequent absence of fiscal responsibility. Apart from the makeup of the legislature and the various state administrations, a contributing factor has undoubtedly been the bonuses from state-owned mineral lands which have periodically bailed the state out of a final reckoning with financial reality. The immense growth in the needs of state and local institutions has created financial requirements which, it would appear, will not much longer permit the capriciousness of past fiscal policy. In any event, the rate of economic growth will be related to the adoption of prudent tax and expenditure measures.

The provincialism of much of the populace of the state, coupled with the vested interests that control the economic complex in so many of the rural areas and smaller communities, has made the reallocation of resources required by rapid economic development difficult. Changes will be inexorably forced in the long run, but a willingness to accept change, even to welcome it, could accelerate economic gains.

The resource base of Louisiana is sufficient to maintain a far more rapid rate of economic development than has occurred in the past. Further, the state has an advantage of location that gives it access to the growing markets of the southern United States and to those of Latin America.

It should be reemphasized that the principal barriers to Louisiana's development are human and institutional, and these change slowly, even under the pressures of modern society. It is to be expected, however, that the changes that are now taking place will continue and that they will be accelerated. The rest of the nation is undergoing the same pressures for more rapid economic growth. The rate at which Louisiana closes the relative gap between its level and that of the nation will probably be, barring unexpected and unpredictable events, a slow and tedious one. In terms of absolute growth, there is no insurmountable barrier to a significant and rapid rise in the level of Louisiana's economic accomplishments.

LOUISIANA'S POPULATION:
ITS GROWTH AND DISTRIBUTION
Roger L. Burford

It has often been said that the most basic and most important resource of any state is its people. Trite as this statement sounds, it is
undeniably true. The people of the state are the source of its labor
force and, at the same time, are the demanders of most of the output
of its economy. In fact, it is the people of the state which constitutes
its *raison d'etre.* Indeed, it is obvious that without people there can
be no economic activity, nor even a state. Thus, the aim of this
essay is to describe and discuss the demographic characteristics,
growth, and geographic distribution of Louisiana's population,
mainly from the viewpoint of their implications for the economic
growth of the state.

AGE, RACE, AND SEX

Table I and Figure 1 contain information on the age, race, and
sex distributions of Louisiana's population in 1960 and the age distribution as compared to the United States. Table I presents the
age-race-sex distribution for the state. Figure 1 compares the age
distribution for the state and the nation. Two things are obvious from
these data: first, Louisiana has a very young population, and second,
Louisiana has a large proportion of nonwhite population. With respect to Louisiana's youth, the median age of the people of the state
was 25.3 years in 1960 as compared to 29.5 years for the nation. Moreover, 35.3 percent of Louisiana's population was under 15 years of
age as compared to 31.1 percent for the nation. At the same time

only 7.4 percent of the state's people were 65 years of age and over, as compared to 9.2 percent for the nation. Moreover, as seen in Figure 1, Louisiana has a larger proportion of its population in every age group under 25 than the nation while it has a smaller proportion in all age groups 30 and over. The median age of population in both the state and the nation declined from 1950 to 1960 but has declined more in Louisiana than in the nation as a whole. Median age in Louisiana in 1960 (25.3 years) was 1.4 years younger than in 1950 (26.7 years). By contrast, median age in the nation in 1960 (29.5 years) was only .7 years younger than in 1950 (30.2 years).

These data have considerable economic significance for the state. They, at the same time, represent problems and promises. The fact that such a large proportion of the population is under labor-force ages means that relatively fewer people must work to support the

Table I

Louisiana Population, by Age, Race, and Sex, 1960

Age-Years	Race and Sex			
	White		Nonwhite	
	Male	Female	Male	Female
Total	1,090,306	1,121,409	501,948	543,359
Under 5	135,001	129,506	79,629	78,587
5– 9	124,155	118,691	72,409	72,638
10–14	110,237	106,407	60,655	60,077
15–19	83,305	86,322	45,426	46,709
20–24	66,854	72,864	30,406	35,203
25–29	69,549	72,167	25,590	30,814
30–34	75,774	77,954	25,051	31,491
35–39	75,722	78,187	25,103	30,317
40–44	69,397	70,256	23,237	27,496
45–49	65,271	65,741	23,667	26,795
50–54	57,630	58,981	21,377	24,168
55–59	48,637	50,870	19,480	21,050
60–64	37,014	40,639	14,599	16,326
65–69	28,762	34,777	14,246	16,773
70–74	20,327	25,729	9,474	11,137
75 and over	19,211	26,713	9,526	10,970
Not reported	3,460	5,605	2,073	2,808
Median Age	26.8	28.3	19.2	21.9

SOURCE: U.S. Bureau of the Census, *Census of Population,* 1960.

FIGURE I

AGE DISTRIBUTION OF POPULATION
LOUISIANA AND UNITED STATES
1960

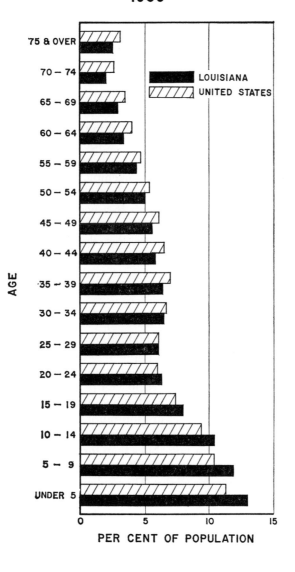

SOURCE   U S BUREAU of the CENSUS, STATISTICAL ABSTRACT
of the UNITED STATES, 1963

whole population. This, in turn, tends to result in low *per capita* income even where *per worker* wages may be high. Moreover, since such a large proportion of the people are school aged, educational costs per worker must be high if education in the state is to keep pace with other areas. Hence, the large proportion of nonproductive people in the state puts more of a financial strain on the productive ages than is the case for the nation as a whole. On the other hand, the population of the state is young and vigorous. The natural increase in working-aged population over the next fifteen years or so that will result from the large proportion of school-aged and younger children will, if educational opportunities in the state keep pace, be favorable to further industrial expansion in the state. In the absence, however, of adequate provision for education and in the absence of substantial industrial growth, the greatly increased labor force is likely to result in either substantial unemployment or a high rate of out-migration from the state among the young people. Most likely, both of these will result. This points to a need for greatly increased business expansion to provide employment for these young people. There is every indication, however, that the economic potential of the state (particularly in the southern part and along the Mississippi River) is virtually unlimited, but most modern industry requires a relatively well-educated labor force. This could conceivably be a limiting factor for the state.[1]

As for race, only two states, Mississippi and South Carolina, have higher proportions of nonwhite population than Louisiana. Mississippi had 42.3 percent nonwhite population in 1960 and South Carolina had 34.9 percent. Louisiana had approximately 32 percent nonwhite population as compared to 11.4 percent in the nation as a whole. This accounts partially for the high proportion of very young people in the state; birth rates are substantially higher for nonwhites than for whites. Consequently, the proportion of very young people is substantially higher for nonwhites than for whites.[2] As is also indicated in Table I, the median ages for nonwhites of both sexes are considerably less than for whites. The median age of nonwhite males in 1960 was 19.2 years as compared to 26.8 for white males. The corresponding ages for nonwhite and white females respectively were 21.9 and 28.3 years.

---

[1] See the discussion below on the educational level of Louisiana's population.
[2] See Table I.

EDUCATION AND INCOME

Louisiana compares rather poorly with the national average with respect to the educational level and the income of its people. Figures 2 and 3, respectively, compare the income and the educational distributions of the population of Louisiana with those of the nation as a whole. The relatively low distribution of income is explained in part by three things: the relatively low education of Louisiana's population (median school years completed by adults twenty-five years of age and over of 8.8 years as compared to 10.6 years for the nation as a whole); the large proportion of young population; and the large proportion of nonwhite population (primarily Negro). Actually, as already indicated, the first two of these are related in some measure to the third. In addition to these three, a larger proportion of the state's population is engaged in agriculture than is the case for the nation, although Louisiana is less dependent on agriculture than are most southern states.

As Figure 2 demonstrates, 23 percent of Louisiana families had annual incomes of less than $2,000 in 1959 as compared to only 13.1 percent in the United States. On the other extreme, 15 percent of the families in the United States had incomes of $7,000 or more, as compared to only 9.9 percent in Louisiana. Moreover, 57.9 percent of Louisiana's families had incomes *less than* $5,000, whereas 58.1 percent of the families in the nation had *higher* incomes than this.

Look now at Figure 3. The comparison of the national and state educational distributions of the adult population in 1960 is very similar to the income comparison shown in Figure 2. For example, 21.3 percent of Louisiana's adult population had less than five years of schooling, and 42 percent had less than eight years. The corresponding national percentages are only 8.3 percent and 22.1 percent. At the same time, 41.1 percent of the nation's adults had at least finished high school as compared with 32.3 percent in Louisiana. Some degree of comfort for Louisianians, however, can be taken from the observation that the percentage of the state's population with at least one year of college was only slightly less than for the nation (13.4 percent in Louisiana as compared to 16.5 percent nationally). This is particularly true for people with four or more years of college (6.7 percent in Louisiana as compared to 7.7 percent in the nation). Hence, it may be concluded that a considerably larger proportion of

FIGURE II

FAMILY INCOME OF FAMILIES IN LOUISIANA AND IN THE UNITED STATES

1959

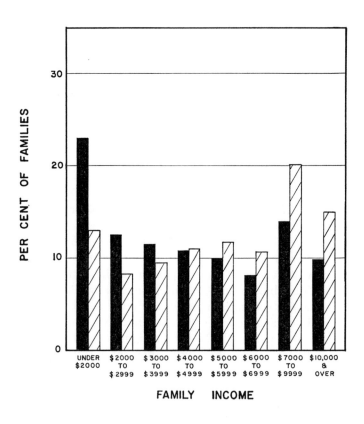

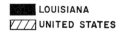

SOURCE   US BUREAU of the CENSUS, STATISTICAL ABSTRACT of the UNITED STATES, 1963

FIGURE III

YEARS OF SCHOOL COMPLETED
BY PEOPLE 25 YEARS OF AGE AND OVER
LOUISIANA AND UNITED STATES
1960

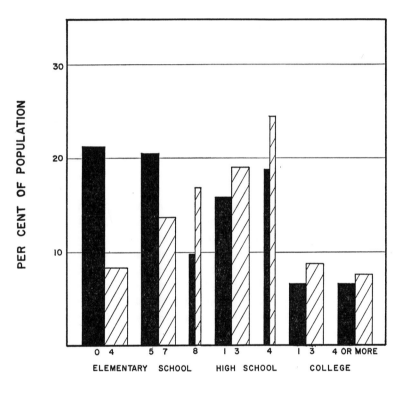

YEARS OF SCHOOL

■ LOUISIANA
▨ UNITED STATES

SOURCE   US BUREAU of the CENSUS, STATISTICAL ABSTRACT
of the UNITED STATES, 1963

Louisiana's high school graduates go on to college than is the case nationally.

As indicated in the last section, continuation of this poor educational comparison (particularly for those with high school educations or less) in the future could act as a serious drag on the state's growth. On the other hand, a young and well-educated populace could be a prime attractive force for future economic development.

OCCUPATION OF EMPLOYED WORKERS

Presented in Table II are data on the occupational distributions of employed workers in Louisiana and the United States for 1960. Actually, the relative distribution of employment among the various occupational groups in Louisiana during 1960 was very nearly the same as the United States. The chief differences were that the percentages who were employed as professional and technical workers; farmers and farm managers; farm laborers; managers, officials and proprietors; and clerical workers were slightly less in Louisiana than in the nation as a whole. On the other hand, Louisiana had larger percentages employed as private household workers, service workers, and laborers other than farm laborers.

These differences in occupational structure account partially for the lower incomes in Louisiana as compared with the nation as a whole. The lowest income occupations are generally private household workers and laborers. On the other hand, the highest income groups are generally professionals, technical, managerial, official, and proprietary groups. Therefore, in order to upgrade the income level in the state, it is necessary to upgrade the state's occupational structure as well. This, of course, is interrelated with the educational problems already discussed.

DISTRIBUTION AND REDISTRIBUTION
OF THE POPULATION

Figure 4 contains data on the geographic distribution of population in Louisiana's parishes in 1960. There were four parishes with populations over 200,000. These were Caddo (224,000), East Baton Rouge (230,000), Jefferson (209,000) and Orleans (628,000). Another three —Calcasieu, Ouachita, and Rapides—had between 100,000 and

200,000. Only four parishes—Caldwell, Cameron, Red River, and St. Helena—had less than 10,000 people. It should be noted that the major population concentrations within the state tend to lie along the major rivers and near the Gulf of Mexico; proximity to water transportation has been and continues to be an important factor in Louisiana's population growth and distribution.

It is interesting to note the similarity of the geographic patterns shown in Figures 4 and 5. Figure 5 presents parish rates of net migration between 1950 and 1960 of population 15–69 years of age in 1960.

Table II

Occupational Distribution of Employed Workers,
Louisiana and the United States — 1960

Occupation	United States[a]		Louisiana[b]	
	Number (1000's)	Percent	Number	Percent
Professional, technical, and kindred workers	7,475	11.2	103,530	10.3
Farmers and farm managers	2,780	4.2	33,080	3.3
Managers, officials, and proprietors	7,067	10.6	91,993	9.1
Clerical and kindred workers	9,783	14.7	120,112	11.9
Sales workers	4,401	6.6	65,809	6.5
Craftsmen, foremen, and kindred workers	8,560	12.8	124,908	12.4
Operatives and kindred workers	11,986	18.0	164,832	16.4
Private household workers	2,216	3.3	61,566	6.1
Service workers	6,133	9.2	94,803	9.4
Farm laborers and foremen	2,615	3.9	28,567	2.8
Laborers, except farm laborers	3,665	5.5	75,965	7.6
Occupation not reported	–	–	42,647	4.2
TOTAL	66,681	100.0	1,007,812	100.0

[a]SOURCE: U.S. Department of Commerce, *Statistical Abstract of the United States, 1963.*
[b]SOURCE: U.S. Bureau of the Census, *Census of Population, 1960.*

FIGURE   IV

POPULATION OF LOUISIANA PARISHES

1960

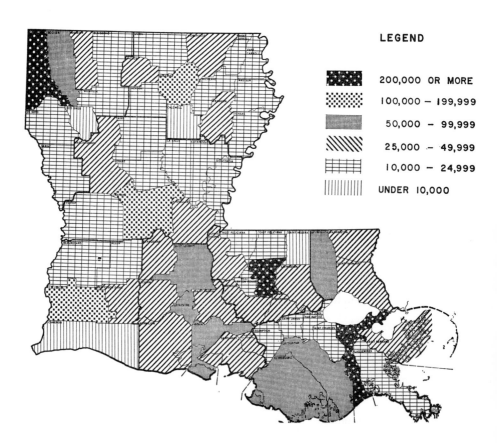

LEGEND

▓▓▓	200,000 OR MORE
⋯⋯	100,000 – 199,999
▦▦	50,000 – 99,999
⧄⧄	25,000 – 49,999
⊞⊞	10,000 – 24,999
‖‖‖	UNDER 10,000

SOURCE: ALVIN L. BERTRAND, LOUISIANA'S HUMAN RESOURCES, PART I, BULLETIN
NO. 548, AGRICULTURAL EXPERIMENT STATION, LOUISIANA STATE
UNIVERSITY, NOVEMBER 1961, pp. 8-9.

Generally, the relatively populous parishes were the ones which gained population by migration while the less populous parishes tended to be the losers. This resulted largely from the fact that most of the parishes with small populations are generally more dependent upon agriculture than are the larger ones; there were rather large-scale movements from farming during the 1950's to other occupations. There has been an increasing urbanization of the population, not only in Louisiana but throughout the nation, for several decades. It has accelerated even more during the post-war period. Hence, migration from farms in Louisiana is just a part of a national pattern of change.

Such patterns of migration (especially among working-aged population) have particular economic significance. In the relatively short run, migration has economic significance mainly in that it is the chief avenue by which the supply of labor in a given labor market (or among labor markets) may be adjusted to the existing demand. Over relatively longer periods of time it has further economic significance. It not only adjusts the supply of labor in various areas to existing levels of demand, but also it tends to modify that demand. Areas with growing population as a result of migration are areas of growing consumer demand. Hence, they are areas of expanding product markets as well as expanding labor supplies. Both of these are important to firms seeking new plant sites. Hence, large-scale inmigration may lead to movement of business into, or expansion of business in, those areas. At the same time, areas having little or no gains in population (and especially those having losses) are generally looked upon less favorably for new business expansion. On the one hand, they are areas of declining or stationary markets. On the other, their labor supply is declining also. Extending the argument still further, such new expansion as may result from net inmigration generally results in still more inmigration, hence still more expansion, and so on. The process is cumulative.

In addition to, or perhaps because of, the role of migration just described, it may be viewed as an indirect indicator of the relative abundance of economic opportunities in any two or more areas at a point in time, or changes through time. Perhaps the most important single factor explaining an area's migration pattern is the state of its relative economic opportunities. It has long been recognized that migratory flows are generally from areas of relatively poor economic opportunities to those having them in relatively greater abun-

FIGURE V

RATES OF NET MIGRATION FROM 1950 TO 1960

AMONG THE POPULATION AGED 15 TO 69 IN 1960

LOUISIANA

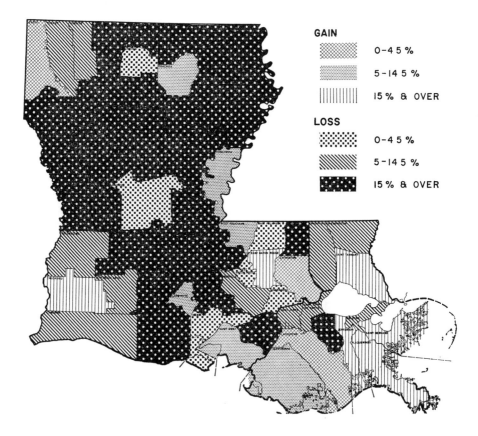

GAIN
- 0-4 5 %
- 5-14 5 %
- 15 % & OVER

LOSS
- 0-4 5 %
- 5-14 5 %
- 15 % & OVER

SOURCE: ROGER L. BURFORD, NET MIGRATION FOR SOUTHERN COUNTIES, 1940-50 AND 1950-60, RESEARCH PAPER NO. 24, BUREAU OF BUSINESS AND ECONOMIC RESEARCH, GEORGIA STATE COLLEGE, JANUARY 1963, pp. 35-37.

dance.[3] Poor opportunities tend to exert an expulsive force on the population of an area, while better opportunities elsewhere represent something of a magnetic attraction. It is this tendency to leave areas of relatively few opportunities in favor of areas having them in greater abundance which makes migration a basic avenue of adjustment or equalization of opportunities to the individuals in different locations.

It was noted above that the tendency to migrate (particularly from rural to urban areas) has been accelerated sharply during the postwar years. This can probably be attributed mainly to three things: a sharp increase in nonfarm employment opportunities (and an even sharper decline in farm employment); a greater awareness of nonfarm opportunities and an increased willingness to move, resulting from improved means of communication and transportation; and a greater ease of moving from one area to another as a result of greater availability of improved highways and automobiles.

PROSPECTS FOR FUTURE MIGRATION
AND ECONOMIC IMPLICATIONS

It is likely that the general pattern of migration during the 1960–70 period will be very similar to that reflected in Figure 5. Moreover, the rates of migration are likely to be greater in the 1960's than in the 1950's. Probably more parishes will have net inmigration during the 1960's than was the case in the 1950's. Those parishes most likely to gain by migration during the 1960's continue to be the urban and especially the suburban parishes, and probably also, those gaining will include several nonurban parishes along the Mississippi River between New Orleans and Baton Rouge, as well as most of the coastal parishes. Those parishes most likely to lose by net migration are the largely rural parishes, especially in the northern part of the state.

[3] See, for example, Carter Goodrich and others, *Migration and Economic Opportunity* (Philadelphia, 1936), 504; C. E. Lively and Conrad Taeuber, *Rural Migration in the United States*, Works Progress Administration Research Monograph XIX (Washington, D.C., 1939), 73, 74, 79, and 80; Donald J. Bogue, Henry S. Shryok, Jr., and Siegried A. Hoermann, *Subregional Migration in the United States, 1935–1940*, Studies in Population Distribution No. 5 (Oxford, Ohio, 1957), I, 8, 9, and 75; Daniel O. Price, "Some Socio-Economic Factors in Internal Migration," *Social Forces*, XXIX (May, 1951), 409–15; and Roger L. Burford, "An Index of Distance as Related to Internal Migration," *Southern Economic Journal*, XXIX (October, 1962), 77–81.

There are many reasons for this outlook; most of them are economic. As noted earlier, people tend to migrate to areas of greatest economic opportunity and these are generally urban or other industrialized or developing areas. Industry, in turn, tends to locate either near its source of raw materials, labor supply, etc.; near its market concentrations (usually urban centers); or near cheap dependable transportation. All of these factors tend to point toward continued growth in the areas indicated above.

In general, the economic outlook for Louisiana is very optimistic, especially for South Louisiana. According to Donald J. Bogue, the whole southern coastal region from coastal South Carolina and Georgia, including all of Florida, and the coastal areas of Alabama, Mississippi, Louisiana, and Texas to the Mexican border is likely to continue as one of the fastest growing regions (in population) in the nation, at least through the end of this century.[4] Moreover, Bogue sees this growth as being based soundly upon an economic foundation. Generally too, the people who are migrating into this region from other parts of the nation are people with higher than average education. They have been mainly professional or managerial people and have contributed significantly to the increasing modernization and progressiveness of the region. Hence, Louisiana, along with at least the southern parts of its neighboring states, may be expected to continue to grow and prosper for the foreseeable future.

Along with such shifts in population, however, come a host of problems. The problems of school crowding (especially in the high schools, colleges, and universities) will continue, and even increase. The problems of providing adequate and safe streets and highways will become more severe, as will the problems of meeting the needs for expanded and improved urban services of all types. At the same time, the areas with declining populations will continue to be faced with a host of other problems peculiar to only such areas. Many of these problems can be solved effectively if they are attacked seriously. They must be faced, no matter how painful or difficult, and the means for their solution must be found.

[4] Donald J. Bogue, "Population in the United States," *Population Bulletin,* XX (February, 1964), 23.

AGRICULTURE IN
THE LOUISIANA ECONOMY

Fred H. Wiegmann

Agriculture is a major contributor to Louisiana's economy. Over the years it has been the dominant factor. In recent years an increase in industrial development in some areas in the state has somewhat decreased agriculture's relative position in those areas. However, the agricultural industry is, in many respects, still the largest of the state's basic industries.

Of Louisiana's 28.8 million acres, about 10.1 million, or 36 percent, were in farms in 1966, and the trend is upward. Another 16 million acres are in commercial forests. It has been estimated that the agricultural industry, including both farm and related nonfarm segments, accounts for approximately 35 percent of all employment. Investment in farm land and buildings alone was over $2.5 billion in 1964. Total investment, including livestock, farm supply inventories, and equipment—plus agriculture supply, processing, and marketing facilities—makes Louisiana agriculture a multi-billion-dollar industry. In 1965 farm "operating" expenses alone, excluding forestry, were over $234 million. Total farm production expenses were over $320 million. Gross farm income (excluding forestry) was over $538 million.

The central unit in the agricultural industry is, of course, the farm. But, in addition to farms, the agricultural sector of the economy includes forestry as a major segment and many closely related nonfarm agriculturally-oriented businesses. The whole complex has been described recently by Dr. John Davis of Harvard's Business School under the more general heading of "Agribusiness." Included by Dr. Davis are those businesses depending directly on agriculture on both sides of the farm—supplying production requirements to the farm in the one case and processing and marketing farm products in the other. Feed, fertilizer, and chemical firms are good examples of the first. Sugar mills, rice mills, cotton gins, milk-processing plants, and meat-packing houses are representative of the second. In many instances ownership and operation of such firms are a part of a highly integrated complex which includes a farm as the central unit of production. Integrated combinations are often found in the sugar, dairy, rice, and cotton producing areas in Louisiana.

While the number of people on farms continues to decrease, the number engaged in agriculturally-oriented businesses continues to increase. A list of the more common agribusiness functions includes advertising, assembling, transporting, grading, packing, storing, financing, and selling agricultural commodities. Other functions include: communications, risk bearing (as in futures markets and insurance), supplying market information, inspection, legal services, and regulation. Dr. Davis estimated in 1957 that nearly 40 percent of the nation's working force was engaged in occupations related to agriculture, either directly or indirectly.

THE LOCATION AND DIVERSITY
OF AGRICULTURAL PRODUCTION

"Type of Farming" areas in Louisiana are shown in Figure 1. These are related generally to the soil type and topography of the land. Cotton is produced primarily in the Mississippi and Red River deltas. Rice is produced in Southwest Louisiana and sugar cane in the southeastern parishes. Beef cattle are concentrated in the rice area and in the Mississippi and Red River delta areas. Commercial dairying is concentrated around metropolitan centers, particularly New Orleans, Monroe, Lake Charles, and Shreveport.

Some agricultural commodities, although only a small part of total production, are very important to the particular area in which they are produced. Of the state's strawberry acreage, 98 percent is found in Southeast Louisiana in Area 10, mostly in Tangipahoa Parish. Strawberry production is of considerable economic importance to that area. Most of the tung nut production is also located in Tangipahoa Parish. The world's total supply of perique tobacco, used in many domestic and European blends, is produced only in Louisiana on about a thousand acres in St. James Parish.

Each type of farming area is characterized by a different set of agricultural enterprises. Major enterprises typically found in each may be summarized as follows:[1]

(1A) UPLAND TIMBER AREA—*Timber, peaches, broilers,* eggs, commercial vegetables, cotton, milk, hogs, hay, Irish potatoes, corn. (1B) NORTHWEST HILL AREA—*Timber, broilers, milk,* beef cattle, hay, cotton. (2) NORTH CENTRAL CUTOVER-PINE AREA—*Timber,* peaches, eggs, broilers, hogs, pecans, cotton. (3) RED RIVER COTTON AREA—*Cotton, soybeans, pecans, hay, beef cattle, broilers,* oats, eggs, hogs, sheep, corn. (4) CUTOVER FLATWOODS AREA—*Sheep, beef cattle,* stumpage, eggs, chickens. (5) MISSISSIPPI DELTA AREA—*Cotton, soybeans, beef cattle, oats, corn,* hogs,

FIGURE 1.   TYPE OF FARMING AREAS, LOUISIANA.

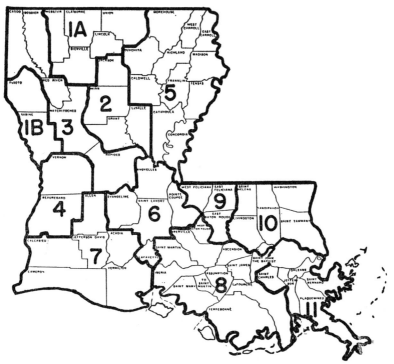

[1] Italics indicate the most important cash products in the area.

pecans, peaches, hay, chickens. (6) CENTRAL MIXED FARMING AREA
—*Cotton, sweet potatoes, corn, hogs,* rice, soybeans, Irish potatoes, sugar cane, chickens, hay, milk, beef cattle, greenhouse and
nursery plants. (7) RICE AREA—*Rice, beef cattle,* soybeans, sheep,
hay, sweet potatoes. (8) SUGAR CANE AREA—*Sugar cane, Irish potatoes, commercial vegetables,* corn, hay, beef cattle. (9) SOUTHEAST
MIXED FARMING AREA—*Beef cattle,* commercial vegetables, Irish
potatoes, sweet potatoes, oats, pecans, greenhouse and nursery
plants. (10) DAIRY, POULTRY, AND TRUCK AREA—*Milk, strawberries,
tung nuts, eggs, broilers, greenhouse and nursery plants, timber,*
commercial vegetables, beef cattle. (11) NEW ORLEANS TRUCK AND
FRUIT AREA—*Greenhouse and nursery plants,* commercial vegetables.

SALES OF FARM
PRODUCTS AND TIMBER

Crops and Livestock

Louisiana shares with a few states the distinction of producing
a wide variety of agricultural products. The major farm commodities,
and cash receipts from their sale in 1965, are shown in Table I. Cash
receipts from sales in 1965 were roughly $485 million. Field crops
made up nearly two-thirds of the total, with livestock and livestock
products making up the remainder. Government payments from various programs added $22,082,000 in 1965, to bring total cash farm
income to $506,905,000, or over half a billion dollars.

The Louisiana Department of Commerce and Industry estimated
that farm products sold in 1959 generated approximately $687,107,000
in additional business in Louisiana, or approximately twice the value
of cash farm receipts of $381 million.[2] Applying the same rule to 1965
production yields an estimate of over one billion dollars in "additional
business" created by the processing and sale of Louisiana farm products.

Changes can take place rapidly in agriculture. For example, the

---

[2] Louisiana Department of Commerce and Industry, *Agriculture—A Basic
Factor in Louisiana's Continued Prosperity* (October, 1961). This is essentially
"value added" in processing and marketing.

value of crop production for 1966 was reported at $357,140,000. Of this amount, $63,148,000 was for soybeans—more than double the previous year.

Table I

Cash Receipts from Sale of Farm Products, Louisiana, 1965.

Item	Farm Income	Percent of Total
Crops		
Cotton and cottonseed	$ 92,047,000	19.0
Rice	88,156,000	18.2
Sugar cane	54,294,000	11.2
Soybeans	31,385,000	6.5
Sweet potatoes	9,709,000	2.0
Fruits, nuts, and vegetables*	12,402,000	2.5
Forest and greenhouse	9,385,000	1.9
Other field crops**	7,358,000	1.5
Total crops	$304,736,000	62.8
Livestock and Products		
Cattle and calves	$ 88,566,000	18.3
Dairy products	52,120,000	10.8
Eggs	18,157,000	3.7
Broilers and chickens	16,095,000	3.3
Hogs	4,163,000	.9
Other	986,000	.2
Total	$180,087,000	37.2
All Commodities	$484,823,000	100.0

SOURCE: Louisiana Crop Reporting Service.

*Strawberries, snapbeans, cabbage, tomatoes, green peppers, cucumbers, watermelons, shallots, peaches, oranges, pecans, other.

**Corn, hay, wheat, white clover seed, oats, Irish potatoes, tobacco, tung nuts, and other field crops.

Timber Harvested

Commercial forests are an important part of Louisiana agriculture. Timber harvested in Louisiana in 1958 was valued at $70,450,000.[3]

[3] Forest Service, U.S. Department of Agriculture, *The Economic Importance of Timber in the United States*, Miscellaneous Publication No. 941 (July, 1963).

This was made up of saw logs, veneer logs, pulpwood, and "other" timber products. Value created (not necessarily all in Louisiana) from this base product was estimated in 1963 at $450 million by the United States Forest Service.

TRENDS IN PRODUCTION

Major Field Crops—Acreage, Yield, and Production

Cotton, rice, and sugar cane have historically been Louisiana's major field crops. Acreage, yield, and production of these and other crops are shown in Figures 2 through 8.

Acreages of cotton and corn have been drastically reduced since the 1930's (Figures 2 and 4). Decreasing cotton acreage (from around two million acres in the 1930's to 352,000 in 1966) primarily reflects government controls and mechanization (which made cotton unprofitable in hill areas). It is likely that cotton acreage, with some yearly variations, will be maintained around the 400,000 acre level, which is slightly above the 1966 level. Greatly reduced corn acreage (from around 1,600,000 acres in the 1930's to 185,000 acres in 1966) reflects the change from mule and horse power to mechanization. Most corn in Louisiana was produced for feeding workstock.

With some variation between years, the acreage of sugar cane has shown a slightly upward trend since 1930. This trend will likely continue. Rice acreage has increased since 1957. Acreage of soybeans has increased spectacularly, from about 40,000 acres in 1950 to over 871,000 in 1966, and is still increasing (Figure 3). Soybeans and pasture have replaced some of the cotton acreage. But a considerable amount of new land has also been cleared for soybeans, particularly in the Delta areas.

Improvements in technology and production practices have brought major increases in yields per acre for all crops (Figures 5 and 6). Thus, production of rice and sugar cane has generally trended up over the years (Figure 8). On the other hand, with declining acreage offset by increasing yields, cotton production has fluctuated around 500,000 bales since 1940 (Figure 7). Corn production has decreased since 1940 but is likely to level off and fluctuate around five million bushels (Figure 7). Potential increases in beef and hog production could cause this trend to be reversed and turn upward, with more corn produced for feeding purposes.

Livestock, Milk, and Poultry Production

Changes in livestock production have been equally as striking as those in crop production, as shown in Figures 9 through 12. While production of hogs and sheep has declined since 1930, beef produc-

FIGURE 2.   COTTON, RICE, AND SUGAR CANE: ACREAGE HARVESTED, LOUISIANA, 1930-1966.

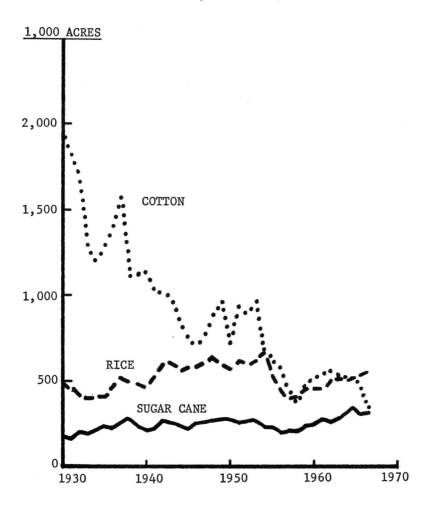

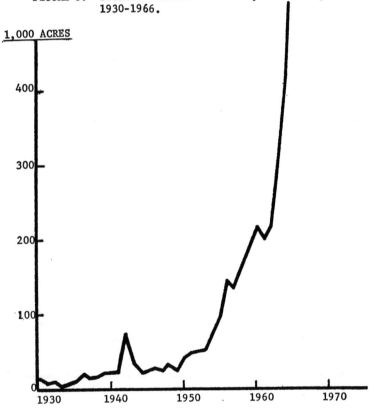

FIGURE 3. SOYBEAN ACREAGE HARVESTED, LOUISIANA, 1930-1966.

tion has increased considerably (Figure 9). Milk-cow numbers have declined also. But increased production per cow has more than offset the decline in numbers so that the total milk production has increased (Figures 10 and 11).

Poultry production, in the form of broilers and eggs, has also become a more important part of the agricultural picture since the 1930's (Figure 12).

FIGURE 4.   CORN, OATS, AND HAY: ACREAGE
            HARVESTED, LOUISIANA, 1930-1966.

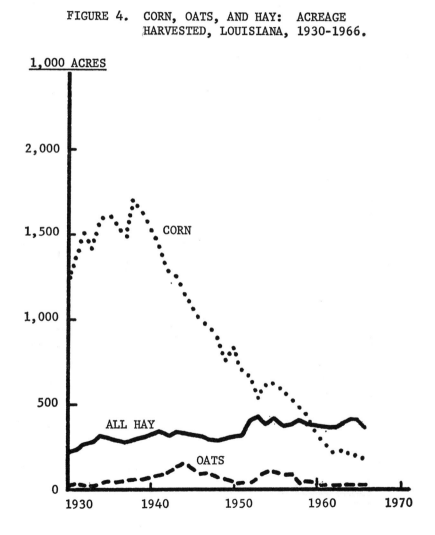

STRUCTURAL CHANGES
IN LOUISIANA FARMING

Farms, Land in Farms, Farm Size, and Capital
Investment in Farms in Louisiana

The Census shows that farms in Louisiana decreased from 124,000 in 1949 to 62,466 in 1964 (Figure 13 and Table II). However, average farm size increased from 96 acres in 1949 to 167 acres in 1964. Total land in farms in Louisiana decreased from about 11.2 million acres in 1949 to 10.4 million acres over the same fifteen years. The value of farmland and buildings alone increased considerably, from $6,983 per farm in 1949 to $38,636 per farm in 1964. This does not include invest-

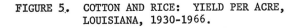

FIGURE 5. COTTON AND RICE: YIELD PER ACRE, LOUISIANA, 1930-1966.

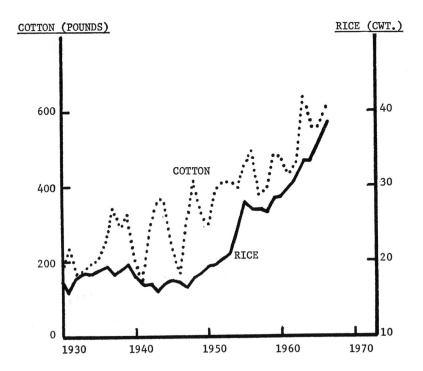

ment in livestock, equipment, or inventories of production supplies on hand.

The rate of change in farm numbers differs appreciably among

FIGURE 6.   SUGAR CANE AND CORN: YIELD PER ACRE,
            LOUISIANA, 1930-1966.

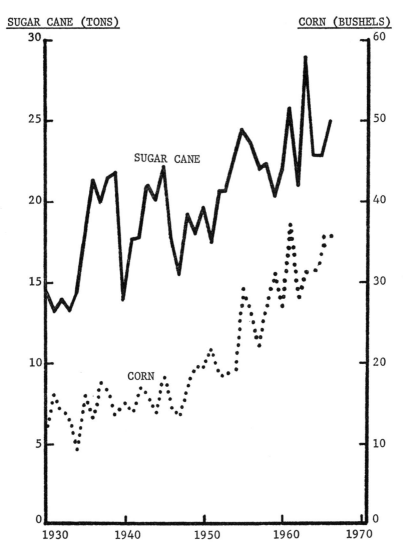

types of farming areas in Louisiana and is closely related to tenancy. For example, in Jefferson Davis Parish, with a relatively low level of tenancy (26.9 percent in 1954), there was a decrease of 158 farms during the twenty years from 1939 to 1959. In Madison Parish, with a relatively high level of tenancy (61 percent in 1954), there was a decrease of 683 farms over the same period. Of this decrease in number, 532 were of nonwhite operators, mostly tenants. Much of the decline in farm numbers is also reflected in an increase in the average size of farms in both parishes. Average farm size increased from 281.5 acres to 463.8 acres in Madison Parish from 1959 to 1964. The increase was from 339.4 to 439.4 acres in Jefferson Davis Parish.

Changes in Farms Measured by Value of Sales

There are fewer farms and fewer people on farms. This is a reflection of technological progress in the agricultural industry. The num-

FIGURE 7.   COTTON AND CORN PRODUCTION, LOUISIANA, 1930-1966.

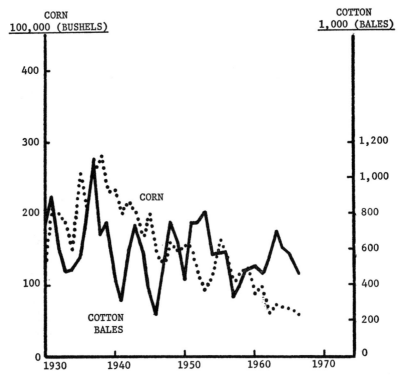

Table II

Land in Farms, Average Farm Size, and Value of Land and Buildings on Farms, Louisiana, Census Years, 1939–64.

Farm Characteristics	1939	1949	1959	1964
Land in farms (million acres)	9.9	11.2	10.3	10.4
Number of farms (1,000)	150	124	74[1]	62
Average size of farm (acres)	67	96	139	167
Value of land and buildings:[2]				
Per farm	$2,359	$6,983	$21,011	$38,636
Per acre	$35	$82	$175	$233

SOURCE: U.S. Census.

[1] Under the 1959 definition of a farm. Part of the decrease from 1949 to 1959 (11, 135) was due to a redefinition of a farm in the 1959 Census.

[2] Does not include investment in livestock, equipment, or inventory of production supplies on hand.

FIGURE 8.   RICE AND SUGAR CANE PRODUCTION, LOUISIANA, 1930-1966,

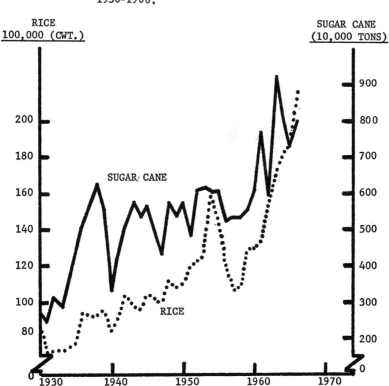

ber of "real" commercial family farms has actually increased, both in Louisiana and the United States. The major decline in number of farms has been among "subsistence" farms, i.e., those having gross sales of less than $2,500 per year (Table III). Many of these were also "phantom farms," as discussed later.

From 1949 to 1964, Louisiana farms with sales of $5,000 or more *increased* from 8,222 to 13,511 (Table III). During the same period, farms with sales of $2,500 or less declined from 51,200 to 6,174. "Other" farms, which includes retirement, residential, and "abnormal" farms, decreased from 53,705 in 1954 to 29,663 in 1964. *Thus, while*

FIGURE 9. CATTLE, SHEEP, AND SWINE NUMBERS, LOUISIANA, 1930-1966.

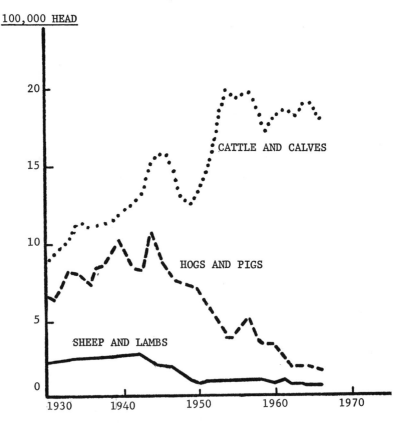

Table III

Selected Categories of Farms by Gross Farm Income, Louisiana, 1949–64.

Farms	1949	1954	1959	1964
Total farms	124,181	111,127	74,438[1]	62,466
Commercial farms	70,476	60,454	34,712	32,834
With sales of:				
$5,000 or more	8,222	11,980	12,497	13,511
$2,500 or less	51,200	34,514	13,011	6,174
"Other" farms	53,705	50,780	39,665	29,633

SOURCE: U.S. Census

[1] Part of the decrease from 1954 (11,135) is due to a census redefinition of a farm.

FIGURE 10.   NUMBER OF MILK COWS, LOUISIANA, 1930-1965.

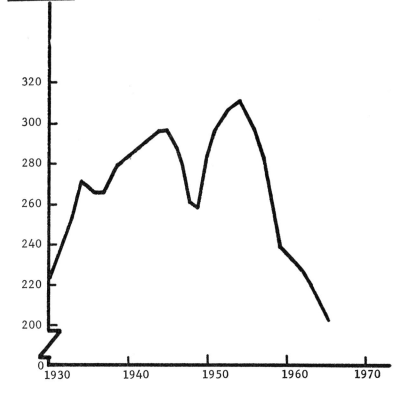

the total number of farms has decreased, the real production base of commercial Louisiana agriculture increased from 1949 to 1964.

Changes in Farm Size

From 1949 to 1964, there was a decrease of 683 farms (about 4 percent) in Louisiana among those with more than one hundred acres

FIGURE 11.   TOTAL MILK PRODUCED AND MILK PER COW, LOUISIANA, 1930-1965.

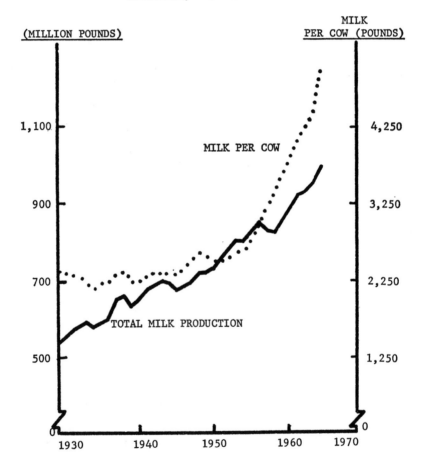

(Table IV). In the same period there was a decrease of 66,145 (or 60 percent) for farms of less than one hundred acres in size. Many of these, again, were tenant or "subsistence" farms. Most of the smaller farms could not support a mechanized operation or provide an ac-

FIGURE 12.   EGG PRODUCTION AND NUMBER OF BROILERS, LOUISIANA, 1930-1965.

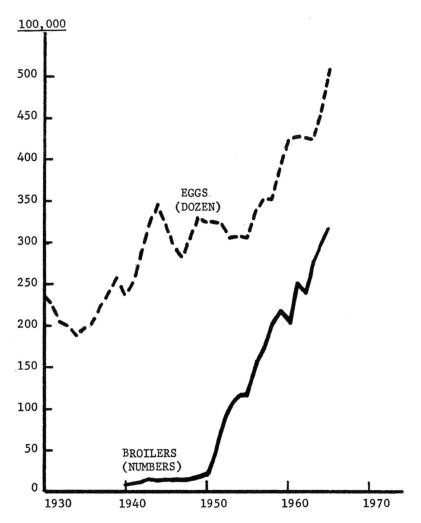

ceptable standard of living. Most of the land on these farms has been combined with other farms and is reflected in the increase in average size of farm and the increase in total land in farms (Table II).

Table IV
Change in Number of Farms, by Size Groupings, Louisiana, 1949–64.

Size of Farm	1949	1954	1959	1964
Farms of more than 100 acres	19,396	21,190	19,999	18,713
Farms of less than 100 acres	109,899	90,037	55,403	43,754

SOURCE: U.S. Census.

Changes in Land Use

The major categories of land use and their relative importance in 1964 are shown in Table V. In 1964 about 10.4 million acres were in farm land. Of this acreage about 3.1 million acres were in cropland (30 percent) and 5.4 million acres (52 percent) in land pastured.

While total acreage has remained relatively constant, land use has

FIGURE 13.   TRENDS IN NUMBER OF FARMS IN LOUISIANA, 1920-1964.

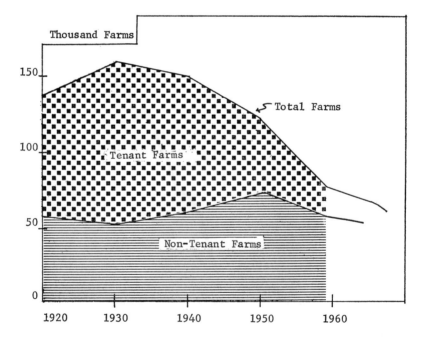

changed through the years. There has been a general decrease in row crop acreage and an increase in pastureland, particularly since 1930. In 1930, 51 percent of Louisiana farmland was in crops and only 24 percent was used for pasture. The increase in pasture and hay crops supports an increasingly important beef producing industry.

The changes in land use differ by areas. Although cropland in hilly areas is still being converted to pasture, timber and idle land in the flat delta and marshlands is still being cleared and/or drained for crop use. There are reasons to believe that acreage in cropland is likely to stabilize at around three million acres over the next few years.

Farm Ownership and Tenancy

Tenancy has decreased drastically in Louisiana. The combined total of full-owner and part-owner farms decreased from 53,159 to 50,057 from 1930 to 1964, or 6 percent (Table VI). During the same period, tenant farms decreased from 107,551 to 12,151, or 89 percent (Figure 13). The proportion of owner-operated farms increased from

Table V
Farm Land Use, Louisiana, 1964.

Category	Total Acreage	Percent of Total Farmland
Cropland		
Harvested	2,672,632	25.7
Not harvested and not pastured	452,612	4.3
Subtotal	3,125,244	30.0
Pasture		
Cropland used only for pasture	1,739,197	16.7
Open	2,003,709	19.3
Woodland pastured	1,719,026	16.5
Subtotal	5,461,932	52.5
Woodland not pastured	1,247,134	12.0
Other	576,735	5.5
Subtotal	1,823,869	17.5
Total	10,411,045	100.0

SOURCE: Compiled from the 1964 U.S. Census of Agriculture.

33 percent to 81 percent (Table VI). Tenancy is expected to stabilize at about 15 percent.

Table VI

Changes in Farm Ownership and Tenancy, Louisiana Farms, 1930–64.

Type of Tenure	1930	1959	1964
Full owners (number)	46,893	44,251	37,440
Part owners (number)	6,266	11,410	12,617
	53,159	55,661	50,057
All tenants (number)	107,551	18,302	12,151
Percent operated by owners	32.9	75.4	80.5

SOURCE: U.S. Census.

These data are particularly significant because they lend emphasis to the point that the owner-operated commercial "family farm" in Louisiana is very much here to stay. Quite the opposite from going out of business, the family farm is maintaining a respectable number as well as growing in average size. The family farm provides a stable productive base for Louisiana agriculture and is a very important segment of Louisiana's economy.

Louisiana's "Phantom" Farms

In Louisiana, and in the South generally, censuses have historically reported an "inflated" figure for "number of farms." A plantation with twelve to twenty sharecroppers has been counted as twelve or twenty separate farms. This is not quite accurate, since the plantation owner generally makes the major managerial decisions for the whole unit. This method of counting still prevailed in 1964 because of the Census definition relating farms and farm operators. [4]

As shown by the Census, farms from ten to sixty-nine acres in size decreased by 750,000 in the United States from 1954 to 1959. Seventy percent of that decrease occurred in the sixteen southern states, mainly because of the decrease in number of sharecroppers and tenants. *Thus, much of the decline in number of "farms" in Louisiana,*

[4] "The term 'Farm Operator' is used to designate a person who operates a farm. . . . He may be the owner . . . or a tenant, renter or share cropper. . . . The number of farm operators is the same as the number of farms," from the definition of "Farm Operator" in *U.S. Census of Agriculture, 1964* (Louisiana), Pt. 35, I, A3.

and in the South, is more fictitious than real. The same farm "managerial unit" is still there, operated now by hired labor rather than sharecroppers and, as a result, now counted as one farm rather than a dozen or twenty. The "phantom farms" are disappearing.

Changes in Technology, Mechanization, and Institutions

It is fairly well recognized that Louisiana agriculture, in common with United States agriculture generally, has undergone many revolutionary changes in recent years. The summary data in Table VII reflect both the degree and rapidity of some of those changes.

Table VII
Selected Measures of Change in Louisiana Agriculture.

Item	1930	1959	1964
Land in farms (1,000 acres)	9,355	10,347	10,411
Percent of land in farms	32.2	35.8	36
Number of farms	161,445	74,438	62,466
Average size of farms (acres)	58	139	167
Farms operated by owners (percent)	33	75	81
Number of tenant farms	107,551	18,302	12,151
Farm land used for crops (percent)	51	28	30
Farm land used for pasture (percent)	24	53	52
Horses and mules	317,185	87,392	—
Tractors	5,016	55,808	60,626

	1919	1940	1964
Cotton (1,000 acres)	1,343		511
Yield per acre (pounds)	109		544
Rice (1,000 acres)	456		513
Yield per acre (pounds)	1,620		3,300
Sugar cane (1,000 acres)	233		318
Yield per acre (tons)	10.4		22.7
Cattle and calves (1,000 head)	804		1,867
Farms with telephones		4,991	42,259
Farms with tractors		6,937	36,101
Percent of farms with tractors		4.6	57

SOURCE: In addition to U.S. census and U.S.D.A. data, some of this information comes from Louisiana Agricultural Experiment Station Bulletin No. 556, 1962.

In 1948 it required 8.48 man hours to produce one ton of sugar cane. Just ten years later, in 1958, this figure had been reduced to 4.08 hours, a decrease of over 50 percent. In 1964 this had further declined to about 1.2 man hours per ton. In 1940 sugar cane crops were harvested by hand. By 1959, 96 percent was harvested mechanically.

In 1950 about 3 percent of the cotton crop was harvested mechanically. In 1960 over 60 percent was harvested mechanically. Since 1953 nearly 100 percent of the rice crop has been harvested mechanically. Many acres of rice are now being planted, fertilized, and treated for insects by airplane. Common cultural practices for cotton production include "flaming" and application of chemicals for weed control, both before and after planting. Cotton "chopping" has been reduced from thirty-six to less than two hours per acre.

In 1955 most of Louisiana's milk production was moved from the dairy farm to the milk plant in ten-gallon cans. Today it is moved in bulk tanks and almost all dairy farms are equipped with mechanical milkers. The introduction of bulk tanks means that most milk handling is completely mechanized and milk is not exposed to the open air, from the cow to the consumer.

Most of the new production practices are speedier, more efficient, more dependable, and less costly than use of hand labor. They are both suited for and required for large acreages. Many have also contributed to increased yields per acre. Thus, these new practices have been widely adopted by progressive farmers as a risk reducing and more economic method of production.

The Impact of Technological Change

Many of the changes on farms have generated other complementary changes. For example, mechanical cotton pickers generally leave more trash in cotton than hand picking. Thus, most gins have had to add new machinery in order to take out the additional trash without loss of grade quality, and many gins have been completely replaced with new ones.

Mechanization and improved technology in agriculture have brought with them many complex and difficult economic and social problems. Their combined impact has been particularly striking and has disrupted many old institutions, tenancy and "share cropping" particularly. (Many people, over the years, have had to move off the land. Most of them were "subsistence" farmers at best, barely earning a reasonable living.) There have also been good results. Farms today are stable farm businesses, increasingly efficient, mechanized, mostly family owned and operated, larger, well-equipped, well-financed, and continually better managed by better educated managers. This kind of change adds strength to any industry.

With 43 percent fewer farms in 1964 than in 1954, Louisiana farmers produced and sold 10 percent more cattle, 392 percent more eggs, 446 percent more broilers, 668 percent more soybeans, 44 percent more sugar, 17 percent more corn, 6 percent more cotton, 7 percent more rice, and 69 percent more milk. The only notable declines during that ten year period were in hogs, sheep, and strawberries.

THE NONFARM SECTOR OF THE AGRICULTURAL ECONOMY

The Importance of Agribusiness in Louisiana

Estimates indicate that Louisiana farmers purchased over $234 million worth of producer goods (including labor) and sold farm products valued at nearly $500 million in 1964. The producer goods were obtained through agribusiness firms domiciled primarily in Louisiana. Other local agribusiness firms financed, assembled, processed, stored, advertised, and distributed farm products to consumers at an estimated retail value of over $1.5 billion.

Fragmentary data show that agribusiness firms engaged in processing and distributing agricultural products in Louisiana had an investment considerably in excess of $300 million in 1959. Some of these investments, by type of service, are shown in Table VIII.

The estimates in Table VIII are out-of-date and incomplete. For example, farm equipment and farm supply firms are not included. Since 1959 there have been sizeable increases in investments in slaughter plants, grain elevators, oil mills, and poultry and lumber processing facilities in Louisiana. Necessary improvements in existing plants, reconstruction, additions, and updating of equipment, constantly add to investment in agribusiness firms.

The types of agribusiness firms shown in Table VIII are just a few of the many types of firms closely allied to farming operations. Other types of businesses, less directly related, include trucking, rail and water transportation firms, sugar and oil refineries, wholesalers and retailers for both producer and consumer goods, and many agriculturally-oriented legal, financing, utility, and regulatory services.

In rural areas particularly, farming and the related agribusinesses support the nonfarm sectors of the local economy. Much of Louisiana is rural. In these areas the economic health and viability of the farm business is of considerable concern and importance to the population generally. A poor crop year is quickly reflected in a general decline in local business, lower tax revenues, and a general decrease in economic activity. A good crop year has the opposite effect.

The importance of Louisiana farmers as customers of agribusiness firms is reflected in the list of selected expenditures in Table IX. Preliminary U.S.D.A. estimates indicate Louisiana farmers spent over $200 million in cash for various production items in 1965. Over $50 million was paid for hired labor. Most of this money remained in the locality where earned to meet family living expenses.

If depreciation, taxes, interest on farm debt, and net rent were added, total production expenses would amount to about $335 million.

Table VIII
Estimated Investment of Some Agribusiness Firms in Louisiana, 1959.

Facility	Estimated Investment
Raw sugar and syrup mills	$ 51,000,000
Livestock auctions and other markets, major slaughter and packing houses	13,000,000
Cotton gins, warehouses and compresses	58,500,000
Oil mills	12,000,000
Canning plants	5,000,000
Rice mills	24,000,000
Grain elevators	21,000,000
Rice driers, rice and grain warehouses	31,000,000
Feed mills	10,000,000
Milk product plants	36,000,000
Poultry processing plants	1,500,000
Lumber mills	50,000,000
Total	$313,000,000

SOURCE: *Agriculture: Leading, Serving, Unfolding*, Louisiana State University Centennial Publication, 1960.

THE FUTURE OF AGRICULTURE IN LOUISIANA

Continued industrial development in Louisiana is bringing a more desirable agriculture-business-industry "mix" to the state's economy. In the past, Louisiana's predominantly agricultural economy has not been very well balanced with business and other industry. As a result, a very poor crop year could have a great and deleterious effect on the general economy. Growth of new business and new industry in Louisiana should add needed economic stability.

However, agriculture will remain an important part of Louisiana's economy in the future. The real basis for a viable agricultural industry remains. Louisiana agriculture is productive and competitive.

Table IX

Selected Expenditures by Louisiana Farmers for
Production Items, 1965

Item	Expenditure
Feed	$ 53,357,000
Seed	8,663,000
Fertilizer and lime	24,723,000
Building materials	23,760,000
Petroleum, feed and oil	18,848,000
Repair parts, tires, batteries, etc.	8,590,000
Miscellaneous hardware	1,673,000
Small hand tools	663,000
Containers	602,000
Building materials	498,000
Pesticides	5,607,000
Veterinary medicines	1,668,000
Greenhouse and nursery supplies	521,000
Dairy supplies	433,000
Harness and saddlery	206,000
Tractors	11,189,000
Trucks	6,012,000
Automobiles	14,410,000
Other machinery and equipment	17,578,000
	$201,507,000
Hired labor (estimated)	50,000,000
	$251,507,000

SOURCE: Mimeo Report. Purchasing Division, Farmer Cooperative Service, U.S.D.A. and Economic Research Service, Service Report #84 (Preliminary), September, 1966.

This fact is quite clear. As noted earlier, there have been rather drastic changes in the methods, institutions, and structure of the agricultural industry in Louisiana over the past thirty years. But, through all this drastic upheaval, the family farm has persisted. The number of owner-operated farms has remained relatively constant, and these farms are now larger, better equipped, better managed, and more profitable than they were thirty years ago at the peak in farm numbers (Figure 13). A considerable proportion of Louisiana's farm land is sufficiently productive to compete favorably with other areas. In addition, in some areas new land is being brought into production by clearing forests and draining marshes.

Farm managers are increasingly better educated, receptive to new technology and methods of production, and alert to the potential for profit from new production possibilities. The tremendous increase in soybean acreage and value in Louisiana over so short a period proves this point (from 216,000 acres and $10,248,000 in 1960, to 871,000 acres and $63,148,000 in 1966).

Any forecast concerning the future of an industry also involves some assumptions as to demand for its product. The increase predicted in population, domestic and foreign, leaves little doubt that future needs for food and fiber will be much greater. Great increases in population are being forecast for those countries least able and least likely to supply their own needs in the future. This country's increasing tendency to adopt a humane and benevolent attitude toward the needs of less fortunate people suggests an increasing future demand for agricultural products. Despite an increasingly productive agriculture in the Western World, some forecasters predict an inability to meet world-wide needs for food and fiber by the year 2000. While the current supply of agricultural products may seem relatively adequate now, it is not unlikely that we may face shortages of essential foods and fibers in the foreseeable future.

It is entirely possible that much land retired from production in past years may have to be brought back into production and "new" land developed. Louisiana is one of the few areas where much potentially productive land is still available for agricultural development.

Implications for Commercial Agriculture

Commercial farms will continue to grow in size and mechanization, although possibly not as rapidly as in the past five years. Fewer, better educated farmers can work together more easily than can large numbers. Thus, more attention will likely be given to farmer co-operatives and bargaining groups in the future as farmers come to realize their role as businessmen in the "new" agricultural industry. There will be more integration, both vertical and horizontal. Marketing orders and contracts will become increasingly feasible for many producers. Farm organizations will become stronger and there will be more interest in developing farmer bargaining power. Farmers will likely do more for themselves and depend less upon government.

New techniques will continue to be developed, both in production and marketing of agricultural products. New techniques will create, at one and the same time, both new problems and new opportunities. Louisiana agriculture will participate in these new discoveries. Those which are worthwhile will be adopted and will contribute to the ability of the Louisiana industry to meet its share of the responsibility for providing food and fiber for a growing population, at home and abroad.

POSTWAR ECONOMIC GROWTH
AND FLUCTUATIONS IN LOUISIANA
Stephen L. McDonald

The fluctuations in economic activity commonly called business cycles are a phenomenon of growth. They result primarily from variations in the rate of real investment, or capital formation, by means of which we increase the stock of plant and equipment and incorporate into this investment the technological innovations that largely account for growth of output and income per employed person. Variations in the rate of investment, in turn, are due to a number of factors, chief among them being uncertainty about the future level of demand in relation to capacity, the tendency of investors to communicate their feelings of optimism or pessimism to each other, and discontinuity in the technological innovations that create major new investment opportunities.

Since the economy of any state is an integral part of the national economy, one expects to find basic similarity between state growth and fluctuations and national growth and fluctuations.[1] Yet each state specializes to some extent by producing goods and services in which it has a comparative advantage and exchanging them for the special- ties of other states. Such specialization makes it possible for a state to grow more or less rapidly and to experience more or less severe fluctuations than the nation as a whole.[2] Given the conditions of

[1] State boundaries do not necessarily define natural economic regions, of course. Interest in state economies per se stems almost wholly from state governments' dependence upon and jurisdiction over economic activities conducted within state boundaries.

[2] It is important to distinguish between growth of aggregate economic activity and growth of per capita income in a state. State economies may grow

supply, the matter depends upon the nationwide growth and cyclical sensitivity of demand for the goods and services involved in a state's specialization. The fast-growing or cyclically unstable areas of the country, for instance, are those areas that have relatively specialized in fast-growing or cyclically unstable industries.

The pattern of local specialization within the national economy naturally changes with the passage of time and the experience of general economic growth. Per capita incomes rise, altering the structure of demands for different goods and services; natural resources in some areas become relatively exhausted; the geographical distribution of population shifts; and technological progress creates new industries and new natural resource bases. Given the distribution of natural advantages among states and regions, growth leadership tends to shift from one area to another as the national economy expands. New patterns of local cyclical fluctuations tend to emerge. Of particular importance here, the areas which benefit especially from the establishment of new growth industries (particularly industries that are capital intensive) tend to experience investment "booms" in the transition phase as the necessary plant and equipment capacity is created. These are followed by investment "lulls" in which demand is allowed to grow up toward the limits of new capacity installed. During such transitional booms, which may span several ordinary business cycles, local economic activity expands very rapidly and business recessions may be relatively mild. During the subsequent lulls, in contrast, local economic growth slows markedly and business recessions may be relatively severe.[3]

There is evidence that in the postwar period Louisiana has experienced a long investment boom, followed by a shorter but pronounced lull, of the type just described, with the principal growth industries involved being the production of oil and gas, chemicals, and light metals.[4] The boom appears to have run from 1947 to 1957,

---

at different rates without producing similar differences in growth rates of state per capita incomes, provided interstate migration of labor and capital is free and sensitive to differential earning opportunities. In point of fact, however, the barriers to migration, particularly over long distances, are substantial. Consequently, there is some correlation between growth rates of aggregate economic activity and per capita income among states.

[3] The idea of long cycles in the process of regional economic growth is elaborated upon in Stephen L. McDonald, *Growth and Fluctuations in the Economy of Louisiana, 1947–1959* (Baton Rouge, 1961), 12–18.

[4] *Ibid.*, esp. 115–18.

the lull from 1957 to 1962 at least. Interstate migration tends to limit inequalities in state per capita incomes despite marked differences in rates of growth of economic activity;[5] but since population movements are not highly sensitive to income disparities between widely separated areas, the relative growth of Louisiana's per capita income reflects the long swing in the state's economic activity from 1947 to 1962. Per capita personal income in the state rose from 66.9 percent of the national average in 1947 to 76.4 percent in 1957. It then fell to 72.2 percent of the national average in 1962, nearly all of the decline occurring between 1957 and 1960. In 1963 the ratio of Louisiana to national per capita income rose very slightly to 72.5 percent.[6]

During the period 1947–63 there were four recessions in general business activity throughout the country. The dates of these recessions, each corresponding to the peak-to-trough phase of a business cycle, were: November, 1948, to October, 1949; July, 1953, to August, 1954; July, 1957, to April, 1958; and May, 1960, to February, 1961.[7] Together with connecting expansions, these recessions identify the fluctuations in economic activity that form the subject matter of the remainder of this essay. Our procedure hereinafter is to compare economic fluctuations in Louisiana with the corresponding fluctuations in the United States as a whole in order to illuminate the distinctive pattern of Louisiana's postwar economic growth. The comparison is made in terms of five series of monthly economic data, corrected for seasonal variation so as to reveal turning points of business cycles proper. Two of the series, total personal income and

[5] The economies of Arkansas, Louisiana, New Mexico, Oklahoma, and Texas have grown at widely different rates in recent decades; yet due to interstate migration, which is relatively cheap between neighboring states, per capita incomes in these states have grown at very similar rates. For additional detail see Stephen L. McDonald, "Some Factors in the Recent Economic Development of the Southwest," *Southwestern Social Science Quarterly*, XLV (March, 1965), 329–39.

[6] Per capita income data from U.S. Department of Commerce, *Personal Income by States Since 1929*; and *Survey of Current Business*, August issues, various years. As the preceding footnote suggests, relative per capita incomes in the other southwestern states have varied in a pattern similar to that observed in Louisiana since 1947. Of the group, only Arkansas has failed to suffer a decline in relative per capita income since 1957.

[7] These are identified as the dates of turning points in general business activity by the National Bureau of Economic Research, a privately endowed research organization of recognized authority on business cycles in the United States. Dates provided in Geoffrey H. Moore, *Measuring Recessions*, National Bureau of Economic Research Occasional Paper 61 (New York, 1958), 260, and subsequent press releases.

total nonagricultural employment, reflect broad aggregates of economic activity. The remaining three series—employment in manufacturing, employment in mining, and employment in contract construction—reflect narrower aggregates of activity that are cyclically sensitive and embrace the major fast-growing industries in Louisiana. Employment in contract construction is the best single state indicator of capital formation. The period covers 1947 through 1963, with initial and terminal years showing periods of high and expanding, but not cyclically peak-level, economic activity.

We shall first examine consecutive business cycles in the general context of economic growth. Then we shall compare typical patterns of cyclical fluctuations in Louisiana and the United States as a whole.

ECONOMIC GROWTH
AND CONSECUTIVE FLUCTUATIONS

Chart 1 shows monthly personal income in Louisiana and the United States, 1947–63. As is true also with Charts 2–5 to follow, the data are plotted on a logarithmic or ratio scale, which gives equal vertical space to equal *percentage* differences. Thus the comparative slopes of the two plotted series indicate the comparative percentage rates of change in the two series. The series with the steeper slope over a given time period is increasing (or decreasing) at the higher percentage rate. The scale for Louisiana data is on the righthand margin of the chart, the scale for the United States on the lefthand margin. The shaded areas on the chart represent periods of general business recession as identified above.

Chart 1 conveys the general impression of quite similar patterns of growth and fluctuations in the Louisiana and national economies. In view of Louisiana's degree of specialization, the observed similarity indicates the interdependence of regional economies and the effective unity achieved through interregional exchange of goods and services. Nonetheless, it is apparent from Chart 1 that personal income grew more rapidly in Louisiana than in the United States as a whole from 1947 to 1957, but less rapidly from 1957 to 1962. In both Louisiana and the nation the depressing effect of business recessions on personal income is clearly discernible, although in about half the instances the effect is only to slow down the rate of growth. In the first two recessions of the period, 1948–49 and 1953–54, growth of personal income was less severely depressed in Louisiana than in

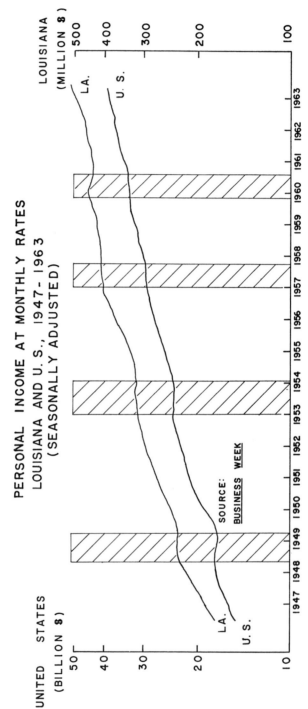

CHART I

PERSONAL INCOME AT MONTHLY RATES
LOUISIANA AND U.S., 1947-1963
(SEASONALLY ADJUSTED)

UNITED STATES
(BILLION $)

LOUISIANA
(MILLION $)

LA.

U. S.

SOURCE:
BUSINESS WEEK

LA.

U. S.

the United States as a whole; in the last two recessions, 1957–58 and 1960–61, the reverse was true. Over the whole period, Louisiana personal income consistently lagged behind national personal income at both peaks and troughs of cycles, suggesting that the Louisiana economy typically responds to cyclical disturbances originating in other sections of the country.

In Chart 2 we have the monthly record of total nonagricultural employment in Louisiana and the United States, 1947–63. Again the marked similarity of growth and fluctuations in the two areas is apparent. It is clear also that, as with personal income, growth of nonagricultural employment was at a higher rate in Louisiana than in the nation as a whole between 1947 and 1957, but at a lower rate in Louisiana after 1957. Indeed, in contrast with the country as a whole, there was no upward trend in nonagricultural employment in Louisiana between 1957 and 1962. All of the recessions of the period produced actual reductions in nonagricultural employment in both state and nation. In the first two recessions, the reductions were relatively smaller in Louisiana than in the United States as a whole; but in the last two recessions, the reductions were relatively larger in Louisiana. The state lagged behind the nation at cyclical peaks and troughs of nonagricultural employment in all recessions of the period except the final one in 1960–61.

In general, the state-national comparison of growth and fluctuations in nonagricultural employment reveals the same pattern of relative behavior as the similar comparison with respect to personal income. By both of these highly aggregative measures of economic activity, Louisiana is shown to have grown more rapidly than the nation from 1947 to 1957, but less rapidly than the nation from 1957 to 1962. By both measures, Louisiana's recessions were relatively less severe than the nation's in the 1947–57 period, relatively more severe in the 1957–62 period. Both measures indicate a tendency for Louisiana to lag behind the nation at cyclical turning points both before and after 1957, although there is no clear lag in nonagricultural employment in the 1960–61 recession. These findings are consistent with the long-cycle hypothesis regarding Louisiana's postwar economic growth, the lag at regular cyclical turning points simply indicating that recessions typically begin and end with industries more characteristic of the rest of the country than of Louisiana. We now see what further insight can be gained from comparisons based on less aggregative economic series.

CHART II

TOTAL NONAGRICULTURAL EMPLOYMENT
LOUISIANA AND U. S., 1947-1963
(SEASONALLY ADJUSTED)

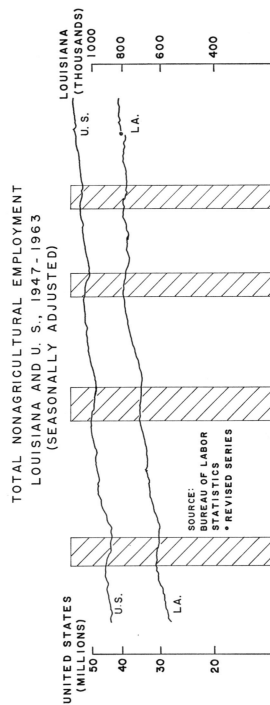

SOURCE:
BUREAU OF LABOR
STATISTICS
• REVISED SERIES

CHART III

EMPLOYMENT IN MANUFACTURING
LOUISIANA AND U. S., 1947–1963
(SEASONALLY ADJUSTED)

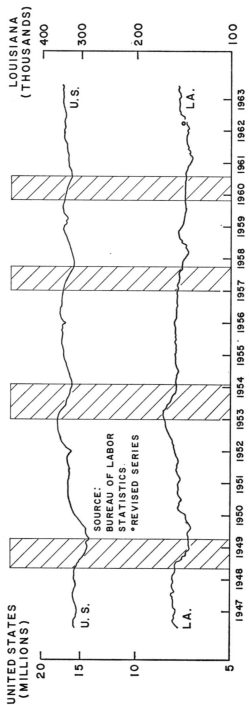

SOURCE:
BUREAU OF LABOR
STATISTICS.
°REVISED SERIES

The record of monthly manufacturing employment in Louisiana and the United States, 1947–63, is depicted in Chart 3. Here the state-national comparison presents a picture that bears a general resemblance to the preceding ones, but there are significant differences. In manufacturing employment, the Louisiana rate of growth was lower than the national rate of growth throughout the entire period from 1947 to 1962. From 1947–55 there was a slight upward trend in the United States as a whole but only a horizontal trend in Louisiana. After 1955 the national trend was horizontal, while the Louisiana trend was distinctly downward. Cyclical reductions in manufacturing employment during the first two recessions of the period were of about the same relative magnitude in both Louisiana and the United States, but in the last two recessions the reductions were relatively less severe in Louisiana. During all four recessions the reductions in manufacturing employment were spread over longer periods of time in Louisiana than in the nation as a whole. Louisiana lagged behind the rest of the nation at cyclical peaks and troughs, particularly the latter, of manufacturing employment. The lag at troughs appears to have lengthened with each successive recession, but this appearance may be due to erratic disturbances combined with the influence of a downward secular trend in Louisiana following the recession of 1953–54. In general, except for the lag at cyclical turning points, the relative behavior of manufacturing employment in Louisiana explains none of the relative behavior of personal income or total nonagricultural employment in the postwar period. Apparently manufacturing employment, as such, contributed neither to the long swing in Louisiana's postwar growth nor to the increased relative severity of the state's recessions after 1957.

Chart 4, which shows monthly employment in mining in Louisiana and the United States, 1947–63, is a study in contrasts. In large measure the contrasts result from the fact that in Louisiana "mining" consists almost entirely of oil and gas production, while in the rest of the country it embraces the extraction of a number of other types of minerals (chiefly coal and metallic ores) in addition to oil and gas. It is relevant also that in oil and gas production most employment is in connection with the drilling and equipping of wells, but in other mineral industries the greater part of employment is associated with extraction proper. Mining employment in the United States as a whole followed a declining secular trend over the entire period after 1947. But in Louisiana the trend of mining employment

CHART IV

EMPLOYMENT IN MINING

LOUISIANA AND U. S., 1947-1963
(SEASONALLY ADJUSTED)

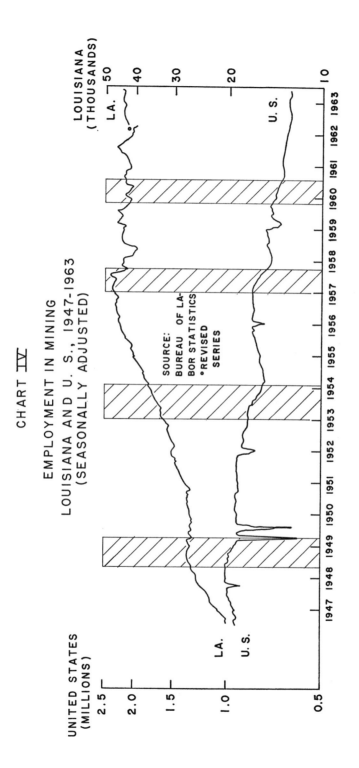

was steeply upward from 1947 to 1957, and then moderately downward for the remainder of the period. The most significant fact for the present purposes is the dramatic change in the trend of Louisiana's mining employment in about 1957. This year obviously marks a major turning point in the state's oil and gas industry, particularly as regards the drilling and equipping of wells. As for cyclical fluctuations in mining employment, the nationwide reductions during recessions were consistent and pronounced throughout the period under study. In Louisiana, however, there has been no consistent pattern of change during recessions. Only in the recession of 1957–58 did mining employment in Louisiana actually fall, and that decline extended well into 1959. It rose steeply during the recession of 1953–54. In the other two recessions, 1948–49 and 1960–61, cyclical behavior is obscured by erratic movements in Louisiana's mining employment, but apparently growth was only checked. It is clear that employment in oil and gas production is not highly sensitive to the business cycle, that the dominant influences on such employment are longer-run growth trends. The sharp change in the trend about 1957 helps explain the long swing in Louisiana's postwar growth rate.

Chart 5 shows monthly employment in contract construction in Louisiana and the United States, 1947–63. This chart throws further light on the decline in Louisiana's growth rate after 1957, and on the tendency of the state to lag behind the rest of the country at cyclical turning points. From 1947 to 1957 the growth of construction employment was more rapid in Louisiana than in the nation as a whole. After 1957, at least until mid-1961, the trend in Louisiana was sharply downward, while in the rest of the country it was approximately horizontal. The cyclical instability of employment in contract construction has been far greater in Louisiana than in the country as a whole during the postwar period. This suggests that business construction, as opposed to personal residential construction, has been relatively more important in Louisiana. The markedly different trends in Louisiana's construction employment before and after 1957, therefore, may well reflect a long investment boom and subsequent lull in the state. In any case, during all four recessions of the period under study the construction employment reductions in Louisiana were more pronounced and longer than in the rest of the nation. Moreover, the peaks and troughs in the state's construction employment consistently lagged behind those of the United States as a whole.

CHART V

EMPLOYMENT IN CONTRACT CONSTRUCTION
LOUISIANA AND U. S., 1947-1963
(SEASONALLY ADJUSTED)

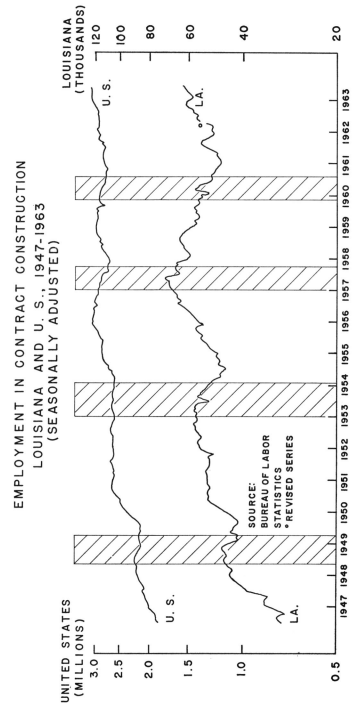

The analysis thus far supports the hypothesis of a long cycle in Louisiana economic activity from 1947 to 1962. The evidence is consistent with the view that the long cycle reflects an investment boom in oil and gas, capital intensive manufacturing, and perhaps other business capacity, followed by an investment lull in which the excess capacity was gradually absorbed. The observed lags in turning points of Louisiana business cycles suggest that the state's principal growth industries are of below-average sensitivity to cyclical disturbances. We now complete our analysis with a comparative study of typical business cycle patterns in Louisiana and the United States.

TYPICAL BUSINESS CYCLE PATTERNS

To measure and compare typical business cycle patterns, it is helpful to express all cycles in common units of measurement and to divide them into comparable phases. A well known and widely used method is employed here.[8] First, each complete cycle, running from initial trough to terminal trough, is identified. We use for this purpose the dates of turning points in general business activity identified above, and the cycles so defined are called "reference cycles." Second, the average of a given series, which may be expressed in terms of dollars, workers, tons or whatever, is computed for each separate reference cycle. Third, the monthly values of the series in each cycle are expressed as percentages of the cycle average. The result is an index number series for each cycle with the cycle average having the value of 100. Since each cycle is thus described in terms of its own average, the procedure has the effect of removing *inter*cyclical trend from the underlying series while leaving in the series its *intra*cyclical trend. Fourth, each cycle is divided into nine periods. Period I is the three months centering on the initial trough; Period V is the three months centering on the peak; and Period IX is the three months centering on the terminal trough. Periods II–IV divide the expansion phase into three parts of equal length—the length of each part depending upon the duration of the expansion phase. Similarly, Periods VI–VIII divide the contraction phase into three parts of equal length. Fifth, and finally, the typical reference cycle for each series is computed by averaging the separate cycle index numbers for each

[8] The method is extensively used in the studies of business cycles by the National Bureau of Economic Research. For a fuller explanation see A. F. Burns and W. C. Mitchell, *Measuring Business Cycles* (Princeton, 1946), Chap. 2.

of the nine periods. The result is one representative cycle for each series showing the average value of the series in each of Periods I–IX expressed as a percentage of the average value for the whole cycle.

CHART VI

PERSONAL INCOME
TYPICAL REFERENCE CYCLE PATTERNS
LOUISIANA AND U. S.

FOUR CYCLES, 1947–1961

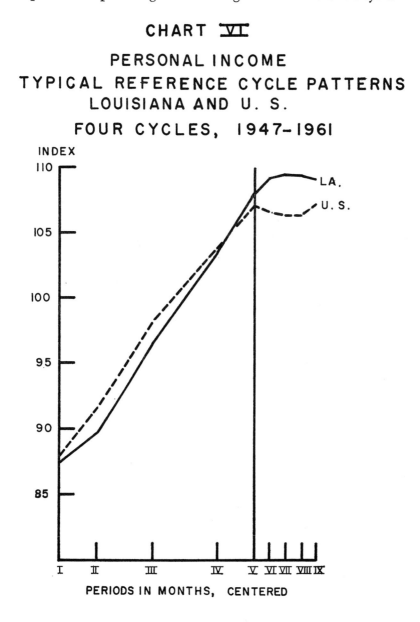

Chart 6 shows typical reference cycle patterns in personal income for both Louisiana and the United States during the four cycles embraced in the period under examination (the last recession occurring in 1960–61). The strong upward trend in personal income in both areas stands out in the chart, the values at the typical terminal trough (Period IX) being far above the values at the typical initial trough (Period I). It is apparent that since 1947, growth typically has been more rapid in Louisiana than in the country as a whole during the expansion phase of the cycle, especially from Period III to Period V. The typical lag of Louisiana at cyclical turning points also is evident. On the average, state personal income has achieved a cyclical peak in Period VII, as compared with Period V for the nation. It then has declined for two periods, VII–IX, during which the national personal income was beginning a new cyclical expansion.

A similar picture of comparative cyclical behavior is given in Chart 7, which shows typical reference cycle patterns in total nonagricultural employment in Louisiana and the United States. Again, we observe faster growth in Louisiana during the last half of the expansion phase and a distinct lag at the upper turning point. Louisiana's lag at troughs is not so clear, but the presence of a lag is suggested by the relatively slow recovery in Periods I–III of the expansion phase. Louisiana's recessions in total nonagricultural employment clearly have been shorter and milder on average than have the nation's during the postwar period. Over the typical cycle as a whole, the state's growth in nonagricultural employment has been markedly faster than has the rest of the country's.

The comparison of reference cycle patterns in manufacturing employment, shown in Chart 8, leads to quite different conclusions. The typical Louisiana cycle in manufacturing employment has a smaller amplitude than the national cycle; it also exhibits a distinct downward trend from initial to terminal trough, in contrast to the slight upward trend in the national cycle. Although state and national turning points coincide at the peak of the typical cycle, some tendency for Louisiana to lag at troughs is suggested by its very slow recovery from Period I to Period II in the expansion phase. However, the most significant impression given by Chart 8 is that of basically similar cyclical patterns in manufacturing employment, except for a smaller amplitude in Louisiana. It is clear that Louisiana's manufacturing industries are relatively insensitive to cyclical disturbances.

As Chart 9 shows, typical reference cycle patterns in mining employment during the postwar period differ widely between Louisiana and the rest of the country. The trend in Louisiana has been steeply

CHART VII

TOTAL NONAGICULTURAL EMPLOYMENT
TYPICAL REFERENCE CYCLE PATTERNS
LOUISIANA AND U. S.
FOUR CYCLES, 1947-1961

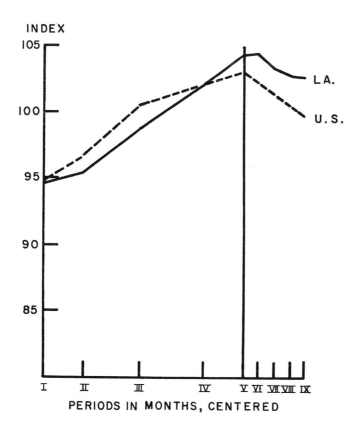

upward, and recessions have been almost negligible on average. In contrast, the trend in the United States as a whole has been markedly downward, and recessions typically have been severe. On the average, the cyclical peak in United States mining employment has been reached in Period III (only half-way into the expansion phase

CHART VIII

EMPLOYMENT IN MANUFACTURING
TYPICAL REFERENCE CYCLE PATTERNS
LOUISIANA AND U. S.
FOUR CYCLES, 1947–1961

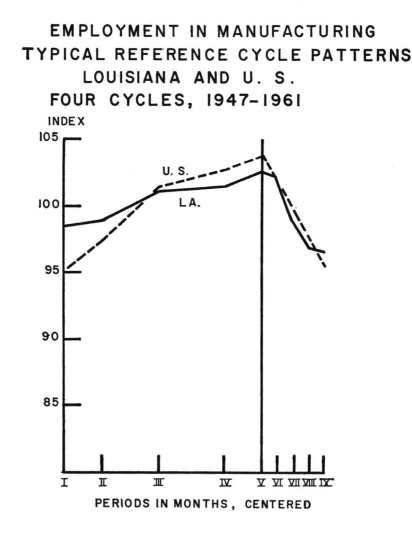

of general business) while the typical peak in Louisiana has been delayed until Period VIII (when recessions in general business were nearing their end). The distinctive cyclical pattern of mining employment in Louisiana obviously helps explain the lagging peaks and mild recessions shown earlier in the state's personal income and total nonagricultural employment.

Finally, Chart 10 shows typical reference cycle patterns for Louisi-

CHART IX

EMPLOYMENT IN MINING
TYPICAL REFERENCE CYCLE PATTERNS
LOUISIANA AND U. S.
FOUR CYCLES, 1947-1961

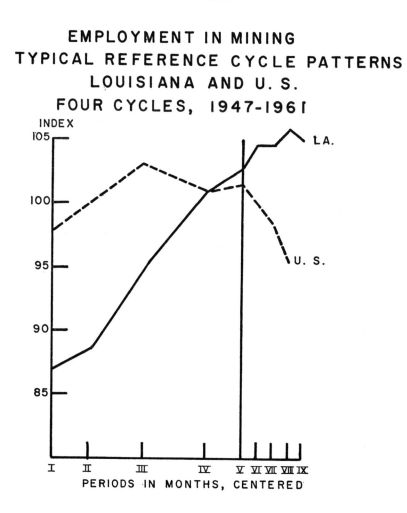

ana and the United States in contract construction employment. Here, again, quite different patterns of cyclical fluctuations are revealed. From trough to trough, on average, growth of construction employment has been faster in Louisiana than in the rest of the nation. Moreover, the amplitude of the typical Louisiana cycle has been much greater than that of the national cycle. While the nation's

CHART X

EMPLOYMENT IN CONTRACT CONSTRUCTION
TYPICAL REFERENCE CYCLE PATTERNS
LOUISIANA AND U. S.
FOUR CYCLES, 1947-1961

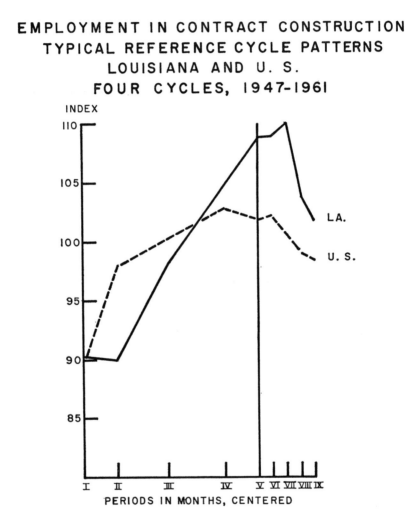

typical peak in construction employment was achieved in Period IV of the cycle, Louisiana's was delayed until Period VII. A shorter Louisiana lag has been typical at the terminal trough, the state's cyclical recovery beginning only with Period II in the expansion phase of general business. So some of the typical Louisiana lag at cyclical turning points in personal income and total nonagricultural employment is traceable to contract construction employment.

SUMMARY

In order to summarize our findings, therefore, we can say that during the postwar period, Louisiana's economic growth appears to have passed through two phases, which together suggest a long cycle superimposed upon and thus shaping the briefer fluctuations commonly called business cycles. In the first phase, 1947–57, Louisiana grew more rapidly than the nation as a whole; in the second phase, 1957–62, it grew less rapidly than the nation as a whole. While the state was growing more rapidly, Louisiana's business recessions were milder than the nation's; but while it was growing more slowly, the reverse was true. Throughout the postwar period, however, Louisiana has lagged behind the rest of the country at cyclical turning points, which suggests that the state's economy typically responds to cyclical disturbances originating elsewhere.

Both the two-phase pattern of growth and the lags at turning points of business cycles seem to be closely associated with two major industries in the state: mining (chiefly oil and gas production) and contract construction. Employment in both of these industries grew more rapidly in Louisiana than in the nation as a whole from 1947 to 1957, but less rapidly in Louisiana than in the nation as a whole from 1957 to 1962. The postwar cyclical behavior of employment in contract construction in Louisiana suggests that, relatively, it has been heavily influenced by business construction. These observations lead to the inference that the apparent long cycle in Louisiana's postwar growth reflects a long investment boom in oil and gas production and closely related capital-intensive industries, followed by a lull during which demand has been allowed to catch up with available capacity.

This analysis should not be taken to suggest that the long boom of 1947–57 must repeat itself. The South Louisiana and offshore oil drilling boom probably cannot repeat itself for obvious reasons. Some of the major new industries locating in the state during 1947–57, such as petrochemicals and light metals, were then relatively young industries in their phase of fastest growth. They may never again experience such high growth rates. If and when a new long boom comes to Louisiana, it is more likely to result from still newer industries attracted by the economic assets of the state than from the reinvigoration of old ones.

PART II
BANKING, INTERNATIONAL
TRADE, AND REGULATION

GROWTH, STRUCTURE, AND ADEQUACY OF COMMERCIAL BANKING IN LOUISIANA

Thomas R. Beard and
Edward B. Selby, Jr.

Few would deny the crucial role of the financial sector in the development of an economy. Any society above a subsistence level depends upon specialization for its very existence. Yet no appreciable division of labor would be possible in an economy without money, and the prospects for substantial development would be slight were there no facilities for the lending and borrowing of funds.

In discussing the role of lending and borrowing, economists are fond of pointing out that debt and credit are the same thing looked at from two different points of view. Both involve an obligation to pay in the future, usually stated in terms of a fixed sum of money. The obligation is a credit from the point of view of the economic unit to which the payment will be made and a debt from the viewpoint of the economic unit that is obliged to pay. Thus, the total amount of debt outstanding at a given time must be equal to the amount of outstanding credit. Judging the optimum volume of debt (credit) is extremely complicated for both the individual economic unit and the total economy. But just as it is possible for individuals, businesses, and/or governments to incur too much debt (extend too much credit) for their own or the economy's welfare, it is also possible for debt (credit) to be inadequate to meet society's needs.

THE ROLE OF FINANCIAL
INSTITUTIONS IN THE ECONOMY

Perhaps the crucial role of financial institutions in the modern economy can best be appreciated by looking backward to an earlier era. In what might be termed a precredit stage of economic development, the dominant form of financing is self-financing.[1] Spending units can acquire goods and services only to the extent of the funds received from the sale of other goods and services. Since large-scale production is a time-consuming process requiring large amounts of capital, the absence of external funds severely limits the construction of productive facilities and the growth of specialized industry. Those who wish to spend less money than they receive and hold the balance in a form which earns an interest return have no suitable outlet for their "surplus" funds. Individuals cannot spread their consumption over time in the manner desired.

The development of credit, however, makes it possible for spending units to augment their internal funds with external funds borrowed from other spending units. The "deficit" units, i.e., those that spend more money than they receive, are partially financed by loans from the surplus units. The payment of interest is involved in the debtor-creditor relationship. At first, external finance is usually *direct*. That is, borrowers issue their debt obligations directly to lenders, or what is the same thing, lenders extend credit directly to the ultimate users of funds.

The development of financial intermediaries adds the final dimension to the debt-credit system. These institutions permit the extensive use of *indirect* external finance. At this stage of development, spending units can deposit their surplus funds at specialized financial institutions and receive from these institutions their promises to pay. The surplus spending units' financial assets (e.g., deposits in a savings and loan association) are the debts of financial institutions. These institutions then lend the funds so acquired to deficit spending units and receive in return their promises to pay. The financial intermediaries' assets (e.g., home mortgage loans) are the debts of the deficit spending units. Thus, the ultimate lenders hold the debts of financial intermediaries, who in turn hold the debts of the ultimate borrowers. By providing a safe and income-producing outlet for funds, even in small amounts, financial intermediaries encourage saving; by pooling saved funds from many individuals so as to make possible larger loans to any one borrower than might otherwise be

---

[1] For a brief and lucid description of the various stages of the credit system, see W. H. Steiner, Eli Shapiro, and Ezra Solomon, *Money and Banking* (4th ed.; New York, 1958), Chap. 4.

feasible, financial intermediaries encourage real investment in homes, plant, and equipment.

The modern financial system is thus a servant of the broader economic system. Financial institutions allow saving and investment functions to be performed separately by those economic units best equipped to do so. While the general characteristics of most financial institutions are determined largely by the needs of the savers and borrowers served, specific decisions by these institutions as to their lending and borrowing policies crucially affect the types of economic activities engaged in and the kinds and amounts of goods produced and consumed.

In his essay on the financial system in California, Roland Robinson lists seven functions of commercial banks and other financial institutions.[2] With perhaps the exception of the fifth function, which applies primarily to a very rapidly growing geographical area such as California, all are applicable to Louisiana, or any other state. These functions are to: (1) allocate capital funds; (2) meet legitimate credit needs; (3) provide a payments system; (4) service the flow of savings; (5) aid in the importation of capital; (6) transmit Federal Reserve credit policies to the various financial markets; and (7) provide various financial services, e.g., trust service, safety-deposit facilities, credit information, and the like.

Of all financial institutions, commercial banks have historically been singled out for the most attention.[3] The reason is not hard to find. While commercial banks are similar to savings and loan associations, insurance companies, credit unions, and other financial intermediaries in many important respects, economists traditionally have stressed that particular facet of their operations that makes them both unique and uniquely important. Unlike other financial institutions, commercial banks are said to *create money* in the form of demand deposits since they generally make loans and purchase securities by

[2] Roland I. Robinson, "Economic Role and Objectives for California Banking and Financial Institutions," in Hyman P. Minsky (ed.), *California Banking in a Growing Economy: 1946–1975* (Berkeley, 1965), 27–62.

[3] In recent years, however, a "New View" has emerged which tends to treat commercial banks much as any other financial intermediary. For the development of this approach, see, for example, John G. Gurley and Edward S. Shaw, *Money in a Theory of Finance* (Washington, D.C., 1960), and James Tobin, "Commercial Banks as Creators of 'Money,'" in Deane Carson (ed.), *Banking and Monetary Studies* (Homewood, Ill., 1963), 408–19. For a defense of the uniqueness of commercial banks as money producers, see Boris P. Pesek and Thomas R. Saving, *Money, Wealth and Economic Theory* (New York, 1967).

expanding their deposit liabilities (subject to the restraint of available reserves). These bank liabilities circulate as money. While in earlier times banks issued circulating notes which were used as pocket currency, this is no longer possible. Because of their role as money creators and the crucial importance of money as a determinant of income levels, prices, and the rate of economic growth, commercial bank operations have been subject to tighter controls than those which exist for other financial institutions.

Thus, in comparison with other types of financial institutions, the distinguishing characteristic of commercial banks is their demand deposit accounts. These bank liabilities, transferable by check, are used throughout the country as money, i.e., demand deposits are generally acceptable as a medium of exchange and in payment of debts. In fact, demand deposits constitute over four-fifths of the total stock of money in the United States, with the remainder consisting of currency and coin issued by the Treasury and/or Federal Reserve System. An even greater percentage of total dollar payments is made via demand deposits. While demand deposits do not possess legal tender powers, they are, nevertheless, just as much money as are currency and coin—money is not a matter of physical characteristics but of general acceptability as a means of payment.

But, of course, commercial banks also have liabilities in a form that is neither payable to the holder on demand nor generally acceptable by the public as a medium of exchange. Commercial banks normally offer savings accounts, usually evidenced by passbooks which the customers present when making deposits or withdrawals, and time deposits, which may be evidenced by book accounts or certificates of deposit. Unlike demand deposits on which the payment of interest has been prohibited since the 1930's, banks pay interest on their time and savings deposits.

In the nineteenth century, banks concentrated their assets in obligations arising out of relatively short-term commercial transactions, e.g., bills of exchange and promissory notes. In recent decades commercial banks have made a wide variety of loans, including commercial loans of varying maturities, consumer loans, loans secured by real estate, and others. They also hold a relatively large volume of investment securities, the majority of which consist of federal, state, and local government debt. In fact, except for limited holdings of corporate bonds and stocks, bank assets represent a broad coverage of the various types of loans and securities outstanding in the economy. In this respect, banks have a greater diversity of assets than do other financial institutions, many of which specialize in but one or two major types.

GROWTH AND STRUCTURE OF
COMMERCIAL BANKING IN LOUISIANA

The structure of commercial banking in Louisiana, as in the nation as a whole, is rather complex. As opposed to the relatively homogeneous banking structure of many European nations—in which, quite often, the banking system is dominated by a few large banks with extensive branches—the system in this country is quite heterogeneous. There are over thirteen thousand individual banks in the United States, and they vary in size from small country banks with assets of less than one million dollars to such multi-billion dollar giants as the Bank of America in California and New York's Chase Manhattan Bank. Furthermore, there is the almost bewildering number of ways to classify commercial banks according to their legal and economic characteristics. Five such classifications are particularly useful in analyzing the growth and structure of commercial banking in Louisiana vis-à-vis the nation as a whole. These classifications are by: (1) type of bank charter; (2) unit or branch banking; (3) membership in the Federal Reserve System; (4) insurance of bank deposits by the Federal Deposit Insurance Corporation; and (5) remission of all checks at par.[4]

National and State Banks

One important method of classifying commercial banks involves the type of charter they hold. National banks operate under federal charters issued by the Comptroller of the Currency; state banks have

---

[4] The complex nature of the U.S. banking system is reflected in the governmental structure of bank supervision. Federal legislation dealing with banking problems has given rise to three federal organizations actively engaged in bank supervisory functions. These organizations are: (1) the Office of the Comptroller of the Currency, which has charter and supervisory authority with respect to the nationally-chartered banks; (2) the Federal Reserve System, which has supervisory authority with respect to its members as well as bank holding companies; and (3) the Federal Deposit Insurance Corporation, which has supervisory authority in connection with insured banks. In addition, the various state banking authorities have supervisory responsibilities with respect to state-chartered banks. In such a complex banking structure, there are necessarily cases of overlapping supervisory responsibilities. By considerable agency cooperation, however, some of the seeming duplication has been avoided; however, many authorities feel that additional simplification is needed.

state-granted charters. In Louisiana, the chartering authority for state banks is the State Banking Commissioner.

Over the last century the relative proportions of state and national banks have varied considerably. Prior to the National Banking Acts of 1863 and 1864, the United States had a banking system composed entirely of state banks. Many (but not all) state banking systems were characterized by both poor banking laws and inadequate enforcement of those laws that did exist. Because of these shortcomings, as well as the desire to assist the U.S. Treasury in financing the Civil War, Congress passed the National Banking Acts. According to the terms of these acts, the Comptroller of the Currency was empowered to grant charters for national banks, a power which is exercised to this day.

Faced with increased competition from national banks and the passage by Congress in 1865 of a 10 percent annual tax on all state bank notes, the number of state banks in the United States declined sharply. Since their major function was granting loans through the issuance of bank notes, many state banks were forced out of business. In 1875, for example, the number of national banks stood at 2,076, while the number of state banks totaled only 586.

But the National Banking System did not spell the end of state banking in the United States. As state banks discovered that they did not have to issue bank notes to operate profitably[5]—since bank customers seeking loan accommodation were generally willing to accept demand deposits in lieu of notes—state banking began a comeback. Encouraged by the fact that the banking rules and regulations in most states were less restrictive than those of the Comptroller of the Currency, the number of state banks increased faster than the number of national banks in the following decades. By 1890 state banks outnumbered national banks, and by 1900 there were 9,322 of the former and 3,731 of the latter. The ratio in Louisiana was a little above the national figure, with 58 state and 20 national banks in existence in 1900.[6] What is perhaps most interesting is the relatively small total of 78 banks in the state as of that date.

[5] National banks were originally granted the right to issue national bank notes in an amount up to 90 percent of the value of their holdings of U.S. Government securities. While today there are a few national bank notes in existence, all are in the process of retirement. No national bank notes have been issued since 1935 and commercial banks are no longer permitted to issue paper currency.

[6] These and subsequent figures on numbers of state and national banks are taken from Board of Governors of the Federal Reserve System, *All-Bank Statistics,*

The first two decades of the twentieth century witnessed an almost astounding growth in the number of commercial banks in both the state and the nation. By 1921 there were 31,076 banks in the nation, of which 22,926 had state charters and 8,150 had federal charters. But the number of commercial banks grew at an even faster rate in Louisiana. By 1920 there were 267 banks in the state, an increase of 342 percent in only two decades. While the number of national banks had risen to 38, the major expansion was in state-chartered banks, which numbered 229 by 1920.

Given the benefits of hindsight, most observers now feel that the rapid expansion in numbers led to a condition of "overbanking" and an excessive number of small, potentially unstable institutions. As both a partial cause and result of worsening agricultural conditions in the 1920's and the Great Depression of the 1930's, the entire banking system was seriously shaken. Bank failures numbered in the thousands, with a substantial portion concentrated in the period from 1930 to the banking holiday in March, 1933. In addition, scores of bank mergers and consolidations took place which resulted in further reductions in bank numbers. By December, 1937, the number of commercial banks in the U.S. stood at 14,882, of which 9,622 were state and 5,260 were national banks. The depression had clearly taken its toll of both types, but the generally smaller-sized state banks were the harder hit.

Louisiana banking, like that of the rest of the nation, was hurt badly by the Great Depression. The decline in numbers began in the 1920's and then accelerated in the early 1930's.[7] State banks were clearly the major victims. From 1920 to 1930 the number of state banks in Louisiana declined by 38 and the number of national banks by 7. By 1937 an additional net loss of 74 state banks had occurred, plus one additional national bank, so that the total number of state banks in existence stood at 117 and national banks at 30. This total of 147 can be compared with the 267 banks in existence in 1920. While state banks, most often the smallest ones, were the hardest hit, it should be emphasized that in 1937 state-chartered banks were still dominant in terms of numbers. Furthermore, a considerably smaller percentage of

---

United States, 1896–1955 (Washington, D.C., 1959), and various issues of the *Annual Report of the Board of Governors of the Federal Reserve System* and the *Annual Report of the Federal Deposit Insurance Corporation.*

[7] For a discussion of bank failures, consolidations, and mergers in this period, see Stephen A. Caldwell, *A Banking History of Louisiana* (Baton Rouge, 1935).

Louisiana banks held federal charters than was the case nationally. These two factors have continued to characterize Louisiana banking until the present time.

Following the banking collapse of the early 1930's, the number of bank failures in the United States declined rapidly and eventually diminished to a mere trickle. In the prosperous decades following the Second World War, bank failures have been rare, testifying to the soundness of the postwar banking system and the wisdom of the tighter bank regulations which came into existence as a result of the Great Depression. As can be seen in Table I, however, the number of commercial banks in the country continued to decline, if somewhat slowly, at least until the first half of the present decade.[8] In view of the tremendous growth in gross national product, population, and total bank deposits, this further decline in bank numbers seems somewhat surprising. In fact, it may be noted that the number of commercial banks in 1965 was well under half the number in existence some forty-five years earlier!

The slight decline in bank numbers since the mid-1930's has resulted from the fact that bank mergers and consolidations have proceeded at a faster pace than has the chartering of new banks. Partly

Table I

NUMBER OF COMMERCIAL BANKS[1] BY TYPE OF
CHARTER IN LOUISIANA AND THE
UNITED STATES, SELECTED YEARS, 1937–65

Date[2]	Louisiana			United States		
	Total	State	National	Total	State	National
1937	147	117	30	14,882	9,622	5,260
1945	151	118	33	14,183	9,166	5,017
1950	165	129	36	14,164	9,206	4,958
1955	175	134	41	13,756	9,064	4,692
1960	190	148	42	13,484	8,954	4,530
1965	214	167	47	13,818	9,003	4,815

[1]U.S. figures also include a small number of nondeposit trust companies.
[2]Dates as of December 31.
SOURCE: *Annual Report of the Federal Deposit Insurance Corporation* (various issues).

[8] The increase from 1960 to 1965 seems largely attributable to the more liberal chartering of national banks by Comptroller of the Currency James Saxon.

because of the then-prevailing view that "overbanking" and "excessive chartering" were partially responsible for the difficulties in the depression era, the Banking Act of 1935 contained generally stronger restrictions on bank entry than had existed in the preceding century. As a result of this statutory change and the strict administrative interpretations of the "need" criteria established by this act, the entry of new banks was severely curtailed in the following twenty-five years.[9]

As can be seen in Table I, Louisiana's experience has been quite different from the national trend. In fact, rather consistent increases have been recorded, particularly since the end of the Second World War. Comparing 1965 with 1937 figures, the number of state banks in Louisiana rose from 117 to 167, national banks from 30 to 47, and total banks from 147 to 214.

While Louisiana has bucked the U.S. trend, it is not the only state to have done so. Using the period 1934–64 for comparison, there were thirteen states that experienced a net gain in numbers; nine of these states, however, are so-called unit banking states which do not (normally) allow existing banks to establish branch offices so that expansion in bank facilities must take place through the formation of new banks.[10] Using a shorter period 1953–62 Louisiana was one of only four states allowing either statewide or limited branch banking to register an increase in bank numbers—the others being Alabama, Georgia, and New Mexico. Louisiana's absolute increase was the largest of the four. While fifteen of the eighteen predominantly unit banking states also registered increases, the amount of increase was less than in Louisiana in at least several cases.[11] During the period 1953–62 some 33 new banks were organized in the state. Coupled with these new charters were an unusually low number of mergers and absorptions (4) and a total absence of voluntary liquidations or suspensions.

The data in Table I indicate that a larger percentage of Louisiana banks have state charters (78 percent in 1965) than is the case in the U.S. generally (65 percent). As mentioned earlier, this relationship was established many years ago and has continued to the present

[9] See, for example, Sam Peltzman, "Banking Entry Regulation: Its Impact and Purpose," *National Banking Review*, III (December, 1965), 163–77.

[10] *Annual Report of the Federal Deposit Insurance Corporation, 1964*, p. 137.

[11] *Federal Reserve Bulletin*, XLIX (September, 1963), 1320. States are classified as unit, limited branch, or statewide branch according to the type of banking that seems to be prevalent and not necessarily on the current status of legal provisions.

time. The high proportion of state banks is neither necessarily good nor necessarily bad; certainly, it is no cause for alarm in view of the state's high standards of bank regulation and the fact that all but one of the banks in Louisiana are insured by the Federal Deposit Insurance Corporation. On the other hand, the well-being of our so-called dual banking system depends to some degree on a reasonably large number of national banks.

Undoubtedly, a great many factors influence the ratio of state to national banks in a particular geographical area. Perhaps one factor is the amount of prestige attached to the designation "national"; in some areas, at least, the prestige factor is considered quite significant. Another factor is the relative ease or difficulty of obtaining a state vis-à-vis a national charter, and this varies among states at any given time according to the prevailing philosophy of the chartering authorities. The stringency of state banking regulations as compared with those applicable to national banks is a further consideration in the minds of those seeking a new charter. Regulations vary with respect to such factors as maximum interest rates on deposits and loans, minimum capital requirements, and reserve requirements against demand deposits and savings and time deposits. Since all national banks must be members of both the Federal Reserve System and the Federal Deposit Insurance Corporation, they must also be prepared to meet all of the regulations involved in such membership.[12]

For national banks, Louisiana state banks, and most other state-chartered banks, there is a direct relationship between the size of the town or city in which the bank is to be located and the amount of capital required. The minimum capital requirement for national banks is $50,000 in towns with six thousand or less population, and this minimum rises (in certain cases) to a figure of $200,000 for cities with more than fifty thousand people. While there are some notable exceptions (no specified minimum capital requirement in Rhode Island and $200,000 in Hawaii), the majority of states have minimum capital requirements ranging from $25,000 to $50,000. In Louisiana, the minimum for state-chartered banks is $25,000 in towns of less than three thousand population. This figure rises to $50,000 in the three thousand to thirty thousand population bracket and to $100,000 for cities of greater population.[13]

[12] For a detailed discussion of commercial bank regulations, see Subcommittee on Domestic Finance, Committee on Banking and Currency, House of Representatives, *Comparative Regulations of Financial Institutions*, 88th Congress, November 22, 1963, pp. 1–64.
[13] *Ibid.*, 5–7.

Minimum capital requirements are also set for the establishment of branches (in those states in which branching is legal). To establish a new branch, a national bank must have the minimum capital stock required for the establishment of a branch by a state bank in the same state. In Louisiana, a state bank must have a minimum capital of $50,000 in order to engage in branch banking within its parish of domicile (and capital and surplus of at least one million dollars to establish branches in a foreign country). The maximum number of branches within the parish is graduated according to capital; additional numbers of branches may be opened only as additional capital requirements are met. For example, capital of $250,000–$300,000 is sufficient for the establishment of seven branches, and an additional branch is permitted for each additional $100,000.[14]

A more important consideration in choosing national- or state-bank status is the level and composition of required reserves. Actually, reserve requirements vary as between banks that are members of the Federal Reserve System and those that are not members; but since all national banks are necessarily members and state banks have a choice of nonmember status, the relative level of required reserves affects the type of charter desired. In many states, reserve requirements are appreciably lower for nonmember state banks. This differential has had a deleterious effect on both the number of national banks and membership in the Federal Reserve System since the forced holding of bank assets in a form which earns no interest adversely affects bank profits. Furthermore, in several states at least, a portion of required reserves can be held in the form of specified interest-bearing securities (U.S. government and/or state and local government obligations), while member banks must hold all of their reserves in the form of noninterest-bearing cash or deposits with Reserve banks.

Member banks must adhere to the reserve requirements set by the Board of Governors. Within the ranges fixed by Congress, these requirements vary according to the type of deposit and also according to the classification of the bank. The range on net demand deposits (i.e., gross demand deposits minus cash items in the process of collection and demand balances due from domestic banks) is 7 to 14 percent for so-called country banks and 10 to 22 percent for reserve city banks. Only banks in relatively large cities, e.g., New Orleans, are classified as reserve city banks. The range on time and savings deposits is 3 to 6 percent without regard to classification. On December

14 *Ibid.,* 8–9.

31, 1965, the requirements in effect were 12 and 16½ percent on net demand deposits and 4 percent on time and savings deposits.

In Louisiana, state (nonmember) banks are subject to somewhat higher reserve requirements on (gross) demand deposits—20 percent —but reserve requirements on time and savings deposits are zero. There is no distinction made between reserve city and country banks. Reserves against demand deposit liabilities must be held in the form of cash in the vault or cash due from other banks.[15]

It is difficult to evaluate the relative severity of reserve requirements on Louisiana banks. A nonmember state bank can count as reserves its balances with other commercial banks, which is something of an advantage since banks would hold some amount of correspondent balances in any case. The absence of reserve requirements against time and savings deposits is also an advantage for state banks. According to a comprehensive congressional study, a total of only six states (as of January 1, 1962) had no required reserves of any type on time and savings deposits; in most states, the requirements ranged from 3 to 6 percent, and in a few cases they went as high as 15 percent. On the other hand, Louisiana was one of only three states with an overall 20 percent reserve requirement against demand deposits. Most states fell in a 10 to 15 percent range, with Illinois operating at the opposite extreme with no reserve requirements of any type.[16] Louisiana's 20 percent requirement, of course, is above that normally applicable to member banks.

While national banks are in the minority in both the state and nation, on the average they tend to be larger in terms of assets and deposits. At the end of 1965, for example, all national banks in the United States held $219.1 billion in assets out of total bank assets of $437.1 billion. In Louisiana, the figures were $2.9 billion out of $4.8 billion in total assets.[17] Thus, in Louisiana, national banks held approximately 61 percent of total bank assets—a figure that was significantly above the overall U.S. average!

On an individual bank basis, the six largest institutions in Louisiana in 1965 were national banks—four in New Orleans and two in Shreveport. Led by the Whitney National Bank with assets of $570 million

[15] *Louisiana Revised Statutes of 1950*, Act 2 of the Extraordinary Session of 1950 (Baton Rouge, 1950), I, 306.

[16] *Comparative Regulations of Financial Institutions*, 16–18.

[17] *Annual Report of the Federal Deposit Insurance Corporation, 1965*, p. 134, and *Annual Report of the Comptroller of the Currency, 1965–1966*, p. 177.

(as of June 30, 1965), the next five banks fell within the range of $140 to $350 million. On the other hand, the two largest state banks had assets (as of December 31, 1965) of $124 and $118 million. Ten national banks, as compared with only three state banks, held assets in excess of $70 million—although from that figure on down the differences began to narrow.[18]

Unit and Branch Banking

Unit banking refers to the operation of a single banking office by a commercial bank while branch banking refers to the operation of two or more banking offices. Historically, considerable debate has occurred over the merits and demerits of branch banking. Its opponents have argued that branch banking leads to an undesirable concentration of economic power and a lessening of competition. Branch managers, it is alleged, may come from outside the community served and thus may not be sufficiently aware of, and responsive to, local problems and needs. Proponents of branching have rejected these arguments. They contend that the unit bank is frequently too small to handle the large borrower; a large bank is usually financially sounder and more efficiently managed than a small unit bank; and a branch is less likely to be embarrassed by a shortage of loan funds since it can draw upon the resources of the whole bank.

In one respect, the opponents of branching have seen their view prevail since no bank is permitted to establish branches outside of the state in which its home office is located (although branches in U.S. territories and foreign countries are not ruled out). This prohibition applies to both state banks and national banks—the latter being "national" only in the sense that they are chartered by the Comptroller of the Currency. There are essentially three ways in which the branching question has been resolved within the individual states: branch banking is not generally allowed, so that unit banking is clearly predominant; branching is permitted within limited areas; and statewide branching is permitted.

Actually, the line of distinction between these three arrangements is not entirely clearcut. Virtually all "unit banking" states have at least a few branches in existence, either as a result of unusual circumstances or because branches were established prior to prohibitory legislation. Texas, Florida, and sixteen other states may be considered

[18] *Statistical Abstract of Louisiana* (2nd ed.; New Orleans, 1967), 230–31.

unit banking states. States in the second group normally limit branching to the county in which the main office is located, or at best include only contiguous counties as well. Louisiana—like Mississippi, Alabama, and Georgia—are members of this second group along with twelve other states.

For all practical purposes, Louisiana should be considered as a state which restricts branching on a parish-wide basis; technically, however, state law appears to allow statewide branching but only under unusually severe limitations. According to the *Louisiana Revised Statutes of 1950*, banks meeting certain capital requirements may establish a branch office in parishes in which there are no state banks, savings banks, and trust companies.[19] Since each parish has generally had one or more commercial banks, the establishment of branches across parish lines has not taken place. There is, however, one major exception. Banks in the parishes of Allen, Calcasieu, Cameron, and Jefferson Davis are specifically authorized to operate branches in any one or more of the other named parishes;[20] the Calcasieu-Marine National Bank of Lake Charles has taken advantage of this provision and established branches across parish lines.

Finally, sixteen states permit statewide branching with only minor, if any, limitations.[21] California, perhaps, is the most notable example. It is the ability to expand statewide over such a large and highly populated geographic area that has enabled the Bank of America to grow to such enormous size. It should be noted, however, that even in these sixteen states where the possibilities of branching are most extensive, banks are not automatically allowed to establish any number of branches they might desire. Rather, in any state, permission to establish a branch is granted only after an application is filed with the appropriate banking authorities. Each application is studied with a view to the public's "need" for the new facility and its possible effect on bank competition. Not all such applications are ultimately approved.

[19] *Louisiana Revised Statutes of 1950*, p. 286.
[20] *Ibid.*, 287.
[21] That some differences in interpretation are possible in categorizing states can be seen by the following figures from *Comparative Regulations of Financial Institutions*, 61. This study listed fourteen states as prohibiting branch banking, nineteen states as allowing branch banking within limited areas, and seventeen states as allowing statewide branching (with some limitations in some of the states).

Regulations as to branching obviously affect the number of banks in a given state—although this is only one among several factors. Other things being equal, unit bank states tend to have a larger number of (smaller) banks, while states permitting widespread branching have fewer, but larger, institutions. Of course, the fact that a majority of states permit at least limited branching does not mean that unit banks are nonexistent in those states or even that they are in the minority. For the nation as a whole, unit banking has continued to be dominant, at least in terms of the total number of unit banks compared to the total number of banks operating branch offices. This dominance has declined somewhat in recent decades, however.

Although the number of the nation's banks has even decreased, the total number of *banking offices* has risen considerably over the period 1937–65. The expanding economy's need for more banking facilities has been met largely by the expansion of branch offices rather than the creation of new banks. On December 31, 1937, there were some 13,958 unit banks and only 924 banks operating branches; all banking offices totaled 18,364. While expansion occurred in the following two decades, the major increase took place in the late 1950's and early 1960's. From 1955 to 1965 total banking offices in the U.S. rose from 20,818 to 29,736. By the latter date there were 3,207 banks operating branches compared with 10,601 unit banks.

The branch expansion situation has been much the same in Louisiana. This is particularly interesting since, at the same time, the state has bucked the national trend by its expansion in bank numbers. In fact, from 1937 to 1965 Louisiana has registered increases in every relevant category—total banking offices, 200 to 462; total banks, 147 to 214; banks operating branches, 27 to 84; and even unit banks, 120 to 130. As the number of banks operating branches has increased, the total number of branch offices has also risen. In 1937 the 27 nonunit banks operated a total of 53 branch offices; by 1965 there were 84 banks operating 248 branch offices. Today, because of branch expansion, bank customers in many areas of the state have come to enjoy a high degree of locational convenience in conducting their financial affairs.

Member and Nonmember Banks

An important method of classifying commercial banks involves their status as members or nonmembers of the Federal Reserve System. All national banks must be members, but state-chartered banks may or may not be members. Some state banks are unable to meet the requirements for System membership, while others simply do not wish to join. Membership requirements include the stipulations that all members must be insured by the Federal Deposit Insurance Corporation, subscribe to Federal Reserve bank stock, and redeem at par all checks drawn by their depositors and presented for collection by out-of-town banks; state member banks are subject to periodic examination by the Federal Reserve authorities.

In deciding whether or not to seek Federal Reserve membership, a state bank necessarily considers both the benefits and the costs of membership. On the one hand, a member bank may obtain loans and advances from one of the twelve Reserve banks, obtain currency free of charge, and have its checks cleared and collected at no cost by the Federal Reserve banks. Another possible advantage is the prestige of membership. On the other hand, a major disadvantage, as discussed earlier, is the fact that in many states the reserve requirements are lower than those set for member banks by the Board of Governors. Furthermore, through the use of member correspondent banks, nonmember banks are often able to obtain the privileges of membership indirectly.

In looking at the nation as a whole, only a small proportion of state banks hold System membership. This pattern has existed for many decades. In 1965 there were only 1,405 member state banks (in addition to the 4,815 national banks); nonmember banks were clearly in the majority, totaling 7,598. But while nonmember banks are the more numerous, well over three-fourths of all bank deposits are held in member banks. This concentration of bank deposits in member banks is a significant factor in the ability of the Federal Reserve authorities to regulate money and bank credit in the interests of economic stabilization.

Obviously, member banks are much larger than nonmember banks —at least on the average. Two factors involved are the larger average size of national versus nonmember banks, and the larger average size of state member versus nonmember banks. In fact, for the nation as a whole, those state banks which choose System membership are even larger on the average than the national banks—a fact which is somewhat difficult to explain.

In Louisiana, only 10 of 167 state banks were members of the

Federal Reserve System in 1965. This number is quite small. Coupled with the below-average number of national banks, it is clear that System membership is considerably less in Louisiana (27 percent of all commercial banks) than in the country as a whole (45 percent). That Louisiana's member state banks also tend to be above average in size is reflected by the fact that seven of the ten institutions in this category maintained branch offices—a ratio far in excess of that of Louisiana's nonmember banks.

Louisiana's fifty-seven member banks fall in two of the nation's twelve Federal Reserve Districts. Member banks in Baton Rouge, New Orleans, and other areas in the southern and southwestern portions of the state belong to the Sixth Federal Reserve District, which is served by the Federal Reserve Bank of Atlanta. Commercial banks in Shreveport and other areas in the north and northwest portions of the state belong to the Eleventh Federal Reserve District, which is served by the Federal Reserve Bank of Dallas.

Insured and Noninsured Banks

Today, more than 97 percent of all commercial banks in the country are insured by the Federal Deposit Insurance Corporation (FDIC). Noninsured banks tend to be among the smallest in size and their deposits total well under 1 percent of all deposit liabilities of U.S. banks. Federal Reserve member banks are automatically insured, and nonmember banks may receive FDIC approval upon meeting certain qualifications. Obviously, the vast majority of them are approved. Since FDIC criteria are at least generally similar to those utilized by the Comptroller of the Currency and the Federal Reserve authorities, the end result is that all but a few commercial banks are subject to certain minimum standards applied at the federal level.

Deposit insurance grew out of the banking collapse of the 1930's. Today, the FDIC insures each deposit account up to a maximum of $15,000. Insured banks pay an annual fee based on the volume of their deposits. The existence of FDIC insurance has probably done much to strengthen the banking system by enhancing public confidence in it, and thereby helping to prevent "runs" on the banks as occurred in the depression years.

Most depositors would probably hesitate to keep their accounts with noninsured banks. The strong competitive pressure from insured banks virtually dictates that any new group seeking a charter will also wish to obtain FDIC insurance. In Louisiana the noninsured bank has almost disappeared. Out of Louisiana's 214 banks in existence in 1965, only one maintained a noninsured status.

(See Table II for details of Louisiana's banking structure with respect to type of charter, branching, System membership, and insured status.)

Par and Nonpar Banks

Undoubtedly, the most unsatisfactory aspect of banking in Louisiana is the large number of state-chartered banks which do not remit all checks drawn on them at par. Nonpar banks normally impose an "exchange charge" of 0.1 percent on checks presented for collection by out-of-town banks. The legality of such an exchange charge is clearly spelled out in Louisiana law, although it is further noted in the law that this percentage is the maximum rate allowable (subject to a minimum charge for small checks) and that an exchange charge cannot be made by banks for the collection of checks deposited with

Table II

THE STRUCTURE OF COMMERCIAL BANKS IN LOUISIANA
DECEMBER 31, 1965

| | | Insured | | | | |
| | | | Federal Reserve Member | | | |
Type of bank and banking offices	Grand Total	Total	National	State	Non-member	Non-insured
All offices	462	461	178	36	247	1
Banks	214	213	47	10	156	1
Unit banks	130	129	17	3	109	1
Banks operating branches	84	84	30	7	47	—
Branches	248	248	131	26	91	—

SOURCE: *Annual Report of the Federal Deposit Insurance Corporation, 1965.*

those banks when the check is drawn on another bank in the same municipality.[22]

Nonpar banks cannot be members of the Federal Reserve System, and in fact, the Reserve banks will not accept their checks for collection (as they will for nonmembers who remit at par and maintain certain deposit balances). Thus, the relatively large number of nonpar banks in Louisiana is undoubtedly related to the state's low percentage of member banks, a fact noted earlier.

While nonpar banking has not been especially important nationwide, it has been quite significant in certain regions of the country. Nonpar banks have been concentrated in the southern states and in such west north-central states as Minnesota, North Dakota, and South Dakota. A slight majority of states do not now have a single nonpar bank. In recent years the number and relative importance of nonpar banks has declined in both Louisiana and the nation.

On December 30, 1950, for example, there were 1,853 banks in the United States that were not on the Federal Reserve's par list. This number constituted about 13 percent of all commercial banks and 26 percent of nonmember banks. By December 31, 1964, the number of nonpar banks had declined to 1,547, or about 11 percent of total banks and 21 percent of nonmember banks.

In Louisiana the concentration of nonpar banks was quite heavy in 1950 when 104 banks were not on the Federal Reserve's par list. This number constituted 63 percent of all banks in Louisiana and an extremely high 88 percent of its nonmember banks! The situation has improved somewhat since that time. By 1964 the number of nonpar banks had declined slightly to 98, while total banks and nonmember banks had increased to 209 and 152, respectively.[23] Still, it may be noted, nearly two of every three nonmember state banks continued to levy an exchange charge on checks presented for collection by out-of-town banks. The nonpar banks are typically below average in size and often located in the smaller one-bank towns where there is less competitive pressure to force them to abandon this practice.[24]

---

[22] *Louisiana Revised Statutes of 1950*, pp. 284–85.

[23] *Federal Reserve Bulletin* (February, 1951), 190; (February, 1965), 325.

[24] Based on a study of North Carolina, Clifton Kreps found that nonpar banks were (1) typically smaller than par banks; (2) generally "small town" banks; (3) ordinarily operated in "one bank" towns; and (4) normally maintained

Most observers condemn the practice of nonpar banking, and in several states there is a move to force all banks to remit at par. (Under a new Minnesota law, all banks in that state must cash checks drawn on them at par after November 1, 1968.)[25] The practice is often attacked as inefficient and inequitable. It limits the usefulness of demand deposits as money, and creates a problem for the banking system in that nonpar checks which cannot travel through Federal Reserve channels are more costly to collect. Since checks sent to out-of-town par banks for collection are paid at par and checks drawn on nonpar banks are paid at less than par when presented by out-of-town banks, a profit margin exists for the nonpar bank. The profitability of the exchange charge seems to be the major reason for the continuation of this practice. Many small, predominantly rural banks argue that the exchange charge is needed as a source of earnings.

THE ADEQUACY OF
BANK FACILITIES IN LOUISIANA

The question of what constitutes "adequate" bank facilities has plagued regulatory authorities for decades. Largely because of the depression experience and the widespread fear of "overbanking" that grew out of it, the (U.S.) Banking Act of 1935 contained strong restrictions on bank entry. State banking authorities also adopted more stringent requirements. In judging an application for a new charter, federal and state authorities are now required to consider such factors as the community's access to other banking facilities, its "need" for a new bank, the talents and character of the proposed officials, the adequacy of the proposed capital stock, and the bank's prospective earnings. In general, the regulatory authorities in this country have exercised rather strong restrictions on new bank entry (although in Louisiana, of course, bank numbers have expanded).

Within the last few years, many students of banking and finance have expressed concern that extremely tight entry restrictions are now outmoded. The earlier fear of overbanking has been replaced by a new concern with the need to maintain vigorous competition in

---

lower ratios of earning assets to total assets than did par banks of the same size. Clifton H. Kreps, Jr., "Characteristics of Nonpar Banks: A Case Study," *Southern Economic Journal*, XXVI (July, 1959), 44–49.

[25] *Wall Street Journal*, May 12, 1967, p. 8.

banking markets. Concern with competition involves not only the question of chartering, but also of bank mergers and holding company expansion.

Admittedly, not all recent scholarly research has pointed in the same direction;[26] the implication of much of it, however, is that bank competition should be given greater weight by the regulatory authorities. Governor George Mitchell of the Federal Reserve Board has suggested that the distinctions between banking and other industries have been overemphasized. Fear of overbanking has led to excessive regulation. In his view the banking industry should be considered a multi-product industry and the operation of banking markets analogous to the operation of markets for other goods and services.[27] Paul Horvitz, in addressing himself to the question of the relationship between bank regulation and the need to strengthen bank competition, has suggested (among other things) that the supervisory authorities can permit easier entry both by new banks and by new branches.[28] In appraising the impact of the sixty-four national banks chartered in the U.S. in 1962, David C. Motter concluded that the entry of the new banks resulted in better service to bank customers at lower prices and a tendency toward payment of higher rates of interest on time deposits.[29] In another study, Motter and Deane Carson examined the impact of liberalized entry regulations on banking performance in Nassau County, New York, and found that bank customers generally benefited from the new entry (via new banks, new branches, and expansion of New York City banks through merger).[30]

Whether or not the "need" criteria now generally employed are undesirably restrictive has thus become an important issue of public policy. Exactly how much competition is necessary or desirable?

[26] For two brief, but comprehensive, summaries of the varied work in the area of bank structure and performance, see Robert Holland, "Research into Banking Structure and Competition," *Federal Reserve Bulletin*, L (November, 1964), 1383–99, and Tynan Smith, "Research on Banking Structure and Performance," *Federal Reserve Bulletin*, LII (April, 1966), 488–98.

[27] George Mitchell, "Mergers Among Commercial Banks," in Almarin Phillips (ed.), *Perspectives on Antitrust Policy* (Princeton, 1965).

[28] Paul M. Horvitz, "Stimulating Bank Competition Through Regulatory Action," *Journal of Finance*, XX (March, 1965), 1–13.

[29] David C. Motter, "Bank Formation and the Public Interest," *National Banking Review*, II (March, 1965), 299–350.

[30] David C. Motter and Deane Carson, "Bank Entry and the Public Interest: A Case Study," *National Banking Review*, I (June, 1964), 469–512.

Furthermore, what constitutes "adequate" bank facilities? In one sense, bank facilities may be said to be adequate when they provide a convenient and safe place for depositors to place their funds, when they meet the "legitimate credit needs" of borrowers, and when they perform other routine services needed by bank patrons. In general, for a facility to be adequate it should be located in the same general area where the customer handles his other business transactions. But even if existing bank facilities in a community are judged "adequate" by these standards, is it not possible in certain cases that the chartering of one or more new banks in the same community could lead to certain benefits through the stimulation of competition?

At present, there is no generally accepted and scientific method of determining "adequacy." Many economic factors are normally considered in addition to the number of existing banks and bank facilities—population, personal income, retail sales, occupational and industrial structure, future growth potential, the composition of bank assets, the concentration of bank assets, etc. Intangible factors, even politics, may enter into the final judgment in the chartering of new banks. In the remainder of this essay, we will consider a few very broad factors that are relevant to this question; however, no attempt will be made to give a definitive answer as to whether or not bank facilities are adequate in Louisiana or in any particular town or parish within the state.

One possible quantitative test of the adequacy of banking facilities is the number of people per banking unit (main offices plus branches) in a given state or area. Other things being equal, the fewer people per banking unit, the greater is the presumed adequacy of banking facilities. From 1920 to 1964 Louisiana consistently exceeded the national average in number of people per banking unit. That this differential is not simply a result of regional characteristics can be detected by comparing Louisiana with other southern and border states. As can be seen in Table III, Louisiana has consistently had more people per banking unit than the majority of these states. Only Alabama, Florida, Texas, and West Virginia had a greater number as of December 31, 1964, and all of these states except Alabama were primarily unit banking states with few, if any, branch offices. Florida, with 12,937, had more people per banking unit than any other state in the nation. Iowa, with 3,079 people per banking unit, had the lowest figure in the nation.[31]

[31] *Annual Report of the Federal Deposit Insurance Corporation, 1964*, p. 144.

It may be noted that the population per banking unit rose considerably between 1920 and 1934 in the U.S., Louisiana, and those states included in Table III. Generally, the figures were even higher in 1950, but more recently the movement has been in the other direction. Since 1950 the decline in people per banking unit in Louisiana has exceeded the national average reduction by a good margin. Because of the state's rapid increase in banking units, Louisiana has been closing the gap in recent years.

Table III

POPULATION PER BANKING UNIT IN LOUISIANA,
THE UNITED STATES, AND SELECTED SOUTHERN
AND BORDER STATES, VARIOUS YEARS, 1920–64

	June 30, 1920	Dec. 31, 1934	Dec. 31, 1950	Dec. 31, 1960	Dec. 31, 1964
All States	3,330	6,643	7,678	7,178	6,469
Louisiana	5,183	10,916	11,091	8,899	7,793
Alabama	6,312	11,519	12,199	9,960	8,647
Arkansas	3,554	7,653	7,610	6,311	5,770
Delaware	3,912	4,048	5,213	5,575	5,337
Florida	3,655	10,434	13,517	15,331	12,937
Georgia	3,602	8,144	7,847	7,482	7,157
Kentucky	4,131	5,830	6,865	6,064	5,631
Maryland	4,544	5,755	7,607	7,351	6,439
Mississippi	5,030	8,415	8,100	6,620	5,979
North Carolina	4,101	10,555	9,170	6,593	5,590
South Carolina	3,537	11,384	10,746	8,161	6,813
Tennessee	4,038	7,175	8,334	6,953	6,448
Texas	2,774	6,426	8,382	9,220	8,811
Virginia	4,475	6,369	7,773	6,735	5,738
West Virginia	4,305	9,972	11,144	10,220	9,766

SOURCE: Data from, or calculated from, *Annual Report of the Federal Deposit Insurance Corporation, 1950*, pp. 226–27; *1960*, pp. 42, 128–35; *1964*, p. 144; and U.S. Bureau of the Census, *1960 Census of Population*, I, Pt. A, 20–9 and 20–10.

Considering the shorter time span 1960–64, it can be seen in Table IV that Louisiana's decrease in population per banking unit in this period was attributable to the increase in both number of banks and number of branches, while in the nation as a whole the population per bank actually rose. In only a few of the southern or border states did the number of people per bank show a decline; in all cases,

however, population per banking unit registered a decline, thus indicating the importance in most states of branch expansion.

Louisiana's recent growth in banking facilities is perhaps best
understood on a town and parish basis. On December 30, 1950, there
were a total of 116 towns with one banking unit; 29 towns with two
units; and 9 towns with three or more units—or a total of 154 towns
with some banking service. By January 1, 1960, the number of one-
unit towns had declined to 107, while the two-unit towns had risen
to 31 and the towns with three or more units had grown to 21, for a
total of 159 towns in all. Additional expansion occurred in the following five years. By January 1, 1965, the figures stood at 116, 44, and 26,
respectively, for a total of 186.[32] The lack of growth in the number

Table IV

CHANGE IN POPULATION PER BANK AND PER BANKING
UNIT IN LOUISIANA, THE UNITED STATES, AND SELECTED
SOUTHERN AND BORDER STATES, 1960–64

	Change in number of banks and trust companies	Change in number of offices operated	Change in population per bank	Change in population per unit
All States	+277	+4,573	+ 591	− 709
Louisiana	+ 19	+ 79	− 549	−1,106
Alabama	+ 14	+ 66	− 206	−1,313
Arkansas	+ 8	+ 52	+ 353	− 542
Delaware	−	+ 12	+2,032	− 242
Florida	+115	+ 118	−2,569	−2,393
Georgia	+ 10	+ 73	+ 597	− 325
Kentucky	− 7	+ 60	+ 520	− 433
Maryland	− 12	+ 111	+4,717	− 909
Mississippi	+ 3	+ 58	+ 520	− 641
North Carolina	− 31	+ 177	+7,024	−1,004
South Carolina	− 12	+ 83	+2,779	−1,347
Tennessee	− 3	+ 76	+ 908	− 505
Texas	+119	+ 141	− 274	− 409
Virginia	− 28	+ 174	+2,799	− 997
West Virginia	+ 2	+ 2	− 456	− 456

SOURCE: *Annual Report of the Federal Deposit Insurance Corporation,
1964*, p. 144.

[32] Data for December 30, 1950, are from a letter to Edward B. Selby from
Charles H. Bradford, Deputy Chief, Division of Research and Statistics,
Federal Deposit Insurance Corporation, May 2, 1966; later data are from Fed-

of one-unit towns is easily explained. While some towns previously without banking facilities have gained a unit since 1950, other towns have moved out of this category into the two- and three-or-more unit categories.

On January 1, 1965, the five cities with the largest number of banking units ranged from New Orleans with forty-nine units to Lake Charles with ten units. Shreveport had thirty-two units; Baton Rouge, twenty-two; and Monroe, twelve units. Given its sizeable (estimated) population, the number of people per unit in New Orleans was 13,541, by far the highest of the five cities.[33] The lowest was Monroe, with 4,892 people per banking unit.

The growth of banking units can also be seen on a parish basis. On December 30, 1950, two parishes, Cameron and Plaquemines, were without banking units; nine parishes had only one banking unit. Seventeen parishes had two units, and the remaining thirty-six parishes had three or more units. By January 1, 1960, the situation had improved somewhat, and by January 1, 1965, there were forty-eight parishes in the state with three or more units. Of the remaining parishes, eleven had two units, only five had one unit, and no parish was without banking facilities.

Forty-seven of the state's sixty-four parishes showed a net decrease in population per banking unit from 1950 to 1965. In thirty-four cases, the number of banking units increased proportionately more than the increase in population; in five cases, banking units increased while population decreased; and in eight cases, banking units remained unchanged while population declined. In the seventeen cases in which there was a net increase in population per banking unit, fourteen resulted from an increase in population coupled with no change in banking units, and three resulted from an expansion in population that was proportionally greater than the expansion in banking units.

The average number of people per banking unit for the state was 7,793 on January 1, 1965. Only twenty-three parishes had a popula-

---

eral Deposit Insurance Corporation, *Operating Banking Offices Insured by the Federal Deposit Insurance Corporation as of January 1, 1960* (Washington, D.C., 1961), 140–45; and *Operating Banking Offices as of January 1, 1965*, pp. 168–75. All data are adjusted to account for uninsured offices. These data are also used in subsequent calculations in this section, as are population estimates from *Statistical Abstract of Louisiana* (New Orleans, 1965), 8–9.

[33] For this purpose estimated population figures were utilized from the *Louisiana Business Review*, XXIX (July, 1965), 20–21.

tion per banking unit greater than the state average. The parishes of Assumption and West Baton Rouge, both single unit parishes, had the highest figures in the state—19,735, and 16,425, respectively. The parishes of LaSalle and Catahoula, with 3,420, and 4,062, respectively, were at the other end of the spectrum.

There are some serious deficiencies encountered when relying too heavily on population and banking unit data; as a minimum, one should also consider income, bank deposits, and bank loans.[34] Obviously, one would expect to find a higher volume of bank deposits and bank loans in a parish with relatively high income than in a low-income parish. In fact, this is the case in Louisiana. Using the least-squares technique on 1964 data, a high coefficient of determination was found between parish income and deposits ($r^2 = .933$) and between parish income and loans and discounts ($r^2 = .935$).[35] These results indicate that 93.3 percent of the variation in deposits and 93.5 percent of the variation in loans and discounts was associated with the variation in income. Correlation, of course, does not demonstrate causation, although on a parish basis (as opposed, perhaps, to a national basis) income may be, to a large degree, the causal factor. That is, increased parish income will lead to increased bank deposits and thus bank assets. (But on the other hand, an increase in bank loans and deposits *could* stimulate the creation of income within the parish.)

Based on 1964 data, an increase in parish income of a hundred dollars was associated with an increase in bank deposits of $80.78. By using the regression equation—which is a statement of the way in which the dependent variable changes with variations in the independent variable—one could readily identify those parishes which deviated the most from the average relationship between income and deposits. If deposits seemed exceptionally low in relation to income, the presumption would arise that banking facilities were less than adequate by statewide standards.

Another comparison could be made with respect to income and bank loans and discounts. If loans and discounts were well below average, this fact could indicate excessively conservative loan policies

[34] See, for example, Leon M. Schur, "Adequacy of Commercial Banking Facilities in Louisiana—A Quantitative Study," *Louisiana Business Review*, XXIV (May, 1960), 20–23.

[35] Parish income refers to *Sales Management* magazine's concept of "effective buying income." Deposits are total bank deposits.

and point to the need for expanding bank facilities. Somewhat similar information might be obtained by computing the ratio of loans and discounts to total bank assets, to total bank deposits, or to demand deposits of individuals, partnerships, and corporations.

SUMMARY AND CONCLUSIONS

The importance of commercial banks to the state's development is well established. In addition to the provision of various financial services, bank liabilities in the form of demand deposits constitute the major component of the public's money supply. Time and savings deposits constitute an increasingly important outlet for savings, and bank loans are an important source of credit.

Historically, Louisiana has been characterized by an above-average proportion of state-chartered banks. In 1930, for example, there were 191 state and only 31 national banks in Louisiana. These state banks held total assets to $399 million, considerably more than the $130 million in assets held by national banks. The depression took its toll, however, and by 1940 the situation was quite different. While state-chartered banks still outnumbered national banks by 116 to 29, the latter held $417 million in assets compared to only $183 million held by state banking institutions. The same general relationship has continued to the present time. In 1965 state banks were in the majority, 167 to 47, but national banks held a much larger volume of assets, $2.9 billion to $1.9 billion.

Neither the above-average ratio of state to national banks nor the below-average percentage of Federal Reserve member banks are necessarily bad. What is somewhat unsatisfactory, however, is the fact that nearly two out of every three nonmember state banks continue to levy an exchange charge on checks presented for collection by out-of-town banks. These nonpar banks are typically below average in size and are often located in areas where bank competition is not strong.

In the last several decades, new bank formation has taken place in Louisiana at a relatively rapid rate, while in many states the number of banks has actually declined due to mergers and consolidations. At the same time, considerable branch expansion has also occurred in Louisiana. As a result, the population per banking unit has been declining. While still above the U.S. average in people per banking unit, the expansion of bank facilities in the state has proceeded at a rate well in excess of the national average. In any particular town or parish, the adequacy of existing bank facilities depends on a number of other factors such as income, loan volume, bank deposits, etc. Unfortunately, not all of the relevant factors can be measured quantitatively.

LOUISIANA AND
THE WORLD ECONOMY
Robert A. Flammang*

Most people take foreign trade for granted. We all eat and wear foreign-produced goods every day. We produce things for sale abroad every day. Only when the normal course of trade is interrupted by a dock strike, an earthquake, or a canal closure do we become aware of how much our jobs, profits, and living standards depend upon market links with other countries. Even then, the effects of the interruption may be delayed long enough that there seems to be no connection between the cause and the effect.

Few states can match Louisiana's involvement in international trade. New Orleans is the country's second-ranked port. Baton Rouge is seventh in terms of waterborne tonnage. Lake Charles is another important outlet. Together they handle well over two billion dollars worth of goods annually. Together they tie Louisiana firmly to the world economy.

LOUISIANA'S INTERNATIONAL PROFILE

The Mississippi River is often compared to the spout of a funnel which channels the produce of America's rich interior to the rest of the world. Similarly, the great waterway funnels back in payment a wonderful variety of goods and services from abroad. Louisiana sits where the two funnels join. It is difficult to conceive of a more favorable commercial location.

* The writer wishes to thank Mr. Robert K. McClammy, formerly of the Division of Research, College of Business Administration, Louisiana State University, and Mrs. Dorothy Y. Ferguson of the U.S. Department of Commerce Field Office in New Orleans for their assistance in gathering data for this essay.

133

International trade came to Louisiana when people came, and it grew with the settlement of the midlands. American history books invariably reproduce drawings of barges laden with cotton and other produce moving downriver to New Orleans, and of steamboats with people and hard goods aboard making the return trip. As the midlands grew, commerce through the state expanded until by 1850 New Orleans was shipping over half of the entire nation's exports. After the Civil War, New Orleans suffered a relative decline as rapid industrial development in the North spurred new trade through East Coast and Great Lakes ports. Revival came with the twentieth century, but the "Old Queen" still lags far behind the Port of New York today.

In addition to serving as a pipeline through which goods flow, Louisiana is both origin and destination for many world-traded products. Traditional Louisiana-produced exports include rice, cotton, petroleum and chemical products, lumber products, and a host of assorted items from lingerie to canned yams. Its major imports are coffee, sugar, aluminum ores, automobiles, bagging materials, rubber, and bananas. The export industries provide direct employment for thousands within the state, and thousands more are indirectly affected because of their ties to these export industries —people in stores, factories, professions, and on farms who sell their products and services to those producing for export. Imports provide Louisiana consumers with more variety, better prices, and often items of better quality than they could have without this trade, and also provide employment and incomes to those who handle, process, distribute, and service foreign products here. In addition to the income and consumer benefits generated by export and import activity, the state and local governments receive added revenues from the trade-broadened tax base.

In 1963 Louisiana ports handled $2,335 million in foreign waterborne commerce—8.37 percent of the national total. Exports accounted for $1,652 million of this and imports for only $683 million. New Orleans led the other ports by a wide margin with 81 percent of the state total, followed by Baton Rouge with 13 percent and Lake Charles with 5 percent. All of these showed substantial export surpluses.[1]

---

[1] Data in this essay are for *waterborne* commerce only. Airborne traffic is very small by comparison, as is overland haulage. Unless otherwise noted, the data

The principal export items in 1963 from *all* sources (in terms of value) were soybeans, corn, wheat, animal feeds, rice, and cotton. Most of these originated in the Midwest and were bound for Europe and Asia, some under the aegis of the Food for Peace program. Wheat shipments to Eastern Europe have generated additional activity in Louisiana ports, helping New Orleans in 1964 to register a 22 percent increase in grain exports over the previous year. In fact, the ports of Baton Rouge and New Orleans together shipped 42 percent of all U.S.-exported grain in 1964.

The top imports in 1963—coffee, sugar, bananas, automobiles, and aluminum ores—came mainly from Latin America, which supplied roughly half of the state's total. Asia ranked second among the supplying regions, and Europe third. New Orleans, with its excellent facilities for handling general cargo, received 88 percent of the imports.

Strangely enough, the best customers of Louisiana ports in 1963 were the three nations aligned against the U.S. in World War II— Japan, West Germany, and Italy. Next in order were the Netherlands, the United Kingdom, and Venezuela. The state's import business went strongly to Brazil, with Mexico, West Germany, Japan, and India following at some distance.

Of all the goods exported from Louisiana in 1963, 22 percent were produced in the state.[2] Manufactured products accounted for 77 percent of the total of $366 million, or $283 million. A breakdown of this amount shows that chemicals and allied products composed 34 percent, petroleum products and primary metals together 36 percent, food and kindred products 20 percent, and paper and related items 4 percent. Agricultural exports were $83 million or 23 percent of state-produced exports, mainly in the form of cotton and rice.

Effects on Income

In recent years, from 20 to 25 percent of Louisiana's agricultural output and roughly 5 percent of its manufacturing output have been

are from U.S. Bureau of the Census, *Foreign Commerce of the United States* (various years); Port of New Orleans, *Statistics Covering Export-Import Commerce, 1963;* and U.S. Department of Commerce, *Survey of Current Business* (August, 1964).

[2] These figures are approximate because the figure used for Louisiana agricultural exports in 1962 is actually for fiscal 1962–63. See U.S. Bureau of the Census, *Agricultural Export Equivalents by States.*

exported, according to a recent study by the Gulf South Research Institute. (This study, not yet published as this was written, is entitled *Financing the Capital Improvements Program of the Port of New Orleans.*) Overall, therefore, it seems likely that from 8 to 10 percent of the state's output of goods is exported in a typical year. And if it is assumed, as seems reasonable, that production of goods for sale abroad supports proportionally about the same amount of related services (transportation, finance, government, storage, and the like) as does production for sale domestically, it may be argued that roughly one-tenth of the state's income is more or less directly due to its exports alone. In addition, of course, incomes are produced by transporting, storing, financing and selling *imports* and by handling products which flow *through* the state. The total impact of international trade upon Louisiana's income is thus considerably greater than 10 percent in the aggregate, and may amount to as much as 15 or 20 percent by the time we take into account imports, flow-through trade, and the secondary income generated when the incomes directly derived from international trade are spent.[3]

Effects on Employment

Income results from the employment of men, machines, and natural resources. Some activities, such as manufacturing, produce a great deal of income per man employed because they make extensive use of capital goods and raw materials. Agriculture produces somewhat less income per man, as do the service industries. Consequently, the direct effects of international trade on employment depend on which parts of the economy are most involved in this trade. Since 77 percent of Louisiana-produced export items are manufactured products, particularly chemicals and petroleum products (which make relatively little use of labor), the direct job-creating effects of the export sector are not as great as would be the case if agricultural exports were more important. However, those who *are* employed by these industries receive relatively high incomes which have strong secondary effects on employment when they are spent. Thus the Baton Rouge auto salesman who sells a new car to an engineer employed

[3] This is only the simplest of calculations, based on incomplete data and should be viewed in that light.

by one of the large petrochemical firms in the area may owe part of his livelihood to the export activities of that firm. Naturally, these employment effects are hard to measure, and a full assessment here is impossible, but they are present and real, nonetheless.

Effects on Prices

Prices are affected by many things—location, number of producers, type of market, finickiness of consumers, flexibility of costs, bank credit policies, effectiveness of competition. It is difficult to pinpoint precisely what causes prices to behave as they do. Yet certain general conclusions may be drawn about the effects of international trade on prices. Economists generally agree, for example, that many of our balance-of-payments problems in the late fifties were caused by hefty price increases in certain of our key industries, particularly in steel. The advent of foreign competition from Western Europe and Japan no doubt helped slow down rising prices, and may be an important factor in explaining this country's relative stability of prices in the early sixties. Auto and steel prices, for example, held remarkably steady and the export-import picture improved markedly at the same time.

Louisiana has experienced a slower rate of inflation than the nation as a whole since the end of World War II. The Consumer Price Index showed a rise of over 38 percent for the country as a whole from 1947 to 1964, while Louisiana climbed only 31 percent. From 1962 to 1964 the disparity increased: the national CPI rose at an annual average of 1.2 percent, while Louisiana registered only .9 percent.[4] Again, various factors may be responsible for this phenomenon—the relative weakness of organized labor, or a relatively slow rate of growth, for example. Yet it seems likely that part of this relative stability can be attributed to the state's involvement in international markets where price competition is brisk. Imported commodities cost less in Louisiana because there is less freight in their prices than there is for the same goods in Denver or Minneapolis. The accessibility of low-cost water transportation keeps prices

[4] These figures are from the *Survey of Current Business*, various issues, and from data compiled by the Division of Research, College of Business Administration, Louisiana State University.

from increasing as they otherwise might. The net effect is a slower rate of erosion of real income and a positive gain in welfare.[5]

Summing Up

Louisiana is a foreign-trading state. Its location has made it a "natural" since the beginning of settlement in the midlands. It has always been an "export" state by a wide margin. International trade contributes a sizeable block of income and employment, directly or indirectly, to the state economy, while acting as a stabilizer to prices. These translate into higher living standards for Louisiana, thanks to the world economy.

CHANGES IN THE PROFILE

Change is the essence of life, deep thinkers tell us. Sometimes it comes so slowly that it passes unnoticed. The period since World War II, however, has been characterized by almost revolutionary changes. Some of this is reflected in Louisiana's changing relationships to the world economy.

Louisiana and the Nation

In 1948 Louisiana accounted for 9.6 percent of the value of the nation's total waterborne exports and imports. By 1955 this share had fallen to 8.8 percent, and by 1963 it had shrunk further to under 8.4 percent. In terms of weight, the state's percentages in the same years were 6.1 percent, 5.6 percent, and 6.6 percent. Louisiana's foreign trade is worth more per ton than the national average, but its value share has been declining while its weight share has held steady or even increased. The trend in value per ton is down.

In terms of export values alone, the state more than doubled its share of the national total between 1946 and 1950 (from 5.8 percent to 11.7 percent), but it has leveled off since then, averaging about 11.2 percent per year. However, Louisiana's share of the

[5] It does not follow that *all* port cities will experience less inflation than areas farther inland. New York, for example, has seen its CPI rise faster than the national average. But New York is also more heavily dependent on domestic trade and has lack-of-space problems which Louisiana ports have been spared.

nation's export tonnage has followed a slow upward trend, with the largest increases coming since 1958—probably due mainly to increased shipping of grain.

Imports are the major factor in Louisiana's relative decline vis-à-vis the nation in total value of waterborne international trade. The state's import share dropped from 8.6 percent in 1949 to only 5.3 percent in 1963. Similarly, Louisiana import tonnage fell from 6 percent of the national total in 1958 to only 3.8 percent in 1963. These are significant changes.

It was mentioned earlier that Louisiana is basically an "export" state. Since the mid-1950's, it has become even more so. From 1948 to 1955 its surplus of exports over imports averaged $374.8 million annually, but this figure jumped dramatically to an annual average of $833.4 million in the 1956–63 period, and has hovered around the one billion dollar mark since 1961. This heavy export surplus has contributed strongly to the overall "favorable" balance of trade the nation has experienced since the war. In fact, in 1953 and 1959 when waterborne imports exceeded exports for the nation as a whole, Louisiana ports still ran sizeable surpluses, and for the 1948–61 period Louisiana ports accounted for approximately 30 percent of the overall trade surplus of the nation in waterborne commerce.

Louisiana and the Gulf Region

Louisiana's strongest competition comes from ports in other Gulf states, particularly Texas. Houston is one of New Orleans' top contenders for the second position among U.S. ports. Galveston, Port Arthur, and Mobile are also major Gulf outlets.

In value, Louisiana's share of waterborne international trade moving through Gulf ports rose from 48.7 percent in 1948 to 50.6 percent in 1955, then fell to 41.6 percent by 1963. In weight, the state's portions in the same years were 33.6 percent, 35.9 percent, and 32.2 percent—again a rise, then a decline. Louisiana has not been keeping pace with its near competitors in recent years.

The state increased its value share of Gulf exports from 1946 until 1954, then lost ground until 1959, regained some by 1962, then dropped sharply in 1963. The same general pattern was repeated with respect to export tonnage. However, Louisiana's slice of Gulf import values dropped rather steadily in the postwar years, from

67.9 percent in 1948 to 45.7 percent in 1963. The import weight picture showed more variation, but the general trend was down, too.

So it appears that the major element in Louisiana's slippage in relation to both the nation and the Gulf region is a relatively slow growth of imports. In fact, state import values held rather steady in absolute terms throughout the fifties, although tonnage increased somewhat. Meanwhile, ports in other areas succeeded in expanding their imports dramatically (particularly from Europe and Japan), leaving Louisiana farther in their wake.

Within Louisiana

Notable changes have also occurred in the relative importance of Louisiana's different ports to the state's aggregate foreign trade. For example, New Orleans accounted for 92.7 percent of the value of the state's waterborne exports in 1948, but only 77.7 percent in 1963. Similarly, its share of state export tonnage declined from 81.8 percent to 64.1 percent in the same period. Meanwhile, Baton Rouge increased its value percentage from 2.5 percent in 1955 to 15.1 percent in 1963, and its weight share from 6.9 percent to 26.0 percent. Lake Charles averaged about 6 percent in value and 7.5 percent in weight during the period, showing no clear tendencies either up or down. Port Sulphur accounted for about 1 percent of Louisiana exports in value and about 5 percent in weight throughout the fifties, but it has been declining in importance during the sixties.

The story is much the same on the import side. New Orleans slipped in the 1948–63 period from 99.5 percent to 88.5 percent in value and 88.7 percent to 45.1 percent in weight. Concurrently, Baton Rouge expanded from .5 percent to 9.5 percent in value and from 9.7 percent to 53.3 percent in weight. Indeed, Baton Rouge has exceeded New Orleans in import tonnage since 1961. Lake Charles' import share has grown, but it still handled only 1.2 percent of the state's total value and 1.6 percent of its weight in 1963. Port Sulphur's import contribution is negligible.

Summing Up

Louisiana's foreign trade has declined in relative importance in the nation and in the Gulf area, basically because its import activity has lagged. Part of the result is a growing surplus of exports over imports—a happy consequence, in light of the nation's balance-of-payments difficulties, but a not-so-happy one if optimum usage of port facilities and shipping tonnage (and maximum local income generation) is deemed desirable.

Within the state, New Orleans has lost ground to its sister ports, particularly Baton Rouge. It still retains its dominant position by a wide margin, but more dramatic growth is being registered by the smaller ports. This is in keeping with a nationwide trend—international trade is becoming less concentrated in major ports.[6]

PORT PERSONALITIES

New Orleans

The Port of New Orleans is a general cargo port which prides itself that it can handle anything that moves in international trade. It covers some fifty miles of developed area along the Mississippi and adjoining deep water canals, including about twenty-five miles of wharves and other waterfront facilities. There are special berths for handling bananas, bulk grain, sacked grain, bulk materials such as ores, and for ship repair. The port is connected to the Gulf by the Mississippi and by a new Mississippi-Gulf tidewater channel which shortens the distance to the Gulf by some forty miles. Inland, it connects with some 12,000 miles of navigable waterways and eight trunk-line railroads.

New Orleans enjoys a number of advantages over competing ports. Great Lakes and St. Lawrence Seaway ports are closed by ice each winter. General cargo handling equipment gives it an edge over smaller ports in the Gulf. Its access to inland waterways is unexcelled. It has been a port for a long time, is well-known throughout the world, and offers regular sailings and a full complement of supporting services. And it has the only Foreign Trade Zone in the Gulf area. This 20-acre zone is free from any tariff or trade restriction whatever, and goods may be brought in, stored, processed, broken into smaller lots, or handled in any manner without being considered as U.S. imports. Only if they move out of the zone into the country proper do they pay import duties. Such zones both attract imports because of the lessened red tape involved and encourage the establishment of small manufacturing operations to process items before

[6] See Lawrence F. Mansfield, "International Trade and District Ports," Federal Reserve Bank of Atlanta *Monthly Review* (September, 1964), 2.

they go through customs. The New Orleans Foreign Trade Zone presently includes a fumigation plant, a battery-manufacturing plant, a casein manufacturing plant, and facilities for packaging Brazil nuts and storing foreign automobiles.

Baton Rouge

The Port of Baton Rouge is much more specialized than New Orleans. Most of its import tonnage is aluminum ore, while its exports are primarily soybeans, wheat, flour, corn, animal feeds, and finished petroleum products. The port itself dates only from 1952, although heavy industry in the area had their own docking facilities earlier, and a municipal dock had existed since 1925. Since the mid-1950's facilities and trade have expanded so rapidly that the port ranked eighth in the nation by weight and twelfth by value in 1962.

Baton Rouge's progress is due both to natural and acquired advantages. It is the farthest inland deep-water port on the Mississippi and the Gulf—a full 230 miles from the river's mouth. It, like New Orleans, is linked to the vast inland waterway system and is served by four major railroads, a developing Interstate highway system, and an extensive pipeline network. A growing industrial complex requiring more and more imported raw materials and shipping increasing amounts of finished products is centered in the area. Like New Orleans, it is ice-free the year around and can rely on a dependable water flow, with a minimum chance of flooding.

The port owns and leases to private businesses grain elevators with a 7.5 million bushel capacity, an 11 million gallon tank terminal, and a bulk-handling terminal and warehouse facility at Burnside. It also has a small general cargo dock, currently undergoing expansion.

Lake Charles

Lake Charles is also a specialized port, with rice as its major export. However, it also exports considerable amounts of petroleum and chemical products. The port comprises some 203 square miles of the Calcasieu basin area, and is but thirty-three miles from the Gulf. It has a small general cargo area, a high density cotton compress, a combination phosphate rock and barite ore grinding plant, and facilities for handling petroleum coke, creosote, and coconut oil.

It connects with the Gulf through the Lake Charles-Calcasieu River Ship Channel, with the Intracoastal Canal, with three major railroads, three federal highways, and the new Interstate highway system. Currently, the ship channel is being enlarged and an industrial canal is under construction.

The Lake Charles Port benefits from its ready access to the rich agriculture of southwestern Louisiana and from the extensive petroleum and chemical installations in the area. It, too, is basically an export port—imports amounted to only $8.3 million in 1963, compared with exports of over $104 million.

WHERE TO?

Louisiana and Brazil have something in common. Brazilians are known for bragging about their country's vast economic potential— but somehow this potential goes on, year to year, never really being tapped, while countries poorer in basic resources outstrip Brazil in growth and per capita income. Similarly, Louisianians like to point with pride to the state's wealth of agricultural, mineral, and industrial resources—but Louisiana stands relatively low among the fifty states in per capita personal income. Some of its cities enjoy high average incomes, but many others are far, far behind. There are reasons for this, of course. Some of the reasons most frequently cited are the lack of a skilled, well-trained labor force (Louisiana imports much of its skilled labor); uncertain political climate; hostility to change in some areas; and proclivity for local capital to seek safe, traditional, conservative outlets. In fact, similar reasons are often given for the lack of speedy, well-distributed growth in Brazil!

The international sector of the Louisiana economy has suffered along with the rest. The evidence shows that exports have grown at the national rate—thanks in part to agricultural surplus disposal operations—while imports have been relatively stagnant. This is not all Louisiana's fault, since most of the imports flow on to other states. But certainly part of it *is* Louisiana's fault and is subject to improvement if the proper decisions are made.

Actually, the Louisiana pattern of heavy export surpluses is merely an extension and magnification of a similar national pattern. For the past century, this country has been extremely "export conscious," anxious to sell but reluctant to buy from abroad. This was understandable a century ago or even fifty years ago, because the U.S. was at that time a debtor nation and it needed an export surplus to repay foreign loans. Since World War I, however, it has been a creditor nation and each year sees that status extended a bit more. Debtor countries complain that they are unable to reduce their obligations because the U.S. is reluctant to accept repayment, i.e., imports. It seems as if we still have with us the old mercantilistic idea—that the road to national wealth (or gold hoards) is through a "favorable balance of trade." There are, of course, good reasons for seeking an export surplus at certain times—when unemployment is a problem, for example, or when the rest of the world is simply unable to pay for the barest necessities of life, as at the end of World War II. But in the long run, exports benefit a nation by paying for its imports— imports which add to its standard of living—and if it refuses these imports but wishes to continue its export surplus, it must enable the rest of the world to buy its goods in some other way, perhaps by means of loans or grants. If it does not, its exports will have to diminish after foreigners exhaust their supplies of dollars and/or gold.

The point is that a heavy export surplus over a long period of time is wasteful. Ships haul goods away and return partially empty. Goods are produced for sale abroad, but few return to bolster the standard of living here. If this results because U.S. citizens want to invest abroad and sacrifice immediate returns in order to derive a larger return in the future, there is no cause for concern—the investment benefits both the lender and the borrower. But if it results because U.S. citizens would rather produce than consume, or because they do not fully understand the basic nature of *trade* with its *two* avenues of flowing goods, it is economically foolish and wasteful. And the U.S., with its tradition of "export consciousness," falls at least partially in the latter category. And Louisiana, to the extent that it beats the drums for exports while ignoring or de-emphasizing the real value of imports, is failing to exploit its real natural advantages.

At the present time there is little pressure on the United States or Louisiana to expand imports. Everyone has heard of the alarming balance-of-payments troubles which have depleted the nation's gold stock by over 30 percent since the mid-1950's and knows of the national government's program of export expansion to curb the deficit. This may seem a peculiar time to discuss the wonderful gains from importing. Treason is not intended here. What *is* intended is that we not lose sight of a basic proposition: exports buy imports in the long run. It is not necessary or desirable that any given state's exports exactly balance its imports, but we must pay attention to the overall contribution of trade on *both* sides and ask ourselves if we are missing any good bets.

Another trend in Louisiana's foreign trade is worth noting—the tendency for its value per ton to decline. Tonnage does not contribute to general well being per se, but value does. Income is nothing more than a flow of currently-produced values, and to the extent that exports and imports drop in value per pound or ton, foreign trade's impact on the economy's overall income is reduced. In 1948 Louisiana's exports were valued about 60 percent higher per pound than the national average; by 1955 they were only 45 percent above and in 1963 only 3 percent above. Louisiana imports rated a premium per pound of 46 percent over the national average in 1948, rose to the 61 percent level in 1955, and fell back to 41 percent by 1963. No doubt a major part of the falling export value per pound can be attributed to the relative weakness of agricultural commodity prices in recent years—Louisiana is heavily dependent on these for exports and is growing in importance as an outlet. There is nothing *wrong* with pushing agricultural exports—far from it—but trade in these goods will not boost state income as much as trade in higher valued, more complex manufactured goods.

Enough has been said on the negative side. What about the positive elements in Louisiana's future relations to the world economy?

Most of the world is hungry and is getting hungrier as population increases. Probably no area of the world is better suited to food production than the vast midlands of North America. These facts alone indicate a rosy future for Louisiana's prime exports. In addition, a larger share of the mid-continent's production seems to be flowing through ice-free Gulf ports. And some of the boomingest markets of the future may well be those of Central and South America, near neighbors of Louisiana who have long done business through the state's ports. As income grows to the south of us, much will be spent for food, and larger numbers of people will add to the demand. Moreover, rising incomes will prompt heavier buying of machinery and durable consumer goods. The current growth of Europe and Japan is also pulling more goods through Louisiana, and no doubt will continue to do so. Again, the potential is there, and there is no good economic reason why the state should not enjoy a prospering export business in the years ahead.

The U.S. population is growing, too, and is developing a healthy appetite for imported goods. Coffee imports will grow, but nontraditional imports such as Chilean shoes, Japanese motorcycles, and Mexican chemicals will grow faster. Over the longer pull, imports of basic raw materials for industry will have to expand as our domestic supplies become more depleted, and much of this will move through Louisiana to feed its plants and those further upriver. Technological breakthroughs which economize the use of these materials may slow down the demand for them somewhat, but are unlikely to cut the need completely off. So the Louisiana import picture in the future appears bright, too.

It is not enough to passively sit back and wait for prosperity. Minor gains may be made, but the fruits will go to those forever on the prowl for new opportunities. Just as sedentary landowners were outdistanced by opportunistic industrialists when the Industrial Revolution began, tradition-bound economies are today being left behind by those sensitive to change and progress. The new is not *always* better than the old, but the odds favor it—if they did not, we would not have progress, but retrogression.

Louisiana is not sitting still while others move. A new 33-story International Trade Mart in New Orleans will tie nations and their commerce closer together. Trade missions of Louisiana businessmen to other countries are growing more numerous. New investments in port facilities are made every day. Educational programs to make businessmen and citizens more aware of the facts of foreign trading are underway. A seaway that would open south-central Louisiana to ocean-going vessels has been proposed. These are encouraging signs of life which deserve active support from the state government, business community, and public generally.

Still more—in addition to emphasizing imports—can be done, however. The smaller ports, Baton Rouge and Lake Charles, are among the fastest growing in the nation—yet they are strongly in need of supporting services which foster trade. These services—international banking facilities, freight forwarding, export management, warehousing and storage, display facilities—can open many doors for would-be traders, but without them trade moves to traditional outlets, or overlooks foreign markets and sources of supply completely.

Perhaps the prime need of the state is for more and better information about doing business with other countries. There is a tendency for old hands in any line of activity to bunch together and keep their knowledge to themselves. This makes for a decidedly parochial environment—and many would-be traders never venture into the fascinating world of international trade. New Orleans abounds with people knowledgeable about how to establish connections abroad, while communities a few miles away are filled with curious individuals who confine themselves to home operations because they do not have the vaguest idea how to even get started on a broader scale. Communication is absolutely essential to any kind of commerce.

Louisiana, the export state, has come far in tying itself to the world economy. It will no doubt go much farther. Most of its people, however, accustomed to the steady throb of daily life, will scarcely notice the effect of its regular foreign trade upon their well-being—unless it should stop.

REGULATION OF PUBLIC
UTILITIES IN LOUISIANA

James P. Payne, Jr.

As the American economy has developed from an agrarian to a highly
industrialized economy, business organization has changed from primarily small, numerous, and highly competitive firms to large industrial corporations with limited competition. Commensurate with
this development has been the emergence of the problem of economic
power and the concentration of control over markets. The resolu-
tion of these problems in the American economy has been, and currently is being, approached in two different, although related, ways.
While the antitrust approach to these problems involves the attempt
to encourage and maintain competition and to eliminate restraints
on trade contrary to the public interest, the public utility concept is
different. The public utility concept formally recognizes that the
technical and economic facts of production in certain enterprises
("natural monopolies") support a degree of economic concentration
and that competition could be inadequate and possibly ruinous.
Coupled with a quasi-monopoly grant by the public is the right to
exercise control over entry, rates, quantity, and quality of service offered by public utility enterprises. In effect, the public utility concept embodies the substitution of the reasoned judgment decision of
regulation for the imperfections of a market mechanism where competition renders an inadequate decision and uncontrolled monopoly
is contrary to the best interest of society.[1]

[1] For a somewhat different point of view of the public utility concept, see
Horace M. Gray, "The Passing of the Public Utility Concept," *Journal of Land
and Public Utility Economics*, XVI (February, 1940), 8–20. For a criticism of
the concept as having some theoretical validity but failing in application and

THE DEVELOPMENT OF REGULATION IN
THE AMERICAN SYSTEM

Regulation of public utilities in the American economy encompasses two different, but interrelated, aspects: the economic and the legal. The legal aspect of regulation is simply the action of the collective whole through its agency, government, over the unlimited expression of the rights of the individual. The source of the power to regulate is found in the police power of the state and the delegated powers (particularly the commerce clause) of the federal government. Under these powers the coercive use of property and the economic power stemming therefrom have been limited for the benefits of both society and the individual.

But the legal aspect of regulation is insufficient to explain public utility regulation; the economic aspect must also be examined. Public utility regulation reflects an intelligent recognition of the economic characteristics of utility production and a realization that the market mechanism would render decisions contrary to sound economic growth and development.[2] Regulatory decisions must be made after careful consideration of the following economic factors: the "natural monopoly" characteristics of the industry; the inadequacy of unrestricted competition to regulate price and service and to efficiently allocate resources; the technical limitations of the market; the relatively low elasticity of demand for some of the services offered; the large investment necessary to render efficient service; the economies of full plant utilization; the economies of size; multi-service production and the associated cost allocation problem; the motive for and the necessity of differential pricing; and the problems of both intra-industry and inter-industry competition.

Prior to the establishment of the regulatory commission type of regulation in the United States, attempts had been made to regulate the utility industry by such means as charter provisions, common law direct regulation by the courts, and direct regulation by statute; but such methods were generally not successful for various reasons.[3]

---

practice and resulting in the promotion of monopoly, see Walter Adams and Horace Gray, *Monopoly in America* (New York, 1955), Chap. 3.

[2] For a more detailed discussion, see Ben Lewis, "The Rationale of Regulation," in Leverett Lyon and Victor Abramson (eds.), *Government and Economic Life* (Washington, D.C., 1940), II, 618–26.

[3] For a detailed discussion of early regulation, see D. P. Locklin, *Economics of Transportation* (6th ed.; Homewood, Ill., 1960), 197–207.

The lack of success with these forms of regulation did not blunt the public's quest for regulation or negate the need for an effective regulatory scheme. Since the power to regulate resided in the legislature, and since such a body was neither experienced nor did it have time to concern itself with the specific application of regulation, the device of the regulatory commission was conceived. While states early formed commissions which enjoyed varying degrees of success, the device achieved fruition when the Interstate Commerce Commission was created by the Act to Regulate Commerce in 1887.

Some authorities view the regulatory commission as a fourth branch of government operating under a new type of law—administrative law—a law, which by all evidences has reached astounding proportions in both influence and application.[4] More specifically, the regulatory commission embodies the functions of all three branches of American government. The commission functions in a quasi-executive, quasi-legislative, and quasi-judicial capacity. In enforcing the provisions of the law under which it operates, the commission is exercising its quasi-executive powers. In investigating and prescribing reasonable practices for the future, it is functioning in a quasi-legislative capacity. In the determination of the reasonableness of past conduct, the commission exhibits its quasi-judicial function. Its relationship to the three branches of government may be summarily stated: the legislature gives it life and direction; the judiciary may review its decisions and require it to function under the law; and the executive furnishes it organization, enforcement assistance, and budgetary needs.[5]

Paramount in the relationship of the commission with other agencies of government is the concept of independence; that is, the recognition that the commission must be awarded independence in reaching its reasoned judgment conclusions in administering the law. Failure to recognize and respect this independence makes the commission subservient to external pressure and renders its decisions subject to a challenge of being capricious, biased, and arbitrary.[6]

[4] See, for example, James Landis, *The Administrative Process* (New Haven, 1938).

[5] There are numerous excellent discussions of the regulatory commission within the American framework of government, among which are: I. L. Sharfman, *The Interstate Commerce Commission* (New York, 1936), I-IV; Landis, *The Administrative Process*; Robert E. Cushman, *The Independent Regulatory Commissions* (New York, 1941); and Locklin, *Economics of Transportation*, Chap. 14.

[6] The case for independence may be found in Sharfman, *The Interstate Com-*

Central also to an understanding of the functioning of the commission is the question of initiative and the exercise thereof. The American concept of public utility regulation leaves the initiative for economic decision-making with the utility in the *first instance*, with the commission only reviewing such action upon a showing of due cause. However, inaction, improper action, or refusal to act on the part of the utility passes the initiative to the commission which must act under the law. Past policies and annunciations by the commission constitute "working rules" which guide and condition private managerial decisions. More succinctly, the functions of the commission do not precede managerial determination; rather, they cover the reasonableness of such action.

DEVELOPMENT OF STATE REGULATION AND THE REGULATORY FRAMEWORK IN LOUISIANA

Development of the State Regulatory Commission as an Agency of Control

One might divide the evolution of the state regulatory commission into three periods: from the 1830's to the Granger movement; from the Granger movement of the 1870's to the Progressive movement of the early 1900's; and from the Progressive movement to the present.

During the primacy of charter regulation, certain supervisory controls or supplementary regulations not repugnant to the charter were assigned by statute to administrative commissions. Such early commissions have been characterized by students of regulation as "advisory type" or "weak type" commissions. Commissions of this nature were established as early as 1836 in Rhode Island, 1844 in New Hampshire, and 1853 in Connecticut.[7]

Unsatisfactory results of control by direct legislation as evidenced

---

merce Commission, IV, 254–74; Landis, *The Administrative Process*, 111–17; Locklin, *Economics of Transportation*, Chap. 14. For the views of a distinguished public servant see Joseph B. Eastman, "A Twelve Point Primer on the Subject of Administrative Tribunals," in G. Lloyd Wilson (ed.), *Selected Papers and Addresses of Joseph B. Eastman* (New York, 1948). For a criticism and an argument that commissions have failed to meet the test of political responsibility in a democratic society, see Marver H. Bernstein, *Regulating Business by Independent Commission* (Princeton, 1955).

[7] Martin G. Glaeser, *Public Utilities in American Capitalism* (New York, 1957), 35 ff.

by the rigidity of the "Granger laws" led to the realization of the need for general statutory enactments of guidelines and for continuous regulation by an agency sufficiently experienced to administer the necessary details. Hence, in the mid-western states and to a degree in the southern states, regulatory commissions were erected with positive powers to prescribe rates and service rules and to enforce them. These commissions have been termed "mandatory" or "strong type" commissions. Illinois established its commission in 1871, followed by Iowa, Minnesota, and Wisconsin in 1874, and by Georgia and California in 1879.[8]

But what was to eventually become the characteristics of present-day commissions was not yet destined to be in the 1870's. The panic of 1873 resulted in financial difficulties for many railroads and was skillfully used by them as evidence that the legislation was an economic mistake. Rightly or wrongly it was effective. With the exception of Illinois, states either abolished their commissions or reduced them to an "advisory" or "weak" commission.

Yet it was during this second period that Congress moved to fill a void created by the U.S. Supreme Court's ruling in the *Wabash* case[9] by establishing the Interstate Commerce Commission—a "strong" type commission. At the state level, Massachusetts established the Board of Gas Commissioners in 1885, the first real attempt to regulate utilities other than the railroads. Although it had comprehensive powers, it still lacked the full powers of an aggressive "strong" commission. Other states moved to restore power to their commissions, yet this period must be characterized as one of largely "weak" type commissions and vacillation regarding the forms of control.

Many authorities date the erection of the modern regulatory commission with the reform movement starting in the early 1900's. More specifically, the initiative of the Progressive movement led by Governor (later Senator) Robert LaFollette of Wisconsin and under the guidance of Professor John R. Commons of the University of Wisconsin culminated in 1907 with passage of legislation in Wisconsin which established a "strong" commission and incorporated provisions which called for continuous supervision under statutory standards of reasonableness. In the same year New York, under the leadership of Governor Charles Evans Hughes, adopted similar legis-

8 *Ibid.*, 63–64.
9 118 U.S. 577 (1886).

lation. So contagious was the movement that by 1913, only three states were without commissions.[10]

Currently all states have regulatory commissions, although the scope of their jurisdiction varies. Extensive regulation is generally imposed upon the following: common carriers by rail, motor, water, and pipeline, including associated facilities; communication common carriers by telephone, telegraph, and cable; and electric, water, natural and manufactured gas, and urban transportation utilities. A limited number of states restrict their commissions to the intercity operations of utilities, leaving regulation of urban utilities to local authorities. Some states leave the control of specific utilities, particularly water and urban transport, to local government entirely. However, most states have not given their commissions authority over municipally owned utilities or over cooperatives engaged in public utility service, such as those financed by the Rural Electrification Administration (REA).

Development of the Commission Type of Regulation in Louisiana

It was not until near the end of the second period in the evolution of state regulatory commissions that Louisiana moved to establish a regulatory agency. The Constitution of 1898, in Articles 283 through 289, provided for the Railroad Commission of Louisiana which was duly organized in Baton Rouge on December 9, 1898. It continued to function until June 30, 1921, when it was superseded by the Louisiana Public Service Commission (LPSC). During its tenure of over twenty-two years, the Railroad Commission issued some 2,426 orders as well as twenty-two annual reports covering a wide range of regulatory problems.[11]

The Constitution of 1921, which created the LPSC, also provided for enlarged powers and extended jurisdiction over those of the old Railroad Commission. All acts of the legislature following the Constitution of 1898 and in effect at the adoption of the 1921 Constitution relating to the Railroad Commission and not inconsistent with the new constitution were retained by Article VI, Section 9. This was

[10] Prior to 1907, state commission jurisdiction was largely confined to common carriers, but following the dissatisfaction with franchise regulation, jurisdiction was extended to all types of utilities.

[11] Pierce A. Frye (comp.), *Louisiana Public Service Commission Laws* (1940). The following discussion rests heavily upon this work.

necessary to make important court decisions relating to the powers and duties of the old commission applicable to the new LPSC.

The new commission came into being on July 1, 1921, with Shelby Taylor as chairman, and Huey P. Long and John T. Michel as members.[12] It immediately issued a general order adopting all of the rates, fares or charges, and the rules and regulations of its predecessor applicable to the common carriers and public utilities under its jurisdiction, thus legalizing and preserving the acts of the Railroad Commission.

The relevant part of the 1921 Constitution concerning the state regulatory agency is Article VI, Sections 3 through 9. Section 3 formed

CHART 1

ORGANIZATIONAL CHART

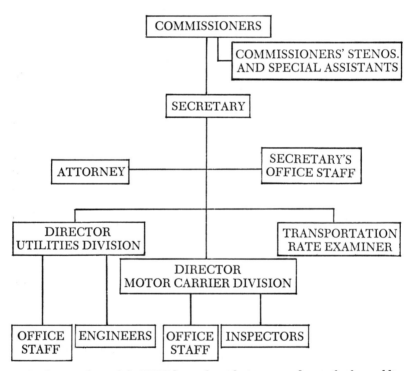

[12] Other members of the LPSC have, through time, moved on to further public service. Among these, the most noted are Jimmie Davis and John McKeithen, who along with Huey P. Long became governor of the state.

the commission with three members to be elected from three public service districts into which the state was divided. The election coincides with the congressional elections. The term of office was set at six years, and no member can be in the employ of or hold any official relation or have any pecuniary interest in any company under the jurisdiction of the LPSC. Initial salary was $3,000 per year and has since been raised to $12,500. The present organization of the commission is shown above.

Extent and Scope of Jurisdiction
of the Louisiana Public Service Commission

It is not the intent of this essay to detail the legislation and jurisdiction of the LPSC but to state in general its field of jurisdiction.

Section 4 of Article VI details the businesses subject to the jurisdiction of the commission and states the powers and duties as follows:

(1) to supervise, govern, regulate, and control all common carrier railroads, street railroads, interurban railroads, steamboats and other water craft, sleeping car, express, telephone, telegraph, gas, electric light, heat and power, water works, common carrier pipe lines, canals (except irrigation canals), and other public utilities in the State of Louisiana (motor carriers were brought under jurisdiction by Act No. 301 of 1938, as amended, and follows the general pattern established by the Federal Motor Carrier Act of 1935);

(2) to fix reasonable and just rates or charges for services or commodities rendered by such companies;

(3) to have authority to affect and include all matters and things connected with, concerning, and growing out of the service by said companies;

(4) to adopt and enforce such reasonable rules, regulations, and modes of procedure as it deemed proper to carry out its duties;

(5) to summon and compel witnesses to appear, to compel production of records, to take testimony, and to punish for contempt.

Section 4 also declares the right of the legislature to place other utilities under the control of the commission and to confer additional powers upon the commission subject only to the limitations of the constitution.

The enforcement and judicial review of commission orders are found in Section 5 of Article VI and may be summarized as follows:

(1) the orders of the commission are to go into effect at a time

set by the commission and remain in effect unless set aside by the commission or by a final judgment of a court of competent jurisdiction;

(2) the district court having jurisdiction may issue a temporary restraining order in cases where the court feels irreparable harm might result pending the final determination of an application for an interlocutory injunction;

(3) appeals from orders and decrees of the commission may be made by filing suit in the trial court at the commission's domicile if within ninety days from the date of the order or decree;

(4) cases under review are to be tried summarily with preference over all cases in the trial and appellate courts, and appeals from decisions of the trial court shall be direct to the Supreme Court.

Penalties for violation of commission orders or decisions within the range of $100 to $5,000 for each violation may be fixed by the commission and recovered through the courts as outlined by Section 6.

Section 7 is most important since it secures to towns, cities, and parishes control and regulation of local utilities vested in such governmental units at the time the constitution was adopted. A majority of qualified voters may vote to surrender such powers and if so voted, such powers are immediately vested in the LPSC. However, Section 7 also contains a "change of mind" provision which permits a local government to re-invest itself of such powers by a like vote. Some doubt regarding the extent of this part of Section 7 was cast by Act No. 19 (November 21, 1934) which revoked regulation of privately owned utilities by local governments and vested such regulation in the LPSC. However, Section 7 of Article VI remained unchanged by the Revised Statutes of 1950 and subsequent court decisions appear to uphold its effectiveness respecting the reservation of jurisdiction in the hands of local governments who had such powers at the time of the adoption of the Constitution of 1921.[13]

Section 8 prescribes the three public service commission districts and enumerates the parishes encompassed in each. Section 9 has previously been noted.[14] Other articles of the constitution apply to regulated enterprises. Article XIII, Section 3 declares railroads to be public highways and requires them to connect with other railroads and to receive and transport shipments without delay or discrimina-

[13] For example, see *City of Monroe v. LPSC*, 223 La. 478 (1956).
[14] See previous pages.

tion. Section 4 of Article XIII requires all railroads and public utilities doing business in Louisiana to maintain offices in the state and necessary records for public inspection. Article XIV, Section 19 provides that the legislature has the power to enact laws authorizing local agencies of government to levy special taxes in aid of railways, water transportation lines, waterworks, and electric light or power plants. Free passes, free transportation, franking privileges, and discrimination are prohibited under penalty to both the seeker and the offerer by Section 15 of Article XIX. Of great importance is Article XIX, Section 18 which says, "The exercise of the police power of this State shall never be abridged."

Numerous acts of the legislature have affected the jurisdiction of the LPSC. Space permits summarizing only two as examples of both additions and deletions. Act No. 254 of 1936 authorizes the LPSC to require electric utilities to extend their services and facilities where reasonable prospects of an adequate return are present. To prevent unnecessary duplication, it further requires that no such utility shall render or extend its services or facilities to customers already receiving service from another electric utility without first obtaining a certificate of public convenience and necessity. It should be noted that certification is required only in areas where some service is already being offered but not in the initiation of service in virgin territory. This act is currently the subject of several cases before the commission and in the courts dealing with the territorial conflicts arising between electric public utilities per se and the REA cooperatives. Act No. 373 of 1946 extends LPSC jurisdiction over the transportation or sale of natural gas by pipe lines, including limited jurisdiction over direct industrial sales necessary to prevent prejudice in rates charged for gas sold to local distributing systems for resale. However, by an amendment to Section 4 of Article VI of the constitution adopted on November 3, 1964 (Act No. 531), the commission was relieved of jurisdiction over "sales of natural gas direct to industrial users for fuel or for utilization in any manufacturing process."

REGULATION IN PRACTICE: A SUMMARY OF THE PRIMARY ELEMENTS OF A FORMAL REVENUE CASE

Regulation is a very complex and intricate process. While much of the regulatory process is routine, day-to-day administration, the impact of regulation is greatest in cases requiring the full breadth of formal proceedings before the commission. It is only through the study of a formal proceedings (preferably by actual observation and the following of a case from origin to conclusion) that a clear understanding and appreciation of regulation can be obtained. It is the purpose of this section to summarize the primary elements presented in two recent and highly significant cases regulating the rates for telephone service in Louisiana.

The cases chosen for review are general revenue cases where the primary concern is the adequacy of the aggregation of earnings to meet the economic and legal tests of reasonableness. The following formula expresses the issues which must be resolved in such cases: $TR = E + (V{-}D)r$. In order for rates to be reasonable, the total revenue (TR) obtained from such rates must be sufficient (and no more) to equate the total costs of rendering the service as measured by the sum of operating expenses (E) and a fair return on the net investment of the utility $(V{-}D)r$. Net investment is computed as the value of the property, both used and useful, devoted to public service (V) less a measure of depreciation of such property (D). The $(V{-}D)$ portion of the formula is more properly termed the "rate base" upon which a reasonable rate of return (r) is to be allowed. The determination of the proper measures to be incorporated in the formula is more critical than might be assumed from the simple symbolic statement. Further, in contrast to most business accounting, interest on the debts of the utility is considered in the return sector of the formula, rather than as an operating expense. Also, the income tax liability of the utility is considered much like an operating expense, since a return held reasonable for the investors is the return remaining after provisions for such taxes.

The decisions of the U.S. Supreme Court in the *Natural Gas* case in 1942[15] and the *Hope* case in 1944[16] established what has become known as the "end result" doctrine which portrays the court's interest in the result of the commission's action rather than the specific techniques used in reaching its conclusions. Standards of reasonableness laid down by the court in these and subsequent cases emphasize revenues sufficient to enable the utility to maintain its credit and to attract capital—that is, the ability to pay interest and dividends.

[15] 315 U.S. 575 (1942).
[16] 320 U.S. 591 (1944).

Hence, much of the recent concern in general revenue cases has centered primarily upon the determination of a fair rate of return and the capital structure of the utility. Following these decisions, numerous approaches or techniques were introduced in regulatory proceedings which purported to develop a cost of capital or cost of money theory as the basis for arriving at a reasonable rate of return.

In two recent Louisiana telephone rate cases, the LPSC adopted a technique which may be best described as an earnings requirement test based upon a modification of the cost of capital approach to the determination of a rate of return. Although various aspects of this technique have been used elsewhere, there are unique factors in the Louisiana cases which deserve direct attention and require comparison with other authorities. Since the method used in the first case, and subsequently upheld by the state supreme court, was used again in the second case and modified somewhat by a second state supreme court review, major reference will be made to the latter.

The Telephone Cases and the Method Used by the LPSC

The first case in which the LPSC gave detailed consideration to the capital structure of the utility and the determinants of the cost of capital resulted in an order by the commission requiring Southern Bell Telephone & Telegraph Company to reduce its annual gross intra-state revenues.[17] The case was subjected to a full review through the judicial system with the state supreme court upholding the ruling of the commission on February 25, 1957. In its decision the court said: "... we are of the opinion that there are presently no exceptional circumstances in this case authorizing a finding that the action of the . . . Commission is arbitrary, capricious, and confiscatory."[18]

The second case began on August 14, 1957, when Southern Bell applied to the LPSC for an emergency increase in revenue and for a full investigation of the rates and charges necessary to provide Southern Bell with a fair rate of return. The case resulted in an order issued in October, 1958, in which the LPSC found an increase in revenues to be justified but, nevertheless, denied such an increase on

---

[17] *Louisiana Public Service Commission v. Southern Bell Telephone and Telegraph Company, Order No. 6993,* 36 Annual Report of the LPSC 43 (1956).

[18] *LPSC v. Southern Bell Telephone and Telegraph Company,* 233 La. 466 (1957).

the grounds that Southern Bell had rendered grossly inadequate service and had arbitrarily curtailed a necessary expansion program, thus failing to perform its obligation as a public utility.[19] Upon appeal, the district court affirmed the commission's order with respect to the findings of a reasonable increase, but overruled the denial based upon inadequate service. The case was then carried to the state supreme court where the commission's method was upheld in general but modified in effect—a fact which can be more clearly shown after a discussion of the method used by the LPSC.

Consideration of the Capital Structure

One of the highly contested issues in the two telephone rates cases was the determination of a proper capital structure for rate-making purposes. A controversy developed between the commission and Southern Bell concerning whether a regulatory commission is bound to the existing capital structure of the utility at or near the time of regulation or whether proper rate regulation requires the use of a hypothetical capital structure that would minimize the total cost of capital. In the first case, the commission had emphatically made its position clear: "The composition of a utility's capital structure affects its operating costs and earnings requirements. Debt capital is much cheaper than equity capital, particularly with the prevailing level of Federal income taxes. A prudent capital structure is one conducive to the lowest cost of service that is consistent with a sound financial posture."[20]

During the test period (entire 1957), the debt ratio of Southern Bell averaged 24.7 percent as compared with a ratio of 45.8 percent in 1947. Company witnesses generally held that a debt ratio of 33⅓ percent was sound as compared with an average ratio of 50 percent for electric utilities and 59 percent for natural gas utilities because of the greater risk faced by the telephone industry. The commission could not agree and refused to be bound by the existing capital structure, holding that: "The evidence is persuasive that Southern Bell's capital structure is imprudent and uneconomical, and subjects the telephone subscribers in Louisiana to an unjust, unreasonable and

---

[19] *Southern Bell Telephone and Telegraph Company, Order No. 7640,* 38 Annual Report of the LPSC 131, 186 (1958).

[20] *Order No. 6993,* p. 52.

unwarranted financial burden."[21] Accordingly, the commission, after considering several alternative forms for the capital structure, adopted as reasonable a capital structure composed of 45 percent debt and 55 percent equity.

Determination of the Cost of Capital

A most critical point at issue in both cases was the determinants of the cost of debt and equity capital. Particularly was it important because of the adoption of a hypothetical capital structure and because Southern Bell as a wholly owned subsidiary of American Telephone and Telegraph Company did not (and does not now) trade its equity in the open market.

In reaching a decision regarding the cost of debt capital, the commission relied heavily upon Moody's average yields on triple-A utility bonds which ranged from 2.62 percent in 1950 to 3.96 percent in 1957, with an average of 3.66 percent in April, 1958. The commission concluded that 4 percent constituted a reasonable current cost of debt and applied this rate to the incremental debt capital necessary to increase Bell's debt ratio to 45 percent. The average actual cost was applied to the prevailing long-term debt portion of the re-formed capital structure, and an average 4 percent rate was applied to the advances from the American company.

Considerable time and discussion was devoted to an appraisal of earnings-price ratios as a measure of the cost of equity capital with the commission quite willing to accept current market conditions as reflecting elements of risks, including the effects of inflation. Although some attention was given to dividends-price ratios and pay-out ratios, the final analysis was based on earnings-price ratios.[22]

Since Southern Bell's common stock was not traded, the commission deemed it reasonable to consider the yields on electric utility common stock as a guide. Witnesses for Bell offered little testimony concerning earnings-price ratios, but the commission's staff offered in evidence seven computations of average earnings-price ratios computed for each of four years from 1954 through 1957, including one for the Bell System operating companies whose common stocks are held in part by the public. As of April, 1958, the average earnings-price ratio for Moody's twenty-four electrics was 6.25 percent; for

[21] *Order No. 7640*, p. 161.
[22] *Ibid.*, 169.

Dow-Jones' fifteen utilities, 6.39 percent; and for the ten leading electrics, 6.36 percent.

Based upon this factual evidence plus other testimony, the commission concluded that a ratio of 6.75 percent was reasonable and would provide adequate dividends and surplus for Bell's investors commensurate with returns on investment in other enterprises having corresponding risks.[23] In applying this ratio to Bell's equity, no specific allowance was made for "cost of flotation" or "market pressure" since in the commission's mind the holding of all of Southern Bell's equity by AT&T at par value of $100 gave rise to no such explicit expense.

Analysis of Earnings with
Proposed Standard of Reasonableness

Table I shows the earnings realized during the test period by Southern Bell compared with the commission's standard of reasonableness. In this computation, credit was given for the reduced federal income tax liability resulting from the increase in debt capital, and the reasonable earnings-price ratio was applied directly to the common equity at its par value of $100 with no application made for the amount of earned surplus in the capitalization of Southern Bell.

Before finalizing the order, the commission made three adjustments. The cost of an advertising campaign conducted by Bell during the rate proceedings was deducted as being abnormal and nonrecurring in character. An upward adjustment in gross revenue was made to reflect the increase in net operating income realized from an increase in directory advertising rates effectuated during the test period. The third adjustment concerned an allowance for a general wage increase granted during early 1958. The result of these adjustments was to increase the initial deficiency in earnings to $1,918,707 from which the commission authorized an upward adjustment in rates.

The Second Supreme Court Case
and the United Gas Case of 1961

As previously noted, the method used by the LPSC and the conclusions drawn from that method were upheld by the state supreme

23 *Ibid.*, 172.

court in the first telephone case. In the second case, however, the court while not per se setting aside the method used by the LPSC (which was identical with that of the first case), did hold that the "end result" of the commission's order was "discriminatory" in that

Table I

Analysis of Earnings Under Present Telephone Rates
Based on a Prudent Capital Structure*
Year Ended December 31, 1957

	Prevailing Debt Ratio 24.7 Percent (1)	*Pro Forma* Debt Ratio 45 Percent (2)
Average Capitalization:		
Long-Term Debt	$ 45,129,300	$ 82,179,000
Preferred Stock	—	—
Common Stock	129,973,690	92,923,990
Earned Surplus	7,521,000	7,521,000
Capital and Surplus	$182,623,990	$182,623,990
Actual Net Operating Income	$ 7,796,227	$ 7,796,227
Federal Tax Saving Resulting from Prudent Ratio (Credit)	—	770,633
Adjusted Net Operating Income	$ 7,796,227	$ 8,566,860
Total Long-Term Debt Interest	$ 1,511,834	$ 2,993,823
Interest on Advances from A.T.&T. ...	55,132	55,132
Preferred Stock Dividends	—	—
Earnings Available for Common Stock	$ 6,229,261	$ 5,517,905
Earnings-Price Ratio Realized Based on $100 per share Paid	4.79 percent	5.94 percent
Earnings-Price Ratio Required to Adequately Compensate Common Stockholders (AT&T)		6.75 percent
Common Stock Earnings Required to Adequately Compensate Stockholders (AT&T)		6,272,370
(Deficiency) in, or Excess, Common Stock Earnings		$(754,465)
(Deficiency) in, or Excess, Gross Operating Revenues†		$(1,680,000)

† (*Based on factor of 0.4498982 as computed by company*)
*source: Southern Bell Telephone and Telegraph Company, Order No. 7640, p. 173.

the rate of return was below the 6 percent which had been allowed other utilities in over thirty previous cases. The court said:

> While we are not prepared to hold and do not hold that an earnings-price ratio of 6.75% on equity capital under a formula of 45% debt and 55% common stock ratio is in itself not just and reasonable when applied *alike to all utilities similarly situated*, we do hold that . . . (such an application) to one utility, while others *similarly situated* are earning 8.5% on equity capital and not less than 6% on property rate base, is discriminatory and for that reason is not just and reasonable. *We believe that a return of not less than 6% on the property rate base as we have revised it is necessary to avoid discrimination. . . .*[24]

The commission was ordered to adjust the rates so that the end results would be a return of not less than 6 percent on the property rate base. This decision gave rise to several serious problems which were clearly stated by Justice Hawthorne in his dissent from the refusal of the court to grant a rehearing. Justice Hawthorne said:

> The Constitution does not require that every public utility be allowed the same rate of return, therefore, I do not think the court should say to the Commission: "You fix the rates . . . to return not less than 6 per cent . . ." The court should . . . concern itself with determining whether the rates fixed by the Commission are just and reasonable, for under the facts and circumstances in one utility company case a return of more than 6 per cent would be just and reasonable, while in others a return of less than 6 per cent would be just and reasonable. Furthermore, I do not think it proper to say that because the Commission has in the past allowed a return of not less than 6 per cent to other utilities, then it should not at the present time, or even in the future, allow a return of less than 6 per cent. Economic conditions change from time to time, and what was a reasonable and just return in the past may not be just and reasonable now or in the future.[25]

In the more recent *United Gas* case,[26] the commission basically used the same method applied in the two telephone cases and concluded that a rate of return of 5.5 percent was just and reasonable. Upon review by the state supreme court, the commission was upheld.[27] At present an apparent conflict in judicial interpretation

[24] *Southern Bell Telephone and Telegraph Company v. LPSC, ET AL,* Supreme Court of Louisiana, No. 44,639 (mimeo), 39. (Italics supplied.)

[25] *Southern Bell v. LPSC, ET AL,* No. 44639 (mimeo), Hawthorne, J., Dissenting from Refusal to Grant a Rehearing, 1.

[26] *United Gas Pipe Line Company, Order No. 8061,* 40 Annual Report of the LPSC 43 (1960).

[27] *United Gas Pipe Line Company v. LPSC,* Supreme Court of Louisiana, No. 45,485, 1961 (mimeo).

exists. In an earlier case, the *Gulf States* case of 1952,[28] the court set aside a LPSC order because it failed to allow a 6 percent rate of return. But in the first telephone case in 1957, the court supported the commission's order although it allowed a return of less than 6 percent. In the second telephone case, as noted above, the court seemed to return, in part at least, to its earlier position, only to again appear to reverse itself in the *United Gas* case in 1961. Justice Hawthorne's earlier remarks still appear to hold: "Thus it is apparent that our recent decisions in these utility company cases are very confusing and leave the Commission, the utility companies, and the district courts of this state in hopeless doubt about this fundamental problem of rate-making."[29]

SUMMARY COMPARISON OF LOUISIANA PRACTICE WITH OTHER PRACTICE AND AUTHORITIES

Regulatory practice as evidenced by the telephone rate cases and by the general overview of the regulatory framework in Louisiana may be compared with practice in general elsewhere and with the views of other authorities.

(1) *Regulatory Framework*

By establishing the Railroad Commission in 1898 and the LPSC in 1921, Louisiana adopted a regulatory scheme composed of a "strong" type regulatory commission with substantial powers and scope of jurisdiction. And, as such, its regulatory framework parallels that existing generally in the several states as well as that at the federal level. Prior trials with other types of regulation by this state closely patterned the experiences elsewhere and, in general, the same reasons for adopting the existing regulatory scheme prevailed in Louisiana.

Following the *Hope* decision in 1944, a majority of the states abandoned older regulatory methods and adopted a method more compatible with that decision.[30] Louisiana early in 1946 became one of these states and continues to follow the pattern then established.

---

[28] *Gulf States Utilities Company v. LPSC*, 222 La. 132 (1952).

[29] Hawthorne, Dissenting, 2.

[30] See Joseph R. Rose, "The Hope Case and Public Utility Valuation in the States," *Columbia Law Review*, LIV (1954), 188–212.

The Louisiana Economy

During the late 1950's and into the 1960's, the effects of the postwar inflation led a number of states to modify their regulatory practice somewhat to reflect this fact, although specific treatment is not uniform.[31]

(2) *The Use of a Hypothetical Capital Structure*

References to state practice support the use of a hypothetical capital structure, especially in cases where the existing capital structure is clearly unsound or is excessively conservative.[32] But agreement is by no means unanimous among regulators, financial experts, lawyers, and economists. Particularly in view of the regulatory treatment given interest payments and the federal income tax liability, it is argued that at any given time there exists a theoretical debt-equity ratio which will minimize the total cost of capital.[33]

(3) *Determination of the Cost of Debt Capital*

Since the return to holders of debt certificates is in the nature of a contractual obligation, it is not surprising to find the historical or actual cost adopted as the measure of the cost of capital attributed to outstanding debt.[34] Where new debt capital is being raised at the time of the proceedings or where an adjustment is made in the actual capital structure which requires the assumption of an increase in the debt portion, current cost of debt capital is used. Such procedures were followed by the Louisiana commission in the telephone cases and in the more recent *United Gas* case.

(4) *Determination of the Cost of Equity Capital*

Determination of the cost of equity capital is replete with difficulties, not the least of which is the question of what motivates in-

[31] Paul J. Garfield and Wallace Lovejoy, *Public Utility Economics* (Englewood Cliffs, N.J., 1964), 73 ff.

[32] See Joseph R. Rose, "Cost of Capital in Public Utility Rate Regulation," *Virginia Law Review*, XLIII (1957), 1085–88.

[33] This is a position long held by most, but it has recently been challenged. See Franco Modigliani and M. H. Miller, "The Cost of Capital, Corporation Finance and the Theory of Investment," *American Economic Review*, XLVIII (June, 1958), 261–97.

[34] See for example James C. Bonbright, *Principles of Public Utility Rates* (New York, 1961), Chap. 15.

vestors.[35] The more commonly used tests of the cost of equity capital are earnings-price ratios and/or dividends-price ratios, with consideration given to proper pay-out ratios, financing costs, and market pressure. More recently, analysts appear to rely more on the earnings-price ratios since studies have seemed to indicate that the market is valuing utility common stocks by reference to total per share earnings, with no clear, consistent tendency to discount retained earnings.[36]

Evidence of the earnings-price ratios experienced by the utility under regulation is generally offered in rate cases, but most authorities rely more heavily upon the ratios of comparative utilities and upon an analysis of the future. Joseph R. Rose emphasizes that since rates are established for the future it is imperative to make some analysis of future anticipated earnings and corresponding earnings-price ratios.[37] For special cases where the stock of the utility is not traded on the market, such as is the situation with most of the Bell operating companies, market data for the parent company are generally offered and analyzed. Louisiana did not follow this practice in the telephone cases, although it did so later in the *United Gas* case.

(5) *Application of the Earnings-Price Ratio and Associated Problems*

The Louisiana commission deviated from common practice in the application of the reasonable earnings-price ratio directly to the paid-in value of the common stock of Southern Bell rather than to book value or to some value in excess of book value; neither did it make any application for the earned surplus. Other analysts have made application to the book value or to some reasonable market value in excess of book value. Critics point out that since utility stocks are generally selling at prices substantially above book value, the application of an earnings-price ratio to the book value would result in a loss to investors and make more difficult and expensive the attraction of capital. Further, the use of earnings-price ratios has a number of other limitations which must be properly treated in order to prevent their misuse and to give them only as much weight as can

---

[35] *Ibid.*, 244–56.

[36] See Fred P. Morrissey, "Current Aspects of the Cost of Capital to Utilities," *Public Utilities Fortnightly*, LXII (August 14, 1958), 217–27.

[37] Rose, "Cost of Capital in Public Utility Rate Regulation," 1093.

be reasonably and accurately defended.[38] The practice commonly followed in most jurisdictions composites the weighted cost of equity and the weighted cost of debt into a differentiated rate of return to be applied to a net property rate base. Louisiana used this procedure in the *United Gas* case in 1961—a case which followed the telephone cases.

(6) *Adjustment for Inflation*

The Louisiana commission made no specific allowance for inflation. Some authorities make an allowance either in the form of a "fair value" rate base or in a specific adjustment to the rate of return. Others recognize the fact of inflation as one of the several factors entering the "judgment" determination of the proper rate of return. Still others make no adjustment in any form.

(7) *"Cost of Capital" and "Fair Rate of Return"*

No complete agreement exists as to whether or not the computations derived from the "cost of capital" techniques constitute a "fair rate of return." As might be expected, much hinges on what is meant by "cost of capital," what specific measurements are used in its derivation, and how it is then applied in the regulatory process. The Louisiana commission held that the method used in the telephone cases resulted in reasonable earnings without consideration per se of a rate of return to be applied against some property rate base. The commission's decision was clearly upheld in the first case, and while upheld in the second case, was modified as to the end results. Following the *United Gas* case, the commission uses cost of capital as a basis for computing a differentiated rate of return to be applied to a reasonable rate base—a procedure upheld as reasonable by the state supreme court. James C. Bonbright, himself a leading authority, states the general view when he says: "Even those public service commissioners and financial experts who derive their conclusions as to a fair rate of return in large measure from their estimate of 'cost of capital' seldom completely identify their conclusions with their estimates. More often than not, the estimated cost is offered as a *minimum*

[38] See Garfield and Lovejoy, *Public Utility Economics*, 126–28, and Bonbright, *Principles of Public Utility Rates*, 254.

standard of adequacy, subject to a 'judgment-made' additional allowance for possible error, for real but immeasurable items of cost, for 'regulatory lag,' and even perhaps as a reward for efficient operation."[39]

As a concluding remark, one might observe that anyone studying the regulatory process in the American economy must conclude that for regulation to be viable, it must be subjected to continual review and revision as economic conditions demand. Such a conclusion is no less true for Louisiana.

[39] Bonbright, *Principles of Public Utility Rates,* 241–42.

PART III
The Public Sector

GOVERNMENT REVENUES AND
EXPENDITURES IN LOUISIANA
Thomas R. Beard

Contrary to much popular opinion, state and local governments collectively spend considerably more on civil (nondefense) functions than does the federal government. Despite substantial increases in the dollar amounts of federal spending in recent years, functions such as education, highways, and hospitals remain primarily state and local responsibilities, while public welfare and health are areas of substantial partnership. In fact, in the period since the Second World War, general expenditures by state and local governments have grown more rapidly than federal general expenditures for all civil purposes.[1]

STATE AND LOCAL GOVERNMENT
FINANCE IN THE UNITED STATES

In comparing expenditures by level of government, an important question concerns the treatment of intergovernmental transfers (primarily grants).[2] When we attribute intergovernmental payments to

[1] General expenditures exclude amounts expended on utilities, liquor stores, and insurance trusts. (These amounts are approximately offset by receipts.) Federal expenditures for civil functions have been calculated by deducting from total direct federal expenditures the amounts spent on national defense and international relations, veterans (not elsewhere classified), and interest on the federal debt. All state and local expenditures are regarded as civil. For an excellent survey of state and local government spending and tax policies in the postwar period, see James A. Maxwell, *Financing State and Local Governments* (Washington, D.C., 1965).

[2] In this paper grants will be used in a general sense as synonymous with intergovernmental transfers. Technically, intergovernmental expenditures

173

the originating level of government, state and local government general expenditures were $63.9 billion in fiscal 1964–65 as compared to federal general expenditures for civil functions of $41.2 billion.[3] By comparison, these figures in 1948 were $15.9 billion and $10.5 billion, respectively; in 1938, $8 billion and $5.8 billion, respectively.[4] In dollar amounts, expansion clearly has been greater at the state and local level. Even in percentage terms, the state and local share has advanced slightly from about 58 percent in 1938 to 60 percent in 1948 and 61 percent in 1964–65. Thus, in terms of general expenditures, state and local government has more than held its own in the last quarter of a century—at least when we eliminate national defense and defense related activities at the federal level.[5]

Of course, state and local general expenditures on civil functions

---

(revenues) are defined as amounts paid to (received from) other governments as fiscal aid in the form of shared revenues and grants-in-aid, as reimbursements for performance of general government activities, and for specific services for the paying government, or in lieu of taxes.

[3] Total federal expenditures of $130.1 billion, however, exceeded total state and local expenditures of $87 billion. In addition to general expenditures for civil functions of $41.2 billion, total federal expenditures included general expenditures on noncivil or defense related activities (defined in footnote 1) of $68.9 billion, and $19.9 billion in insurance trust expenditures.

Unless otherwise noted, most of the data utilized in this essay are from U.S. Bureau of the Census, *Governmental Finances in 1964–65* (Washington, D.C., 1966) and *Compendium of State Government Finances in 1965* (Washington, D.C., 1966). Bureau of the Census figures are on a fiscal year basis. Financial statistics for 1964–65 relate to government fiscal years ending June 30, 1965, or at some date within the twelve previous months (July through June). Fiscal year 1965 refers to government fiscal years ending during the calendar year. Normally, there is little difference in figures for 1964–65 and 1965.

[4] Historical data are found in U.S. Bureau of the Census, *Historical Statistics of the United States: Colonial Times to 1957* (Washington, D.C., 1960). See also Maxwell, *Financing State and Local Governments*, Chap. 1.

[5] It might be noted, however, that the state-local share declined from 64 percent in 1963 to 61 percent in 1964–65.

The 1930's brought a major intergovernmental redistribution of expenditures for civil purposes. Prior to the great depression, the federal government played a small role vis-à-vis state and local government. In 1927 state and local government accounted for 82 percent of general expenditures for civil functions. With the shift in social philosophy and the difficulties of state and local government in meeting relief and welfare needs during the depression years, federal civil expenditures increased both absolutely and relatively. By 1938 the state and local share had declined to 58 percent. In the World War II period, state and local expenditures were placed on a standby basis. Although federal spending on all functions rose from roughly $10 billion in 1940 to slightly over $100 billion in 1944, virtually all of this expansion was for military, rather than civilian, purposes.

would appear even larger if we attributed expenditures to the level of government making final disbursements, i.e., if we included federal grants to state and local government in the latter's expenditures. Since the amount of federal grants totaled $11.1 billion in 1964–65, state and local expenditures by this measure would rise to $75 billion as compared to only $30.1 billion at the federal level. This approach of measuring so-called direct expenditures, however, has some obvious drawbacks because it conceals the size of federal grants. If we are trying to analyze the power of the states vis-à-vis the federal government or the ultimate responsibility for certain civil functions by level of government, it seems more appropriate to include federal grants with other types of (direct) federal spending on civil functions.

The upsurge in the dollar amounts of state and local activity which began after World War II has continued unabated to the present time. The biggest expansion has been for education, the major single function of state and local government throughout this century. In 1948, excluding federal grants, state and local expenditures on education totaled $5 billion; in 1964–65 these expenditures were $27.3 billion. Including federal grants, the figures were $5.4 billion and $29 billion, respectively. Not only have federal grants continued to be relatively small in percentage terms, but direct expenditures at the federal level are still quite modest. In 1964–65 state and local expenditures as a percentage of total expenditures on education were 90.9 percent, excluding federal grants, and 96.5 percent when federal grants are included. (See Table I.)

Some of the postwar expansion in education expenditures is attributable to price inflation and the resulting higher costs of construction, materials, and personnel. But much is attributable to the facts that population has expanded, children are a larger portion of the population, a greater percentage of children goes to school and for longer periods of time, and subject matter is more complex and involves more plant, equipment, and better trained teachers. Perhaps as never before the public also has come to recognize the crucial importance of education for reasons of both personal welfare and national survival.

Highways are another traditional function for which state and local spending has increased dramatically. The construction and maintenance costs have risen, the affluent society has purchased more automobiles and driven greater distances for both business and pleasure, and the transportation of goods by truck has expanded. Excluding federal grants, state and local government expenditures on highways have risen from $2.7 billion in 1948 to $8.2 billion in 1964–65. Including federal grants, the figures are $3 billion and $12.2 billion, respectively. By either means of comparison, highways are the second most important function of state and local government—but it must be emphasized, it is a very poor second.

Public welfare expenditures first grew into prominence in the 1930's. By 1948 state and local government spent $1.4 billion on this function, excluding federal grants, and $2.1 billion when such grants are included. While the dollar amounts of these expenditures have more than doubled since that time, neither the absolute nor the percentage increase has been as large as those in education, or even in highways. Nevertheless, state and local outlays for public welfare in 1964–65 were $3.2 billion, excluding federal grants, and $6.3 billion, including such grants. Thus, it might be noted, slightly over half of all funds dispersed on public welfare at the state and local level were financed from federal grants. Direct (nongrant) spending by the federal government was quite small.

The closely related functions of health and hospitals have also expanded significantly in the postwar period. Hospitals are primarily

Table I

General Expenditures for Selected Civil Functions
By All Levels of Government, 1964–65
(amounts in millions of dollars)

| Function | All levels of government | State and local government | | | |
		Including federal grants	Percent of total	Excluding federal grants	Percent of total
Education	$ 30,021	$28,971	96.5	$27,294	90.9
Highways	12,348	12,221	99.0	8,224	66.6
Public welfare	6,420	6,315	98.4	3,217	50.1
Hospitals	5,865	4,525	77.2	4,397	75.0
Health	1,805	836	46.3	672	37.2
All others	48,622	22,086	45.4	20,088	41.3
Total	$105,081	$74,954	71.3	$63,892	60.8

SOURCE: *Governmental Finances in 1964–65*, pp. 22–24.

a state and local responsibility and accounted for $4.4 billion, excluding grants, and $4.5 billion, including grants, in 1964–65. Health expenditures, which are smaller, are substantially a shared function. Excluding federal grants, state and local expenditures were only 37 percent of total health expenditures by all levels of government in 1964–65.

In addition to the five functions discussed above, state and local governments spend considerable sums on other civil functions, and in general these expenditures also have risen in the last two decades. Such functions include: police and fire protection, sewerage and sanitation; local parks and recreation; natural resources; housing and urban renewal; air and water transportation; correction; libraries; general public buildings; interest on general debt; financial administration; and general control. In 1964–65 the total of state and local expenditures on all these various functions was $20.1 billion, excluding federal grants, and $22.1 billion, including federal grants.

While all levels of government can and do borrow and there are certain nontax sources of revenue, tax collections are the primary source of revenue to support governmental functions. Federal expenditures, of course, are not confined solely to civil functions. Partly because of large federal expenditures for noncivil purposes, as well as (smaller) intergovernmental grants to state and local government, the majority of all tax collections are now at the federal level. In 1938 state and local government still collected roughly 59 percent of all general tax revenue, even after the expansion of federal activities in the depression years.[6] Of the combined state and local collections, local units continued to dominate (35 percent of all general tax revenue). The war period dramatically changed the level at which tax collections took place. In 1948 state and local governments collected only 26 percent of general tax revenues. In that year state and local collections stood at $13.3 billion, as contrasted with federal tax receipts of $37.9 billion.

While general tax collections at the combined state and local level have risen both absolutely and relatively since 1948, federal collections were roughly 64 percent of the total in 1964–65. The other 36 percent was split fairly evenly between the state level and the

[6] General revenue excludes utility revenue, liquor store revenue, and insurance trust revenue. In addition to general tax revenue, governments also collect certain nontax general revenues which are called "charges and miscellaneous general revenue."

local level of government. (See Table II.) In dollar amounts, federal tax collections were $93.7 billion, compared to combined state and local collections of $51.6 billion ($26.1 billion at the state level and $25.5 billion at the local level).

By type of tax, income taxes (personal and corporate) are dominant at the federal level, accounting for $74.3 billion in 1964–65. The dominance of the federal government in this area has left relatively little room for extensive use of income taxes by state ($5.6 billion) and particularly local levels of government ($0.4 billion). Consumption-type taxes in the form of general and selective sales and gross receipts taxes are dominant at the state level, accounting for some $15.1 billion in 1964–65. While the federal government does not levy a general sales or gross receipts tax, collections from selective consumption-type taxes amounted to $15.8 billion. Property taxes have retained their historical role as by far the major source of local government revenue. In 1964–65 property tax collections were $22.2 billion, a figure representing 87 percent of all general tax collections at the local level. Property tax collections are now relatively small at the state level and the federal government does not operate in this area.

Table II
General Tax Collections by Type and Level of Government
1964–65
(amounts in millions of dollars)

Type of tax	All levels of government	Federal	State and local government			State-local as percent of all levels
			State	Local	State-local	
Income	$ 80,272	$74,253	$ 5,586	$ 433	$ 6,019	07.4
Sales and gross receipts	32,904	15,786	15,059	2,059	17,118	52.0
Property	22,918	—	766	22,152	22,918	100.0
Other	9,191	3,670	4,714	807	5,521	60.1
Total	$145,288	$93,710	$26,129	$25,451	$51,578	35.5

SOURCE: *Governmental Finances in 1964–65*, p. 20.

Certainly, it is clear by this point that the extent of state and local government expenditures and taxation is not only large but has grown considerably in the postwar period. Projections of future expenditures and revenues have all indicated continued growth. Many prognosticators, in fact, have forecast an alarming divergence between growth in the demand for schools, roads, and other public services and growth in the ability of state and local government to provide such services.

In addition to projecting the need for rapidly rising public expenditures, some pessimism has been expressed concerning the revenue side of the budget. It is clear, of course, that tax receipts will rise as gross national product (GNP) expands. But the important question is whether the revenues from existing state and local tax sources, at current rates and bases, will be sufficient. A pessimistic answer is based on the lower income elasticity of taxes at the state-local level as compared with the federal level. (Income elasticity refers to the percentage change in tax revenues divided by the percentage change in gross national product.) State-local revenues depend primarily on sales and property taxes. The yields from these taxes are less responsive to economic growth than are the yields from income taxes, which are prevalent at the federal level. If, on the average, the income elasticity of state-local taxes is in the range of 1.0 to 1.2, then an increase in GNP of 10 percent will automatically bring forth additional revenues from existing tax sources of 10 to 12 percent. If income elasticity at the federal level is around 1.5, as has been suggested, the same increase in GNP will result in an automatic 15 percent rise in federal tax revenues. Thus, given existing tax rates and bases (and assuming defense expenditures do not rise as a percentage of GNP), it appears easier for the federal government to finance much of the expected increase in civil expenditures—expenditures which traditionally have been largely the responsibility of state and local government.

Demands for expanded federal assistance are one reflection of the view that needed expenditures on education, highways, and other services cannot be financed solely from state and local revenues. In recent years programs of new and enlarged federal grants have been passed into law. As a result, intergovernmental expenditures by the federal government have risen from $7.7 billion in 1961–62 to $8.5 billion in 1962–63, $10.1 billion in 1963–64, and $11.1 billion in 1964–65. Some observers estimate that the size of federal grants will reach $18–$22 billion by 1970. Yet many feel that conditional federal grants, tied to specific purposes, stimulate an undesirable degree of centralization and, perhaps ultimately, federal control. Thus, increasing attention also has been given to the possibility of extending general assistance in such a way as to leave the final decisions on the allocation of funds and program content to the state and local levels of government. Some of the suggested devices for intergovernmental financial coordination have involved general purpose or untied grants-in-aid, tax sharing and tax supplements, and federal tax credits. The latter may well have the greatest possibilities. Under a system of tax credits, taxpayers could be allowed to offset part of their payments of certain state taxes against their federal income tax liability. This would make it possible for states to raise additional revenue without increasing the total tax payments of their residents.[7]

LOUISIANA—AN OVERALL VIEW

This brief survey of state and local government finance has set the stage for a more intensive investigation of Louisiana's pattern of receipts and expenditures. What is true for state and local government finance in general is not necessarily the case for Louisiana or any other individual state. While one can point to certain broad general patterns of state and local finance, as has been done above, there exists such a diversity in the financial affairs of the various governmental units that it would be hazardous to attempt to isolate a single state or group of states as being "typical" in all respects. All states have certain unusual features. Nevertheless, as we shall discover, Louisiana varies to such a degree from the average in several important respects that one is tempted to emphasize its unusual features.

In earlier years Louisiana had a relatively simple tax structure at the state level.[8] The major source of tax revenue at the local level was the property tax. In 1920 only four major state taxes were collected— the ad valorem or property tax, the severance tax, occupational license taxes, and vehicle licenses. The ad valorem tax alone accounted for almost three-fourths of total state tax revenues of $12.5

---

[7] For an excellent discussion of tax credits and similar devices, see James A. Maxwell, *Tax Credits and Intergovernmental Fiscal Relations* (Washington, D.C., 1962).

[8] This brief history of Louisiana's tax structure draws heavily on compilations by the Public Affairs Research Council (PAR), *Louisiana State Tax Handbook, 1964* (Baton Rouge, 1964).

million in 1921. Since that time it has declined considerably in relative importance, although at the local level the property tax has remained the major source of tax revenue. In 1920 a special state excise license tax on insurers doing business in Louisiana was also in existence; the rates were based on amounts of premiums and types of insurance. An inheritance tax was also collected, although prior to 1921 this tax was levied by state law but collected and used locally for public school purposes. Since that date, it has been collected locally with the revenues assigned to state use.[9]

Two relatively important taxes were added in the 1920's—a one-cent gasoline tax in 1921 and a tobacco tax in 1926. Most of the present taxes were passed in the 1930's, as Louisiana, like other states, sought new sources of revenue in the depression era. Among the more important taxes levied during this period were the alcoholic beverage tax and dealer permits, beer tax, corporation franchise tax, electric generation tax, income tax, lubricating oil tax, power use tax, public utilities tax, general sales tax, and soft drink tax.[10] In addition, a number of lesser revenue producers were instituted in this period. In 1940 the gas gathering tax (declared unconstitutional by the Louisiana Supreme Court in 1959), horse racing tax, and use fuel tax were introduced. No new major taxes have been levied since that time, although some relatively minor ones have been added and rate increases have taken place in many cases.

The most significant rate increases were in 1948. The general sales tax was raised from one to two cents and there were substantial increases in most of the severance tax rates. Tobacco tax rates were increased to levels presently in effect. The tax on liquor was raised, and the tax on beer was increased from $1.50 to $10 a barrel. The gas gathering tax was doubled, and the gasoline and use fuel taxes were hiked from seven to nine cents a gallon. In 1952, however, some tax rates were reduced, including a reduction of two cents a gallon in the gasoline and use fuel taxes. In 1956 a constitutional amendment was adopted which has made it significantly more difficult to levy new taxes or raise the rates on existing ones. This amendment requires a

[9] In 1932 an estate transfer tax was added. This tax is designed to capture the difference between the total of state inheritance and estate taxes paid and the maximum 80 percent federal credit.

[10] Unemployment compensation taxes were also introduced during the 1930's. However, this and other types of insurance trust revenues, as well as insurance trust expenditures, are generally ignored in this study.

two-thirds vote of the elected members of both legislative houses to effect tax increases. Since that time only a few minor taxes have been added. Perhaps the only significant rate increase has been in the gas severance tax.

As one would expect, Louisiana has followed the upward trend in general revenues and expenditures characteristic of state and local government in the postwar period. Considering the *state level* only, the upward trend in general revenues, by Bureau of the Census major breakdowns, can be seen in Table III. Both tax and nontax sources of revenue are included. Increases in tax revenues, of course, are attributable largely to the expansion in economic activity; in certain cases, however, changes in tax rates and tax bases are partially responsible.

The rapid rise in general revenues is apparent from the figures in Table III—an increase from $150.5 million in 1946 to $364 million in 1950, $768.1 million in 1960, and $1,046.9 million in 1965. Most revenue sources have experienced periodic gains. The rates at which the various tax and nontax revenues have grown, however, have varied significantly; thus the relative importance of specific revenue sources has changed appreciably over the last two decades.

One notable development has been the decline of tax revenue as a percentage of total general revenue. In 1946 the figure was 75.2 percent; in 1948, 66 percent. In 1965 the figure had fallen to only 55.5 percent. That is, little over half of the general revenue at the state level came from tax sources. In this respect Louisiana's reliance on tax revenues was well below the U.S. average.

Many of the major types of taxes have declined in relative importance over the last two decades. Selective sales taxes—a Bureau of the Census category which includes Louisiana's various excises on motor fuels, alcoholic beverages, tobacco products, insurance, public utilities, and pari-mutuels (horse racing), as well as the levies on lubricating oil, soft drinks, and the unique power use tax—have suffered a significant decline. In 1946, 33.5 percent of total general revenues at the state level were generated by selective sales taxes. In 1965 this figure was only 15.7 percent.

License taxes—a category including Louisiana's corporation franchise tax, as well as general occupational license taxes and license taxes on motor vehicles, motor vehicle operators, alcoholic beverages, and hunting and fishing—have fallen from 8.1 percent in 1946 to 4.3 percent in 1965. Similar figures for the income tax, which includes

Table III

General Revenues of State Government in Louisiana,

Selected Years 1946–65

(in millions of dollars)

Types	1946	1948	1950	1955	1960	1965
Total general revenue	150.5	215.8	364.0	539.3	768.1	1,046.9
Total tax revenue	113.2	142.4	240.9	303.5	452.7	581.3
General sales and gross receipts	12.9	19.1	45.0	64.8	88.5	119.3
Selective sales and gross receipts	50.4	59.2	94.1	112.0	136.0	164.6
License	12.1	15.6	17.7	27.3	38.0	44.6
Income	11.0	16.4	18.8	19.1	30.8	50.9
Property	8.8	10.3	11.5	11.2	14.9	17.6
Severance	16.3	20.4	52.3	66.9	137.2	179.1
Death and gift	1.6	1.4	1.5	2.3	7.3	5.2
Intergovernmental revenue	22.7	30.7	85.8	95.0	204.4	291.4
From federal government	21.7	29.4	84.1	89.0	200.4	284.7
From local government	1.0	1.3	1.7	6.0	4.0	6.7
Charges and miscellaneous general revenue	14.7	42.7	37.3	140.8	111.0	174.2

SOURCE: Bureau of the Census, *Revised Summary of State Government Finances, 1942–50*, p. 21; *Compendium on State Government Finances in 1955*, pp. 8–16; *1960*, pp. 12–14; and *1965*, pp. 19–23.

both personal and corporate receipts, are 7.3 percent and 4.9 percent, respectively. Over the last two decades the state property tax has continued its long-run decline in importance, and accounted for only 1.7 percent of total general revenue in 1965.

The two major individual state taxes, however, have bucked this trend. Due partly to the hike from one to two cents in the late 1940's, receipts from the general sales tax accounted for 11.4 percent of general revenues in 1965 as compared with 8.6 percent in 1946. At the more recent date, general sales tax receipts stood at $119.3 million, second only to severance tax collections of $179.1 million. The severance tax is not only now the major single source of tax revenue, but its relative importance, with some minor fluctuations, has generally risen over the last two decades. Severance tax receipts now account for 17.1 percent of total general revenues, up from the 10.8 percent figure in 1946.

Despite the behavior of these two major taxes, total tax revenues have declined in relative importance, as previously noted. The combined categories of intergovernmental revenues (primarily federal grants) and "charges and miscellaneous general revenue" (in Louisiana, primarily royalties and bonuses) have risen in importance. In percentage terms intergovernmental revenues were 15.1 percent in 1946, 23.6 percent in 1950 (when public welfare expenditures were relatively large), 17.6 percent in 1955, and 27.8 percent in 1965. The dollar amounts of these revenues have risen fairly consistently over the years. Expanded programs of federal grants in the last decade are evident by the rise from $89 million in 1955 to $200.4 million in 1960 and $284.7 million in 1965. Today, one might say, federal grants are the state's major "single" source of revenue.

The year to year behavior in the Bureau of the Census category "charges and miscellaneous general revenue" has been quite erratic, reflecting the quite volatile nature of Louisiana's royalty and bonus income from public property. But despite pronounced fluctuations in these earnings, the overall movement has been in an upward direction. In 1946 state government collected only 9.7 percent of total general revenue from this source. In 1955 this figure was an amazingly high 26.1 percent; in 1965 it was 16.6 percent. As we shall see later, Louisiana's earnings from this source are quite high compared to most other states.

As revenues have increased, so have expenditures. Considering the *state level* only, the upward trend in general expenditures by major function can be seen in Table IV. It should be noted that these figures include both direct state expenditures and intergovernmental transfers by the state to the local level. The figures also include funds received from federal grants and expended by state government.

In Louisiana, as in other states, expenditures on civil functions held relatively steady in the early 1940's as the bulk of overall government spending was devoted to the war effort. With the cessation of hostilities it was clear that a considerable "catching up" period would be necessary. Such was the case. Not only was it necessary to meet some of the more pressing backlog of needs, but Louisiana was faced with rising costs, an expanding population, and generally increasing demands for more and better public services. These factors led to a more than doubling of the level of state government expenditures in Louisiana from 1946 to 1950. Education expenditures, alone, rose almost three-fold; highway spending more than quadrupled from the relatively modest base at the end of the war period.

The most startling increase, however, was in public welfare expenditures after 1948—an increase that perhaps was attributable to both the prevailing political philosophy and the availability of federal grants for welfare activities. In 1948 public welfare spending was $26.2 million; in 1950 it stood at $105.8 million. This constituted a rise from 13.2 percent to 29.8 percent of total general expenditures. Looked at another way, public welfare expenditures reached a level

Table IV
General Expenditures of State Government in Louisiana,
Selected Years 1946–1965
(in millions of dollars)

Types	1946	1948	1950	1955	1960	1965
Education	32.3	64.1	95.0	142.3	242.2	334.7
Highways	13.8	41.0	56.9	82.3	184.2	235.3
Public welfare	18.4	26.2	105.8	107.3	162.6	202.9
Health and hospitals	12.3	15.2	25.9	35.6	52.0	69.3
All others	39.6	51.7	71.2	108.0	144.7	194.1
Total	116.5	198.2	354.7	475.5	785.6	1,036.4

SOURCE: *Bureau of the Census, Revised Summary of State Government Finances, 1942–50*, p. 21; *Compendium of State Government Finances in 1955*, p. 22; *1960*, p. 24; and *1965*, pp. 28–33.

in 1950 that exceeded even spending on education and was almost double that on highways.

In the 1950–60 decade, general expenditures of state government continued to rise at a rapid pace, increasing from $354.7 million to $785.6 million. The expansion has continued to the present time, with expenditures of $1,036.4 million in 1965. The great bulk of these expenditures go for the three major functions—education, $334.7 million; highways, $235.3 million; and public welfare, $202.9 million.

While the amounts of spending on all major functions have risen substantially since 1950, one might note the interesting changes that have evolved in the relative weights attached to these functions. Expenditures on education as a percent of total general expenditures have gradually risen from 26.8 percent in 1950 to 32.3 percent in 1965. The percentage spent on highways has also risen from the relatively low level of 1950 (16 percent), and now stands at 22.7 percent. On the other hand, while rising in absolute dollar amounts, public welfare expenditures have fallen percentagewise from the unusually high figure of 1950. By 1965 these expenditures had declined to some 19.6 percent of the total—a figure, however, which is still above that of 1946 and 1948.

The figures in Tables III and IV reflect only the situation at the state level. To obtain a complete picture of the fiscal situation in Louisiana, it is necessary, of course, to consider revenues and expenditures at the local level as well. Some relevant figures for state and local finance are shown in Tables V, VI, and VII.

In 1964–65 total general revenue at the combined state and local level was $1,363.1 million. At the state level, the figure was $1,046.9 million; at the local level, $609.6 million. (See Table V.) Obviously, there is some double counting involved in these figures, and this is the result of the complex system of intergovernmental transfers among the levels of government. More meaningful concepts are obtained through measuring general revenue either by the originating level of government or by the final recipient level of government. (See Table VI.)

In 1964–65 the state level in Louisiana collected $755.5 million in general revenue from its own sources. As noted earlier, it also received a quite sizeable $284.7 million in grants from the federal government, plus relatively small intergovernmental transfers of $6.7 million from local government. These figures total the $1,046.9 million in general revenue from all sources at the state level. Out of

Table V

General Revenues of State and Local Government in Louisiana By Source, By Level of Government, 1964–65
(in millions of dollars)

Level of government	Total general revenue	Intergovernmental revenue		All general revenue from own sources	Taxes			Charges and Miscellaneous general revenue
		From federal government	Local-state and state-local		Total	Property	Other	
State and local	1,363.1	309.9	—	1,053.2	784.7	174.6	610.1	268.5
State	1,046.9	284.7	6.7	755.5	581.3	17.6	563.6	174.2
Local	609.6	25.2	286.7	297.7	203.4	156.9	46.5	94.3

SOURCE: *Governmental Finances in 1964–65*, p. 32.

these revenues, however, the state level made substantial intergovern-mental transfers of $286.7 million to the local level, thus leaving it with total general revenue by final recipient level of government of $760.2 million.

Local units, on the other hand, collected slightly less general revenue from their own sources, some $297.7 million, than from various intergovernmental transfers (primarily state). As in most states throughout the country, the major source of tax revenue at the local level is the property tax. Over three-fourths of local tax revenues in Louisiana are attributable to this single source, thus at-testing to its continued predominance. In addition to their own re-sources, local units were the recipients of a very substantial $286.7 million in transfers from the state level and $25.2 million from the federal level, thus pushing total general revenues from all sources to $609.6 million. Out of this figure, local units made relatively small transfers to the state level of $6.7 million, leaving them with total general revenue by final recipient level of government of $602.9 million.

It might be noted in passing that owing to the rough similarity between grant monies *received* by the state level and those *disbursed* from the state level, there is actually little difference in the state level's share of total revenues, whether that share is computed by originating or final recipient level of government. Obviously, this is not the case at the local level where the difference between the two concepts is quite striking.

Table VI

General Revenues of State and Local Government in Louisiana
By Origin and Allocation, By Level of Government, 1964–65
(amounts in millions of dollars)

Level of government	By originating level of government (before transfers among governments)		By final recipient level of government (after intergovern-mental transfers)	
	Amount	Percent	Amount	Percent
Total	1,363.1	100.0	1,363.1	100.0
Federal	309.9	22.7	—	—
State	755.5	55.4	760.2	55.8
Local	297.7	21.8	602.9	44.2

SOURCE: *Governmental Finances in 1964–65*, p. 49

On the expenditure side, we find that combined state and local direct expenditures were $1,383.7 million in 1964–65. After netting out the various intergovernmental transfers from total spending, direct general expenditures by the state level totaled $730.5 million; direct local expenditures were $653.2 million. (See Table VII.) Practically all public welfare expenditures in Louisiana were made directly by state government, as were a very large percentage of highway and combined health and hospital expenditures. However, the bulk of direct education expenditures—with the notable exception of higher education—are local in nature. Such functions as police and fire protection, sewerage and sanitation, and local parks and recreation are either wholly or primarily local.

The figures on state and local revenues and expenditures are not only revealing in themselves, but are especially enlightening when we compare Louisiana with other states. Taken together, they indicate that Louisiana receives relatively large amounts of federal grants, and in turn displays a high degree of fiscal centralization within the state. Local units raise relatively small amounts of funds from their own sources. Despite substantial intergovernmental transfers to local government, direct local expenditures vis-à-vis those at the state level are still well below the U.S. average.

The following interstate comparisons bear out these conclusions. When we compare the percentages of total state and local *tax* revenues raised at the state level, Louisiana recorded an extremely high 74.1 percent. This percentage was topped by only four states— Delaware, New Mexico, North Carolina, and South Carolina. The average for all states was 50.7 percent. When we consider *all* gen-

Table VII

Direct General Expenditures of State and Local Government in
Louisiana, By Level of Government, 1964–65
(in millions of dollars)

Level of government	Total	Education	Highways	Public welfare	Health and hospitals	All others
State and local	1,383.7	435.0	270.1	203.6	79.1	395.9
State	730.5	115.4	215.2	202.9	65.6	131.4
Local	653.2	319.6	54.9	0.6	13.5	264.6

SOURCE: *Governmental Finances in 1964–65*, pp. 36–37.

eral revenues (tax plus nontax) raised from their *own sources*, Louisiana's relative standing was even higher. Only two states—Delaware and New Mexico—topped Louisiana's 71.7 percent.

State and local governments, of course, receive federal grants in addition to revenues generated from their own sources. In Louisiana the percentage of total state and local general revenue raised via federal grants was relatively high, but perhaps not unusually so. Some 22.7 percent of general revenue came from the federal level, a figure well above the national average of 14.8 percent but below that in thirteen other states. By comparison, the percentage of *total* general revenue (from own sources plus federal grants) raised at the state level in Louisiana was 55.4 percent. This figure is quite high and was exceeded only by that in Delaware, Hawaii, North Carolina, and South Carolina. The national average was 41.2 percent. To complete the picture, Louisiana's percentage of total general revenue raised at the local level was a lowly 21.8 percent. The national average was 44 percent. In only two states did a smaller percentage of total general revenue originate at the local level—the new state of Alaska, where there has been little chance for local units of government to develop, and New Mexico.

Thus, whether the comparison involves the state level's share of tax revenues, all general revenues (tax plus nontax) from own sources, or total general revenues (including federal grants), the same conclusion emerges. The state level is unusually strong, and the local level is unusually dependent. Whatever the merits of "home rule" as a political slogan in Louisiana, it is clear that local government can have little real power without a better developed financial base. The relatively small amount of revenue collected by local government from its own sources virtually dictates a considerable degree of centralization within the state. In Louisiana the state level either performs directly or indirectly finances through intergovernmental transfers many services that in other states are left to local government.[11]

GENERAL EXPENDITURE AND REVENUE COMPARISONS

A study of the fiscal structure of the fifty states indicates a wide variance in the division of responsibility between the state and local

[11]Two further comparisons might be offered—total general revenue by final recipient level of government and local government percentage of direct state

levels of government. For example, in 1964–65, the state government percentage of direct state and local general expenditures varied from under 30 percent in California, New Jersey, New York, Ohio, and Wisconsin to 74 percent in Alaska and 65.9 percent in Hawaii. Because of this divergence, interstate comparisons which focus only on the state level may be quite misleading as indicators of revenue effort and levels of government services. This is quite true for Louisiana because of its considerable degree of fiscal centralization. All too frequently critics have exaggerated the size of government in Louisiana by focusing on the state level only.[12] Fairer and more revealing comparisons can be made of combined state and local expenditures and revenues.

Interstate comparisons are traditionally made in per capita terms and per thousand dollars of personal income. The first measure is often deemed to be particularly useful for expenditure comparisons since it points up the relative levels of services provided on an appropriate per person basis. Yet total population figures have limitations in that certain groups in the population—for example, the elderly, the blind, and dependent children—legitimately need more public services than do other groups. Furthermore, per capita computations make no allowance for differences in price or quality of the services provided or in the efficiency of the governmental units in providing them. While a per capita expenditure measure is admittedly imperfect, it nevertheless is useful and a more refined measure would be difficult to construct.[13]

---

and local expenditures. Both measures, of course, reflect intergovernmental transfers in the local government percentages. By the first measure, local (state) government in Louisiana received 44.2 percent (55.8 percent) of general revenue *after* grants; by the second measure, local (state) government in Louisiana made 47.2 percent (52.8 percent) of *direct* general expenditure. Again, the figures for local government are well below the national averages. Even when Louisiana's sizeable state grants are included in local figures, local government does not improve its relative standing appreciably, ranking fifth from the bottom in the first case (followed by Alaska, Hawaii, Vermont, and West Virginia) and sixth from the bottom in the second (the above four states plus Oklahoma). No matter what specific comparisons are drawn, the conclusions appear to remain roughly the same.

[12] The tendency to exaggerate Louisiana's tax burden, due in part to its highly centralized tax structure, was justly criticized over a decade ago in William D. Ross, "The Federal-State-Local Tax Structure in Louisiana," *National Tax Journal*, VII (December, 1954), 371–76. Some of the early confusion was probably due to the fact that figures for local government finance were not generally available on a yearly basis.

[13] One question, however, is whether to include federal grants or exclude them from per capita expenditure figures. In this section, such grants are included.

To compare taxes on a per capita basis would be highly misleading, however, if one were interested in the "revenue effort" made by
the states (or, depending on the point of view, the "burden" on their
citizens). Relatively rich states can raise the same amount of revenue
per capita as poor states with much less effort or burden. If one assumes that ability to pay is related (proportionately) to income,
revenue per thousand dollars of personal income is a much better
measure. But here, too, this measure is not perfect, although it is relatively simple and useful for making rough comparisons.

Consider first Louisiana's general expenditure pattern in comparison with that of other states. (See Table VIII.) On a per capita
basis, combined state and local expenditures in 1964–65 placed
Louisiana squarely in the middle of the rankings in twenty-fifth
position. Thus, it might be argued that Louisiana was about average
in the provision of services to its residents—although it should be
noted that above-average amounts of federal grants helped it to
achieve this ranking. It would be clearly erroneous, however, to focus
on general expenditures at the state level only, where Louisiana oc-
cupied the rather lofty position of ninth.

While the overall level of per capita expenditures was average for
the country as a whole, the state varied from the norm strikingly in
two major categories, namely public welfare and education. Louisiana's public welfare expenditures in 1964–65 were $57.60 per capita,
second only to Oklahoma and over twice that in the median state
($28.24). Educational expenditures, on the other hand, ranked only
thirty-seventh in the nation at $123.08 per capita, well below the U.S.
median of $146.05.

The relative weights attached to the education and welfare functions is striking. This divergence can be seen in yet another way.
When total general expenditures at the state and local level are
compared per thousand dollars of personal income, Louisiana's overall rank rose to sixth, owing to its relatively low level of personal income. In public welfare, Louisiana still ranked second in the nation
with expenditures of $31.26 per thousand dollars personal income—
almost three times that in the median state.[14] Highway expenditures

Since Louisiana receives above-average amounts of grants per capita, its overall
rank is higher when federal grants are included. The systematic exclusion of
grants from all expenditure comparisons, however, would not materially affect
the general conclusions.

[14] It might be noted that Louisiana's sister southern state Virginia ranked at
the very bottom in this category with public welfare expenditures of only $5.79

were also well above the median (and considerably above the U.S. arithmetic average of $24.89). Of the three major functions, education received by far the less emphasis, and Louisiana's rank of twenty-third barely exceeded the median.

Comparisons of state and local expenditures per thousand dollars of personal income point up the fact that even the provision of a "normal" amount of overall governmental services is unusual in a state such as Louisiana where the level of personal income is well below the U.S. average. This also can be shown in two other ways. First, comparisons can be made on the revenue side of the budget after eliminating federal grants from total general revenue. On this basis Louisiana ranked third in the nation based on general revenue from *own sources* per thousand dollars personal income. This is a standard measure of effort by the states.[15] By this criterion Louisiana appears to be making a major revenue effort to attain an average level of government services.

Second, the state's general expenditure rank (25) can be compared with its per capita personal income rank, which in calendar year 1964 was forty-fourth. In contrast to U.S. per capita personal income of $2,566, Louisiana's figure was $1,877. This figure exceeded the level attained in only six other southern states—Tennessee, Kentucky, Alabama, Arkansas, South Carolina, and Mississippi.

The latter type of comparison is interesting for several reasons. When economists have attempted to isolate and measure statistically the significant variables which explain per capita expenditures, the most important variable discovered has been income. On the average more will be spent by state and local government in a relatively rich state than in a state with low per capita income. Of course, this is not an unexpected result. However, this general relationship has a great many exceptions. Including federal grants in expenditure figures, some examples can be cited. Among the relatively high income states, Connecticut (2), Illinois (7), and New Jersey (8) ranked only twenty-first, twenty-ninth, and thirty-second, respectively, in per

---

per thousand dollars personal income. One scholar summed up this striking difference of an earlier date by suggesting that "a safe guess" would be that the explanation lies in "differences in the political philosophy of the Byrds and the Longs." Glen W. Fisher, "Determinants of State and Local Government Expenditures: A Preliminary Analysis," *National Tax Journal*, XIV (December, 1961), 353.

[15] For example, see Maxwell, *Financing State and Local Governments*, 41–43.

Table VIII

General Expenditures in Louisiana and the United States, Per Capita and Per $1,000 Personal Income, 1964–65

(dollar amounts)

	Total general expenditures	Education	Highways	Public welfare	Health and hospitals
Per Capita:					
State-local					
Median state	391.53	146.05	70.51	28.24	23.51
Louisiana	391.53	123.08	76.43	57.60	22.37
Rank	(25)	(37)	(21)	(2)	(27)
State (only)					
Median state	213.89	76.42	59.75	25.08	13.75
Louisiana	293.26	94.70	66.59	57.42	19.63
Rank	(9)	(11)	(16)	(2)	(11)
Per $1,000 personal income:					
State-local					
Median state	162.26	62.48	33.20	11.82	10.04
Louisiana	212.54	66.81	41.49	31.26	12.14
Rank	(6)	(23)	(12)	(2)	(14)
State (only)					
Median state	97.22	35.96	25.93	10.42	N.A.*
Louisiana	159.20	51.41	36.15	31.17	N.A.
Rank	(4)	(6)	(13)	(2)	N.A.

*N.A.–Not available

source: *Governmental Finances in 1964–65*, pp. 45–47, 50; *Compendium of State Government Finances in 1965*, pp. 13, 14, 18

capita general expenditures. Maryland, Ohio, Pennsylvania, and Missouri also had significantly higher income than expenditure rankings. In addition to Louisiana, several states had appreciably higher expenditure rankings. Interestingly, all of the more notable ones, with the exception of Vermont, were west of the Mississippi River— Wyoming, Montana, Utah, New Mexico, Idaho, North Dakota, and South Dakota. Thus, while in the minority, Louisiana is not really so unique in the considerable divergence that exists between its expenditure and personal income rankings.

Louisiana *is* somewhat unique, however, from a regional point of view. Of the ten states with the lowest per capita personal incomes in 1964, nine were southern states (the other was South Dakota). Excluding Louisiana, these states ranked 42, 43, and 45 through 50 in per capita expenditures.[16] Given the relatively low income levels of this southern group, only Louisiana was willing to make the effort required to maintain an expenditure level that was about average by U.S. standards. Even the somewhat higher income states of Florida (29), Virginia (30), and Texas (32) did not match Louisiana's per capita general expenditure level.

In looking at the country as a whole, what factors other than per-capita income can help explain the diversity in expenditure levels among the fifty states? Economists have attempted to quantify these factors with the use of regression techniques. Traditionally, such variables as population per square mile and percentage of the population living in urban areas have been used as explanatory variables. In recent studies a number of additional variables have been added. Sacks and Harris, for example, used per capita federal aid to state governments and per capita state aid to local governments as additional independent variables; they concluded that federal aid, notably for welfare, was an important determinant of state and local expenditures in 1960.[17] Fisher used five independent variables in

[16] These states, ranked by per capita personal income and expenditures (in parentheses), are as follows: Georgia, 41 (42); North Carolina, 42 (48); Tennessee, 45(47); Kentucky, 46(43); Alabama, 47(45); Arkansas, tied 48(49); South Carolina, tied 48(50); and Mississippi, 50(46).

[17] Seymour Sacks and Robert Harris, "The Determinants of State and Local Government Expenditures and Intergovernmental Flows of Funds," *National Tax Journal*, XVII (March, 1964), 75–85. The Sacks-Harris results have been strongly criticized by Elliott R. Morss on methodological grounds. Since state and local governments must spend virtually all the federal aid they receive, he argues, it is hardly surprising to find that aid and expenditures move together in a manner that is "statistically significant." See Morss, "Some Thoughts on the Determinants

addition to the population density and urbanization measures. One of these, percent of families with less than two-thousand dollars income, served as a substitute for per capita income and yielded relatively good results for 1960 data.[18]

Unfortunately, the empirical results of the various studies have not been entirely satisfactory and much has been left unexplained. Furthermore, there are certain drawbacks in cross-sectional analysis of the type utilized. The most significant variables for the fifty states as a group may not fit well the particular situation in a given state. This is quite likely the case with Louisiana. On the other hand, variables that are important in a particular state may not appear statistically significant in cross-sectional studies of the entire country because of wide social, political, and other variations among states. Differences in political philosophy may be very important but difficult or even impossible to quantify.

Perhaps a partial explanation of Louisiana's expenditure level lies in an anatomy of the revenue side of the budget. That is, the *manner* in which the state raises its funds may affect the *level* of its expenditures. It may be recalled that by one set of standards—i.e., per capita expenditures compared with revenue from own sources per thousand dollars of personal income—Louisiana appears to generate a considerable revenue effort to achieve an average level of government services. But Louisiana's lofty rank of third in this revenue category may not be truly reflective of fiscal "effort," or "burden," at least in a relevant political sense. Other things being equal, it seems reasonable that the less burden the average citizen-voter feels in meeting his fiscal obligations, the higher will be the level of government expenditures. In this respect Louisiana seems to enjoy significant revenue sources that represent little or no direct burden to the average voter

of State and Local Expenditures," *National Tax Journal*, XIX (March, 1966), 95–103. This objection to the Sacks-Harris approach has obvious merit. For an attempt (in the case of highways) to replace aid variables stated in dollar amounts with variables reflecting the *determinants* of federal and state aid, see L. G. Gabler and Joel I. Brest, "Interstate Variations in Per Capita Highway Expenditures," *National Tax Journal*, XX (March, 1967), 78–85.

[18] The other variables were as follows: the yield of a representative tax system for each state as a percent of the U.S. average; percent increase in population for the previous decade; an index of two-party competition; and the percent of population over twenty-five with less than five years schooling. Glenn W. Fisher, "Interstate Variation in State and Local Government Expenditure," *National Tax Journal*, XVII (March, 1964), 55–74.

and this may partially explain the state's relatively high expenditure level.

Excluding grants, state and local revenues come from either tax or nontax sources—the latter being termed "charges and miscellaneous general revenue" by the Bureau of the Census. As can be seen in Table IX, Louisiana ranked fifth in this category. In the country as a whole well over half of these revenues accrue to local units; in Louisiana the relationship is quite the opposite. In a substantial majority of states such nontax revenues consist mainly of "current charges," i.e., amounts received for performance of specific services benefiting the person charged or from sales of commodities and services.[19] This includes such things as fees, assessments, and the like, and at the state level these are collected in large measure via institutions of higher education, highway toll facilities, and hospitals. It is not entirely clear how taxpayers view these charges. One may assume that since such charges are payments for direct services voluntarily purchased, perhaps they are considered less burdensome than tax payments where the benefit is less clear. On the other hand, current charges may be identified by the public as a clear alternative to tax payments—e.g., states can meet rising higher education costs by raising college tuitions or by increasing direct appropriations; they can finance highway construction through general tax revenues or by building toll facilities.

If one cannot safely generalize about the psychological burden of current charges, the situation in Louisiana is rather unusual in that the state collects large sums from bonuses and royalties on state property. In 1964–65 this source yielded $115.1 million. This is a windfall resulting from the state's spectacular endowments of mineral resources and represents virtually no recognizable burden to the typical taxpayer. Only Texas collected more from this source, and "rents and royalties" (the Bureau of the Census category) exceeded $10 million in only two other states, California and New Mexico. Thus, not only did Louisiana rank fifth in the country in total "charges and miscellaneous general revenue," but about 43 percent of its substantial collections in this category came from a seemingly painless source.

With nontax revenues excluded, Louisiana's rank drops to ninth

[19] This does not include sales by government owned utilities and liquor stores, as these are excluded from the concept of general revenue.

Table IX

General Revenues in Louisiana and the United States, Per Capita and Per $1,000 Personal Income, 1964–65

(dollar amounts)

	Total general revenue	From federal government	From own sources	Taxes	Charges and miscellaneous general revenue
Per Capita:					
State-local					
Median state	388.95	62.39	315.73	254.61	60.66
Louisiana	385.71	87.70	298.02	222.04	75.98
Rank	(26)	(12)	(31)	(36)	(11)
State (only)					
Median state	214.56	56.26	156.72	133.23	24.26
Louisiana	296.25	80.56	213.78	164.48	49.30
Rank	(10)	(13)	(5)	(9)	(7)
Per $1,000 personal income:					
State-local					
Median state	160.07	27.35	130.42	104.43	25.89
Louisiana	209.39	47.60	161.78	120.54	41.24
Rank	(6)	(8)	(3)	(9)	(5)
State (only)					
Median state	101.46	24.66	69.02	57.75	10.90
Louisiana	160.82	43.73	116.05	89.29	26.76
Rank	(4)	(9)	(2)	(2)	(4)

SOURCE: *Governmental Finances in 1964–65*, pp. 45, 50; *Compendium of State Government Finances in 1965*, pp. 11, 12, 18

in tax collections per thousand dollars personal income. But even this rank may imply a greater psychological tax burden than that experienced by the average taxpayer (if not the oil and gas industry). The main reason for this is the state's substantial collections from the severance tax of $179.1 million in 1965, a figure topped only by Texas. Only four other states were fortunate enough to collect as much as $10 million from this source. Furthermore, Louisiana's combined income, property, and sales tax collections from individuals are among the lowest of any state.

Not only is the severance tax not levied directly on the typical taxpayer-voter, but it is quite probable that a relatively high percentage of the tax is ultimately shifted to residents of other states largely through the prices paid for exported products. In the language of public finance a portion of the tax is "exported" to other states. Of course, all states have both export and import taxes of various kinds, and for many states it is probably reasonable to assume a rough cancellation takes place. It also seems reasonable, however, to expect a state with abundant mineral resources to be in a better position than most to export taxes. In addition to its heavy reliance on the severance tax, Louisiana's property tax collections are concentrated to a high degree on nonresidential property. While some portion of the taxes on manufacturing, railroad, utility, and mineral properties are undoubtedly exported, this is not the case for residential property.

All taxes considered, it seems probable that Louisiana's export rate is one of the highest in the country. Although this is only an "educated guess," it does conform to the results of a recent study by Charles McLure. While interstate incidence is difficult to measure and any conclusions are based on very restrictive assumptions, McLure estimated Louisiana's short-run export rate in 1962 at 31.7 percent.[20] (This includes an allowance for exports to the federal government through deductibility of state-local taxes on federal income tax returns.) This rate was topped only by Delaware, Nevada, and Texas and was significantly above the overall rate of 25 percent

[20] Louisiana's high overall export rate critically depends upon the export rate assumed for the severance tax alone. McLure assumes a rate of 50 percent. If this rate is reduced to 25 percent, the overall export rate for Louisiana falls to 26 percent. Most of the exporting of property taxes that takes place is attributed to manufacturing and public utility properties; Louisiana is one of ten states whose short-run property tax export rate is estimated at more than 28 percent. Charles E. McLure, Jr., "The Interstate Exporting of State and Local Taxes: Estimates for 1962," *National Tax Journal*, XX (March, 1967), 49–77.

for all states.[21] Since tax exporting lowers the cost of public under-
takings to any one state, it may well create an incentive for that state
to expand its public sector.[22]

On occasion, students of the state's fiscal situation have suggested
other explanations for Louisiana's historically high level of expenditures relative to its per capita income. For example, it has been
suggested (if somewhat casually) that "the number of state taxes,
pressure for exemptions, extensive dedications, and centralization of
taxation and spending at the state level have contributed to the high
level of spending and taxation in the state."[23] While the last two
reasons are suggestive, there is no conclusive evidence that either
the degree of centralization or tax earmarking is a major influence on
relative expenditure levels in the various states.[24] Furthermore, if
carried too far, this type of reasoning might lead one to attempt to
lay the blame for high spending on the variety of alleged shortcomings
in the state's fiscal structure. Fiscal reforms with respect to nuisance
taxes, earmarking, and centralization may well be desirable even if
they are largely unrelated to the overall level of state and local expenditures. Furthermore, whether spending is excessive or not is
largely a matter of value judgments and not the state's relative
rankings. Being average or typical is not necessarily desirable.[25]

EDUCATION EXPENDITURES

As shown in the previous section, the relative weights attached to
the education and welfare functions in Louisiana are striking. Of

[21] The high export rates in Delaware and Nevada were largely attributed to
the corporation income and franchise taxes in the former and the gambling tax
in the latter. The high rate in Texas was attributed largely to the severance tax
and the property tax on petroleum reserves. Certain other high export states
placed heavy dependence upon taxes on manufacturing. Many of the states with
low overall export rates relied heavily on property taxes of a type that are
assumed not to be exported. *Ibid.*

[22] That this is only a partial explanation, however, is seen by the fact that
Texas with its higher per capita personal income and roughly similar export rate
ranked well below Louisiana in per capita expenditures.

[23] "Louisiana's Complex Tax System," *PAR Analysis*, December, 1959, p. 6.

[24] On the possible relationships between earmarking and expenditures, see
Elizabeth Deran, "Earmarking and Expenditures: A Survey and a New Test,"
National Tax Journal, XVIII (December, 1965), 354–61.

[25] Because of space limitations, this study does not consider the question of
state and local debt. In Louisiana per capita debt outstanding at the end of 1964–
65 was $554.13, ranking the state eleventh in the nation and well above the
figure for the median state of $425.30. As is the case in most states, the majority
of debt in Louisiana is at the local level—some $1,356 million out of a total
$1,958 million.

the three major functions of state and local government—education, highways, and public welfare—the first receives below average support relative to other states while support of the third function appears relatively generous. In this and the following section, expenditures on education and public welfare will be considered in greater detail.

One of the most interesting facts about public education in Louisiana is the high degree of centralization that exists owing to the abnormally low level of local support and the sizeable transfers to the local school systems through the state-administered equalization program. In 1965 over two-thirds of all state intergovernmental transfers to local units went to education—the bulk of the remainder going to "general local government support" and a small amount to highways. State transfers for education totaled $219.2 million, or roughly 69 percent of all local direct expenditures on this function. Only two other states, Delaware and New Mexico, financed a larger portion of local spending in this manner. The U.S. average was 37 percent.

As can be seen in Table X, education spending does not appear unusually centralized when compared with the state's expenditures on public welfare and highways. Virtually all of Louisiana's welfare expenditures are made directly by the state government. So are the bulk of highway expenditures, with only relatively moderate amounts originating from local sources or from intergovernmental transfers by the state government. But these comparisons are rather misleading

Table X
State and Local Expenditures on Education,
Highways, and Public Welfare in Louisiana, 1965
(in millions of dollars)

Category	Education	Highways	Public welfare
State-local direct	435.0	270.1	203.6
State total	334.7	235.3	202.9
State direct	115.4	215.2	202.9
State intergovernmental transfers to local units	219.2	20.1	—
Local direct	319.6	54.9	0.6

SOURCE: *Governmental Finances in 1964–65*, p. 36; *Compendium of State Government Finances in 1965*, pp. 28, 30, 31

since a high degree of centralization is customary in these areas. Furthermore, since final spending on *local* schools is almost invariably *local* in nature, centralization in education takes the form primarily of state grants to local units, while in both highways and welfare, centralization may also take the form of direct state expenditures.[26]

In public welfare, for example, Louisiana is one of sixteen states in which no intergovernmental transfers were made by the state level, while in another half-dozen or so such transfers were trivial. Thus, Louisiana can hardly be considered unique in this respect. Some states, of course, do rely heavily on intergovernmental payments to local government, and in such states as California, Maryland, Minnesota, and New York, direct local expenditures account for over 95 percent of all welfare dollars. These wide differences in approach to welfare spending do not occur in the highway area. In this case intergovernmental transfers are usually less than one-fourth of total highway expenditures at the state level and direct local spending averages less than one-half that at the state level. To be sure, Louisiana is somewhat more centralized than average, but several states exceed Louisiana in the percentage of highway expenditures financed at the state level. In any event, one is not likely to be as impressed by the degree of centralization in this area as in the field of education.

Given the substantial support of public education at the state level, it is not surprising that many observers would like to see the state's sixty-seven school systems make a greater effort to finance local schools from their own resources.[27] Certainly the school systems have not utilized property taxation to the fullest extent possible.[28] Local school boards (except in Orleans) have authority to levy up to 19 mills for school operating and maintenance purposes. In fiscal year 1964–65 only one school board levied this amount; thirty-one levied 10 or fewer mills. Orleans Parish had authority for 18 mills for all

[26] Direct state expenditures in education are primarily for institutions of higher learning, thus largely reflecting the relative weight attached to higher education in a state. Expenditures on higher education are not explicitly considered in this essay.

[27] These include each of the state's sixty-four parishes plus the cities of Monroe, Bogalusa, and Lake Charles.

[28] See, for example, the recommendations in PAR, *The Economic Status of Teachers in Louisiana* (Baton Rouge, 1963). For an emphasis on improving the property tax assessment process in order to expand local support for education, see B. F. Sliger, "Financing Public Education in Louisiana," *Louisiana Business Review*, XXIV (March, 1960), 20–23.

Table XI

Current Expenditures Per Pupil in Average Daily Attendance
and Average Annual Salaries of Instructional Staff in
Public Elementary and Secondary Day Schools, Louisiana
and the United States, Selected Years,
1945–46 to 1963–64
(in dollar amounts)

	1945–46	1949–50	1955–56	1959–60	1963–64
Current expenditures per pupil in average daily attendance:[1]					
U.S.	136.41	208.83	294.22	375.14	460.24
Louisiana	101.36	214.08	281.68	371.94	390.30
(Rank)	(38)	(27)	(29)	(22)	(37)
Average annual salaries of instructional staff:[2]					
U.S.	1,995	3,010	4,156	5,174	6,240.[3]
Louisiana	1,537	2,983	3,885	4,978	5,304.
(Rank)	(36)	(23)	(25)	(24)	(34)

SOURCE: Tax Foundation, *Facts and Figures on Government Finance, 1967*, pp. 245–46
[1] Beginning in 1959–60, U.S. totals and Louisiana rank include Alaska and Hawaii
[2] Includes supervisors, principals, teachers, and other instructional staff
[3] Partly estimated

school operating and capital purposes and levied a total of 13 mills.[29] Added to the relatively small amount of support at the local level is the overriding need to expand funds for education and, in particular, to raise the salaries of school teachers and other school employees to more competitive levels.

As noted earlier, in 1964–65 Louisiana ranked thirty-seventh in the country in per capita expenditures for education. Not only is this low rank significant in itself, but it is interesting to note the relative decline in the state's position that took place in the preceding five years in such measures as current expenditures per pupil in average daily attendance and average annual salaries of instructional staff in public elementary and secondary schools.

As can be seen in Table XI, educational expenditures were well below the nation's average at the end of the Second World War. During the first complete administration of Governor Earl Long, the figures rose to approximately U.S. average levels in school year 1949–50 and then maintained a roughly similar position throughout the 1950's. However, a serious decline in the state's relative position took place in the early 1960's. While average U.S. expenditures per pupil were rising by about $85 from 1959–60 to 1963–64, the increase in Louisiana was on the order of only $18. Increases in the relative salaries of instructional staff showed similar disparities, and by the latter date the average salaries in Louisiana were more than $900 below the U.S. figure. That the sharp relative decline did not cause greater consternation is perhaps partly due to the self-defeating tendency of many to compare Louisiana only with other southern states. In this respect, Louisiana was still in a somewhat "satisfactory" position.

In November, 1964, however, a special session of the Legislature did adopt proposed statewide salary increases for teachers and other school employees. Act 28 called for increases averaging $1,100 per teacher and 10 percent for others. (Act 27 applied to school bus drivers.) Interestingly, the special session provided state funds to pay for only one-half of the proposed salary increases during the last half of school year 1964–65, and the following legislative session continued this level of support.[30] Under state law the 50 percent im-

[29] "Louisiana Public School Revenues to 1976," *PAR Analysis*, February, 1966, pp. 7–8.
[30] Full implementation was attained, however, in the 1967 legislative session.

plementation became, in effect, the state minimum salary schedule. At the same time, the 1964 special session authorized local school boards to levy a local sales tax, with taxpayer approval, to provide additional funds for teacher pay (Act 29). This was the first state-wide grant of such authority to local school boards. The Legislature pledged that no revenues from the local sales tax would be counted as local support of the state's school equalization program.

This new development, coupled with the operation of the school equalization program and the acknowledged need for additional support for education, created an interesting fiscal situation. In its November, 1966 report, the Public Affairs Research Council (PAR) found that twenty-eight of Louisiana's sixty-seven school systems had obtained voter approval to levy or share in local sales taxes.[31] All but two of the twenty-eight were in the southeast and southwest portions of the state. (Another five in this area had unsuccessfully sought voter approval.) Of the thirty school systems lying above the lower Vernon-Rapides-Avoyelles boundary, only two had been authorized to levy school sales taxes and three others had sought voter approval but had been turned down.

At the time of the PAR report, there were some thirty school systems paying full Act 28 or higher salaries; another seven were paying above the state minimum but less than Act 28. The remaining thirty school systems—all but a few being in the northern part of the state—were following the state minimum schedule.

What seemed to be most paradoxical about this situation is the fact that most of those school systems not levying local sales taxes to provide higher salaries and meet other operating costs were generally: (1) among the highest spending school systems per pupil in 1964–65 (the year before local sales taxes became fairly common); (2) among those systems receiving the highest amounts of state equalization aid per pupil; and (3) among those systems providing the smallest portions of their school operating revenues locally. It seems clear that most systems not paying the full Act 28 teacher salary schedules were ones which relied heavily on state aid and were among the highest spenders per pupil.

All of this seems rather confusing. According to PAR, a part of the explanation is related to the method of distributing state equalization

[31] "Key Issues of 1966 Special Session," *PAR Analysis*, November, 1966, pp. 5–15.

funds. In computing the minimum foundation program, certain items of local school revenue are counted as local support—the revenues from 5 mills of property tax, school boards' share of parish severance taxes, and one-half of any amounts received from rent or lease of school lands. The state makes up the difference between the cost of the minimum foundation program and the total of local government revenue counted as support for the program.

The amount of state equalization aid per pupil varies widely among school systems. In 1964–65 it varied from a low of $121 to a high of $371 per pupil; the state average was $250. Some of the variations are due to differences in mineral wealth and property assessments. But a very significant reason, according to PAR, is a strong bias in the equalization formula which heavily favors small over larger schools. "Because they have many small schools, the parishwide pupil-teacher ratios which result from application of the formula are lower in the school systems which get larger amounts of state equalization aid than they are in the systems with low state aid."[32] This system is said to be in need of overhaul. Although state equalization aid is supposed to provide a minimum foundation program of education for every public school child, the equalization formula has worked to provide the highest spending per pupil in the supposedly poorer parishes. It is further suggested by PAR that continued local support of teachers salaries should be encouraged and that the very high proportion of school support which continues to come from the state has tended to dampen local initiative in and control of school affairs.

It must be pointed out, however, that it would be extremely difficult to devise an equalization formula that would please all parties and be entirely equitable. No magically simple formula seems possible.[33] Some consolation may also be taken from the fact that problems of state transfers to local units are not unique to Louisiana. In fact, in many parts of the country the problems may be equally as severe because of the continued existence of excessive numbers of local school districts—a problem that does not exist in Louisiana. In these cases, state aid has often tended to perpetuate inefficient units rather than promote needed consolidation. Of course, what magnifies

[32] *Ibid.*, 12.
[33] For a discussion of the many problems of implementing the equalization objective in state grant-in-aid programs, see Richard Rossmiller, "The Equalization Objective in State Support Programs: An Analysis of Measures, Need and Ability," *National Tax Journal*, XVIII (December, 1965), 362–69.

any deficiencies in the equalization formula in Louisiana is the fact that such a large share of education funds comes from the state as opposed to the local level of government.

PUBLIC WELFARE EXPENDITURES

Public welfare expenditures cannot be discussed without some consideration of federal grants since the latter play such a major role in the public assistance programs of the various states. In fact, over half of all public assistance expenditures of state and local government in 1965 were financed by federal grants. The percentage of welfare expenditures financed in this manner is above that for highways and considerably above that for education.[34]

In a very general way, per capita grants are inversely related to per capita personal income, i.e., low income states tend to receive higher per capita grants. However, the coefficient of correlation, while negative, is not very high. Some high-income states, e.g., Nevada and Alaska, receive relatively large per capita grants; some of the poorer states, e.g., North Carolina and South Carolina, receive relatively small grants. One reason for the deviations is that in certain cases Congress has allotted grants to the states on the basis of such criteria as area, road mileage, public land acreage, etc.—factors that are unrelated to state income or population.

One might expect to find a particularly close (negative) relation between state per capita income and federal grants for public welfare. In this program, attention is normally given to differences in the fiscal capacity of the recipient states so that a minimum program is feasible even in the poorer ones. This is evidenced by the wide interstate variations in the percentage of public assistance expenditures financed by federal grants. In such relatively low income states as Alabama, Arkansas, Georgia, Kentucky, Louisiana, Mississippi, North Carolina, South Carolina, and Tennessee (plus a few others), the federal percentage ranged between 70 and 79 percent in calendar year 1964. In a number of high income states, the federal share was less than 45 percent.[35]

[34] The most rapid expansion, however, is probably taking place in the education area. In Louisiana, for example, federal grants to the State Department of Education (Public School Fund) rose from $14.4 million in 1964–65 to $51.6 million in 1965–66.

[35] Tax Foundation, *Facts and Figures on Government Finance, 1967* (New York, 1967), 146–47.

Partly because of the equalizing characteristics of public assistance programs, welfare grants are generally higher in the states with relatively low per capita incomes. But even here, there are many exceptions. Since federal grants require some type of matching funds, those low-income states which have chosen to spend only small amounts of their own funds for welfare, e.g., South Carolina, consequently receive only moderate amounts of grants.

Table XII

State Intergovernmental Revenue[1] from Federal Government
Louisiana and the United States, 1965

	Total	Educa-tion	High-ways	Public welfare
Dollar amounts (per capita)				
Median state	56.26	7.53	24.18	14.42
Louisiana	80.56	5.94	28.31	40.34
Rank	(13)	(38)	(19)	(1)
Percentage of state-local general expenditures:				
Median state[2]	14.4	5.2	34.3	51.1
Louisiana	20.6	4.8	37.0	70.1

SOURCE: *Compendium of State Government Finances in 1965*, p. 12; percentages computed using Table VIII.

[1]Smaller amounts of direct federal grants to local units are omitted in per capita dollar amounts and in percentage calculations.

[2]Estimated by dividing per capita intergovernmental revenues in the median state by per capita state and local expenditures in the median state.

As can be seen in Table XII, Louisiana ranked first in 1965 in terms of per capita federal grants to state government for welfare purposes.[36] These grants were almost three times that in the median state.[37] Not only is Louisiana in a position to finance a substantial

[36] This discussion generally ignores the much smaller amounts of direct federal grants to local units.

[37] In 1964–65 welfare grants to combined state and local government were $40.84 per capita in Louisiana and $15.75 per capita in the median state. A substantial portion of Louisiana's aid was concentrated in the old age assistance program—some $29.09 per capita as compared with $5.58 in the median state. Louisiana was clearly first in this category. It ranked seventh in grants per capita in the aid to families of dependent children program and second and fourth, respectively, in the smaller programs of aid to the blind and aid to permanently and totally disabled. *Social Security Bulletin, Annual Statistical Supplement, 1965*, p. 107.

portion of its welfare costs through federal monies, but it has been willing to commit more of its own funds for this purpose than have its sister southern states. Furthermore, Louisiana's commitment to the welfare function largely explains why it is able to rank thirteenth in per capita grants received for all purposes. Certainly, its grants for education and highways are not responsible. In fact, if one subtracted the welfare component from total federal grants per capita, Louisiana would vary little from the median state despite its relatively low level of personal income.

What factors account for the state's substantial commitment to welfare spending? Obviously, the answer to this question is not a simple one. In part, it may reflect Louisiana's abysmal ranking in functional illiteracy and its poor showing in median grades completed per adult; these factors, in turn, are related to its large non-white population. Low educational attainment and job discrimination make for a high rate of dependency. In addition, it appears that the state has been exceptionally lenient in its eligibility requirements for the main public assistance programs.

The major public assistance programs in the United States are old age assistance (OAA)—$2.1 billion in 1965—and aid to families with dependent children (AFDC)—$1.8 billion in 1965. The other programs—aid to the blind (AB), aid to permanently and totally disabled (APTD), medical assistance for the aged (MAA), and general assistance (GA)—are considerably smaller in total dollar outlays. In Louisiana at least four of these six programs are relatively well supported; in particular, the state has placed considerable emphasis on OAA.

As can be seen in Table XIII, the state had a recipient rate in OAA over four times the U.S. average in 1965. Virtually half of Louisiana's population aged sixty-five and over received old-age assistance payments—the highest recipient rate in the country.[38] The even lower income states of Alabama and Mississippi ranked second and third, respectively, in this category; but even in Alabama the recipient rate was less than four out of ten. In the fourth ranking state of Oklahoma, it was roughly three out of ten. Louisiana's relatively liberal eligibility requirements for the OAA program are clear from these com-

[38] Louisiana has consistently had the highest recipient rate in the country in recent years. In June, 1953, for example, Louisiana's recipient rate under OAA was 604 as compared to the U.S. rate of 191. As the number of recipients under the self-financed Old Age, Survivors, Disability, and Health Insurance program has expanded, the recipient rate under OAA has gradually declined.

parisons. It might also be noted that the recipient rates for AB and APTD were well above average (ranking sixth among the states in both cases) as well as that for AFDC (where Louisiana ranked seventh).

While the recipient rates were generally high (except in the relatively small MAA and GA categories) the average monthly payments per recipient were not unusually so. In the important AFDC category, the size of monthly payments was well below the U.S. average; it was only slightly above average in the OAA category. In comparison with the other low income southern states, however, the average monthly payments often appear relatively generous.

One additional factor should be mentioned with respect to Louisiana's OAA expenditures. This is the amount of coverage of elderly citizens under the Old-Age, Survivors, Disability, and Health Insur-

Table XIII

Public Assistance Recipient Rates and Average Monthly Payments, Louisiana and the United States, 1965

	Recipient rates (per 1,000)[1]		Average monthly payments (dollars)[2]	
Category	U.S. average[3]	Louisiana	U.S. average[3]	Louisiana
OAA	115	490	80.36	84.93
AFDC	47	56	33.83	23.08
AB	76	129	87.88	81.34
APTD	5.5	10.8	84.65	58.75
MAA	18	1.9	190.48	159.13
GA	4	2.6	31.33	47.25

SOURCE: *Social Security Bulletin, Annual Statistical Supplement, 1965,* p. 105; *Social Security Bulletin* (October, 1965), 42–43.

[1]OAA and MAA recipient rates per 1,000 population aged 65 and over; AFDC, children receiving per 1,000 population under 18; AB, per 1,000 population aged 18 and over; APTD, per 1,000 population aged 18–64; GA, per 1,000 population under age 65–all recipient rates as of December, 1965.

[2]Includes cash plus vendor payments for medical care per recipient as of June, 1965.

[3]No APTD program in Nevada; MAA average based on forty-seven states with program in operation; GA average based on data for forty-six states.

ance (OASDHI) program. This social security program, of course, is financed by a tax levied against insured employees and their employers and is administered solely by the federal government. In an important sense, it is a substitute for OAA, although the coverage is considerably broader under OASDHI and it is possible to receive payments under both programs in certain cases. In February, 1965, some 752 per thousand population aged sixty-five and over in the United States received benefits under OASDHI; in Louisiana, for whatever reasons, only 614 received benefits and the state ranked behind every other state in this respect. Clearly, the relatively low rate of OASDHI benefit recipients is related to, and partially causes, the relatively high rate of OAA assistance. Future expansion in OASDHI coverage should lead to a reduction in OAA recipients.

Louisiana's relatively low rates of OASDHI coverage for the elderly is a fact not generally appreciated by the state's many critics of welfare spending. (Neither, perhaps, is the fact that over two-thirds of welfare spending is financed via federal grants.) On the other hand, it must also be noted that Louisiana had the highest recipient rate in the country for those aged sixty-five and over receiving *both* OASDHI and OAA benefits (216) and was third in those receiving either one or both types of benefits (894). Some 35 percent of those receiving OASDHI benefits also received OAA payments, and this was the highest percentage in the country.[39]

TYPES OF TAXES

While federal grants and other nontax sources are important, Louisiana still must rely primarily on tax revenues to finance most governmental activities. In 1965 tax collections at the state level constituted 55.5 percent of total general revenue. The major tax sources at the state level (in millions of dollars) were as follows: severance, $179.1; general sales, $119.3; motor fuels, $77.3; tobacco, $31.1; corporation income, $27.4; alcoholic beverages, $24; individual income, $23.5; property, $17.6; corporation franchise, $17.3; insurance, $13.5; and motor vehicle licenses, $11.4[40] In addition, sizeable but lesser sums were collected from general occupational license and other

[39] *Social Security Bulletin, Annual Statistical Supplement, 1965,* p. 14.

[40] Revenue figures are based on Bureau of the Census concepts and may differ slightly from those in Division of Administration, *State of Louisiana, Financial Statements.*

license taxes, death and gift taxes, a tax on the generation and sale of electricity, public utilities tax, power use tax, lubricating oil tax, soft drinks tax, and a pari-mutuels tax. The state also collected a number of very minor taxes, most of which could be eliminated with little loss of revenue.[41] Some of the more important taxes will be considered in this section.

Severance Tax

Severance taxes are paid when natural resources are severed from the soil or water. In Louisiana severance taxes are collected, at varying rates, on pulpwood and other timber, oil, distillates, gas, sulphur, salt, sand, gravel, shells, and a number of lesser revenue producers. In 1964 sulphur, which is also assessed in the ground, bore a severance tax rate of $1.03 a long ton. The rate on distillates, condensates, and similar resources was 20 cents a barrel. The two most important revenue producers, of course, were oil and gas. The rate on oil varied from 18 cents a barrel to 26 cents a barrel, with the stipulation that rates were cut to one-half these amounts for oil from wells incapable of producing more than an average of six barrels per day. The severance tax rate on gas stood at 2.3 cents per thousand cubic feet, with a somewhat lower rate on marginal wells. Unlike sulphur, however, oil and gas in the ground were both exempted by the constitution from the ad valorem tax—although a property tax was imposed on production equipment and inventories.[42]

Not only is the severance tax the state's leading source of tax revenue, but Louisiana collects a more sizeable percentage of its total revenues in this manner than does any other state, Texas included. This heavy reliance on the severance tax has certain advantages. For one thing, as noted earlier, it makes it easier for a relatively low-income state to provide a level of public services that is roughly average by U.S. standards. A related advantage is the below-average reliance on sales, license, and income taxes that is made possible by the abundance of severance tax collections.

---

[41] PAR reported that in fiscal 1962–63 there were twenty-four separate taxes yielding less than one million dollars each. Several yielded less than $15,000. Two taxes on the books at that time actually produced no revenue at all—a bank tax and a royalty gas excise (dry gas) tax. PAR, *Louisiana State Tax Handbook, 1964*, p. 2.

[42] *Ibid.*, 77–82.

But this emphasis on the severance tax may also have certain disadvantages. It is often alleged by industry spokesmen, as well as others, that the oil and gas interests are subject to a higher rate of taxation than is imposed in neighboring states. While tax rates in Texas, Oklahoma, and New Mexico are stated as a percent of value (rather than per barrel and per thousand cubic feet), Louisiana's severance tax rates have been appreciably higher considering the oil and gas prices that have prevailed in recent years. It is argued that this tax differential hinders industrial development by discouraging new industry from locating in the state. Not only are oil and gas producers affected, but industrial users in Louisiana must bear part of the incidence of the gas tax in their higher costs of power. It is further noted that in addition to the severance tax, industry is taxed heavily in other ways. Industry is subject to a significant portion of state-local property taxes, and Louisiana collects both a corporate income tax and a corporate franchise tax, as well as a sales and use tax.[43]

It is difficult to assess the importance of these contentions. While there is certainly some limit to the extent in which industry can be taxed without adversely affecting industrial expansion, it is not easy to compare the overall tax burdens in the various states. As emphasized by students of industrial location, comparative tax burdens may not be nearly so important as availability and cost of raw materials, transportation facilities, markets, and similar factors. What is also crucial is the degree to which the tax burden can be exported to residents of other states.

Heavy reliance on the severance tax may have one other disadvantage. This pertains to the long run rather than to the immediate future. The development of competing energy sources in other parts of the country, e.g., coal, shale oil, and atomic energy, could well cut into the petroleum market. Louisiana would suffer significantly from any such development since the severance tax would become a less reliable revenue producer. While income and sales tax collections will expand at reasonably predictable rates, long-run projections of severance tax collections are less reliable. Given the state's current tax structure, a rapid development of alternative energy sources could well strike a crippling blow to Louisiana's ability to meet rising demands for public services.

[43] See, for example, PAR, *Factors Affecting Louisiana's Industrial Development* (Baton Rouge, 1962).

General Sales Tax

The general sales tax is the second biggest source of tax revenue at the state level in Louisiana and for the nation as a whole is the leading tax source of state government. It is currently levied at a rate of 2 percent in Louisiana. Unlike many states which have raised their rates in the last decade, Louisiana has not increased its rate since 1948. Within the last few years, however, Louisiana has embarked on a unique system of collecting at the wholesale level what is essentially a state retail sales tax.

According to State Collector of Revenue Ashton J. Mouton, an audit program revealed that the majority of small retail sales tax accounts paying less than a hundred dollars a month were substantially underpaying their tax liabilities. Certain types of businesses were generally paying about half of the tax that they actually collected from the customer and owed to the state. As a result of this appalling situation, the state turned to a wholesale or advance collection system as a means of obtaining additional revenue. The system now covers all purchases of tangible personal property for resale at retail. The retailers pay the wholesalers when they make purchases from them and then receive a refund in the form of a credit against their sales tax liabilities when they file their monthly sales tax returns. The result has been a surprising expansion in sales tax collections of $10 million, or even more.[44]

State sales taxes are now very common throughout the country. In 1965 Louisiana was one of thirty-seven states with a general sales or gross receipts tax, and the number has since increased. Per capita revenues in Louisiana amounted to $33.76, somewhat below the median of $43.39 for those states collecting the tax. Furthermore, Louisiana was near the bottom in the percentage of its total state tax revenues collected from this source—a fact partially attributable to the concentration of tax collections at the state level.

The amount of Louisiana's below average per capita collections is explainable in several ways. Sales tax collections depend on the

[44] Ashton J. Mouton, "Collection by the Wholesaler of the Retail Sales Tax," *Proceedings of the Fifty-Eighth Annual Conference of the National Tax Association*, 286–90. As an example of the extent to which funds had been diverted from the state coffers under the previous system, Mouton stated that some taxpayers paid more tax the first month that the new act went into effect than they had reported in sales the previous month. This means that these particular taxpayers were reporting less than 2 percent of the tax they actually collected!

volume of sales, and these are below average in a relatively low-income state. Furthermore, Louisiana's tax of 2 percent is below that in the majority of states which employ a general sales or gross receipts tax. As of September 1, 1966, seven states had rates of 4 percent or higher and another twenty-five states set rates of (mainly) 3 or 3½ percent. No state having the tax maintained less than a 2 percent rate.[45]

In addition to the rate, however, an important factor is the breadth of coverage. States vary considerably in this respect, and it is often difficult to generalize about them. It does appear that Louisiana has a relatively broad based tax. Many of the items exempted in Louisiana are exempted by a majority of states; some items exempted by other states are covered in Louisiana.

Perhaps the most important type of inclusion or exclusion is food products sold for home consumption. One of the most frequent criticisms of a sales tax is its regressive nature, i.e., low-income groups pay a larger fraction of their income in sales taxes than do higher income groups.[46] Recent studies indicate, however, that when food exemption is introduced much of the regressivity is eliminated because food purchase is a major budget item that declines as a percentage of income as income rises.[47] Some twelve states employ a rather general exemption of food products; more limited exemptions apply in several others. Louisiana does not exempt food, so that its overall sales tax burden is undoubtedly regressive.

Although the state sales tax rate has remained unchanged since 1948, local governments in Louisiana have greatly expanded their use of this revenue source in the last decade. The first local sales tax in Louisiana was a one cent levy in New Orleans in 1936; Baton Rouge followed with a city sales tax in 1951, and Jefferson and East Baton Rouge parishes levied sales taxes in 1954 and 1956, respectively. Since 1957 a significant number of municipalities and parishes have introduced sales taxes; in early 1963 the number stood at twenty-six.[48] More recently, as noted earlier a number of local school boards have

[45] Tax Foundation, *Facts and Figures on Government Finance, 1967*, p. 188.

[46] For an evaluation of the advantages and disadvantages of Louisiana's state sales tax, see George W. Fair and B. F. Sliger, "The Louisiana Sales Tax," *Louisiana Business Review*, XXV (October, 1961), 20–24.

[47] For a succinct summary of the results of recent studies concerning equity, see Daniel C. Morgan, Jr., "Equity Considerations of Retail Sales Taxation," *Proceedings of the Fifty-Eighth Annual Conference of the National Tax Association*, 278–80.

[48] "Local Sales Taxes in Louisiana," *PAR Analysis*, January, 1963, pp. 1–2.

enacted sales tax levies to finance education. Although local governments now levy sales taxes in a number of states, Louisiana is still in the minority in this respect.

Selective Sales Taxes

Louisiana collects a wide variety of selective sales or excise taxes. As in most states, the major revenue producer is motor fuels, with tobacco and alcoholic beverages next in line. Motor fuels alone accounts for roughly one-half of selective sales tax collections. The traditional rationale for the motor fuels tax has been the benefit principle. That is, the taxpayer should pay for public services that yield particular and measurable benefits to him. Taxes on alcoholic beverages and tobacco are so-called sumptuary taxes. In part, "taxing the vices" may be undertaken to diminish consumption, but little of this is actually accomplished, given the relatively inelastic demand for these commodities and the states' desire for large revenues. In effect, consumers are paying a penalty in order to enjoy their vices.

Following Oregon's lead in 1919, every state in the union had passed a motor fuels tax by 1929. All states collect this tax today, with rates ranging from a low of 5 cents to a high of 8 cents per gallon. Louisiana imposes a rate of 7 cents per gallon, identical to that in twenty other states (as of September 1, 1966).[49] Interstate variations in per capita revenue collections are less pronounced than with any other major tax. In 1965 Louisiana collected $21.86 per capita from this source, slightly below the median state figure of $24.22.[50]

Louisiana's per capita collections from both tobacco ($8.81) and alcoholic beverages ($6.80) were slightly higher than those in the median state ($6.88 and $4.39, respectively). Every state except North Carolina levies a cigarette tax (as of September 1, 1966). Rates vary from 2½ cents per package in Virginia and Kentucky to 11 cents in New Jersey, Texas, and Washington. The rate in Louisiana is 8 cents per package. The state is also one of seventeen to tax cigars and/or smoking tobacco and the rates on these items are relatively

[49] Tax Foundation, *Facts and Figures on Government Finance, 1967*, p. 190.
[50] It should be noted, however, that many states make a considerably greater use of motor vehicle license fees than does Louisiana. The state's extremely low fees resulted in per capita collections of only $3.23. Only two states—Alabama and Hawaii—collected less on a per capita basis in 1965, and the U.S. median was $10.06.

high. Rates on distilled spirits, wines, and malt beverages also display considerable interstate variations. Louisiana's tax of $1.68 per gallon on distilled spirits is neither unusually high nor low, while rates on wines are relatively low. The beer tax in Louisiana is by far the most lucrative of the alcoholic beverage levies, and only six states, all southern, impose a higher rate. The state's $10 a barrel tax amounts to roughly 3 cents per twelve-ounce container, or $.726 per case.[51]

In one respect interstate comparisons of selective sales tax collections on alcoholic beverages are somewhat misleading. This is because states have chosen two different methods of controlling and gathering revenue from the sale of distilled spirits, and often wine. The majority of states, like Louisiana, have chosen the so-called license system and raise revenues primarily from gallonage excises and, to a lesser degree, license charges. On the other hand, seventeen states have chosen a monopoly system of state-owned stores (county-owned in North Carolina) and raise their revenues primarily from profits. Although some monopoly states also levy excise taxes in addition to store markups, most revenue is attributable to the markup. While liquor store revenues are excluded from the concept of general revenue on which this study focuses, the "socialization" of the retail liquor business has often proven to be quite profitable in the monopoly states.

Income Taxes

Louisiana is one of thirty-six states levying an individual income tax, although in New Hampshire and Tennessee the tax is limited to interest and dividends and in New Jersey to the income of nonresident commuters. For the nation as a whole, the individual income tax is third among the major sources of state tax revenue. Its rapid growth in recent decades is due partly to the widespread adoption of withholding, higher rates, and broader bases, but also partly due to its high income elasticity.

General sales and individual income taxes have sometimes been viewed in political debate as alternative revenue sources. Yet in almost half of the states, as in Louisiana, both taxes are levied simul-

[51] Tax Foundation, *Facts and Figures on Government Finance, 1967*, pp. 192–96.

taneously. Surprisingly, however, Louisiana collected less revenue per capita from these two taxes combined in 1965 than did all but ten states—and this includes those states which utilized only one of the taxes (or neither, as in Nebraska).

Obviously, Louisiana's collections from the individual income tax are relatively low. Excluding the three states which tax only particular types of income, Louisiana's per capita collections of $6.65 were second from the bottom of the list. Only Mississippi was lower. Among those states taxing individual incomes, the median state collected $21.46, with several receiving in excess of $60 per capita.

The major explanation for Louisiana's low yield is the extremely high personal exemptions and modest rate structure. Single persons receive a $2,500 exemption and married couples and heads of families receive $5,000. Over half of the income tax states fall in the range of $600–$1,000 in the first category and $1,200–$2,000 in the second. While Louisiana's additional exemptions of $400 per dependent are moderate, the revenue potential of the tax is largely crippled by the high initial exemptions. Rates start at 2 percent on the first $10,000 of net income—which is a very broad initial bracket—and then progress to 4 percent on the next $40,000 and 6 percent on net income above $50,000. As in eighteen other states, Louisiana permits deduction (only partial in three states) of federal income taxes.[52]

Thirty-eight states employ a tax on corporation net income. For the nation as a whole, this is a less productive tax than on individual income. Such is not the case in Louisiana. The state's per capita collections from corporation net income were $7.74 in 1965, only slightly below the median state figure of $8.32 for those states tapping this revenue source. Louisiana fixes a flat 4 percent rate on corporation net income, with federal income taxes deductible.

Property Tax

The property tax has long ceased to be a major source of state government revenue in the United States. Many state governments have abandoned it altogether or collect only negligible sums from it; in only three states do property tax collections amount to as much as 10 percent of tax revenues.

The property tax, however, continues to provide the great bulk of

[52] *Ibid.*, 182–83.

local tax revenues—some 87 percent in 1964–65. The extreme dependence of local governments on property taxation rests squarely on the fact that few good alternatives are available. Local taxation of business and income invites shrinkage of the tax base. There are narrow limits on the levels to which local sales taxes can be pushed. Real property, however, is immobile, and differential tax rates are less likely to induce migration out of a particular geographic area.

The plight of municipal and parish governments in Louisiana is inextricably bound to the relative unproductiveness of property taxation in the state. In 1964–65 local governments collected $156.9 million in property taxes and the state government collected another $17.6 million. Together, these property tax collections accounted for only 22 percent of combined state and local tax revenues in Louisiana. This figure was well below the U.S. average of 44 percent. Only four states—Alabama, Alaska, Delaware, and Hawaii—relied less heavily on property taxation at the combined state and local level.

In recent years the issue of unequal property tax assessments has been a source of considerable controversy in the state. As a result of a comprehensive three volume study by the Public Affairs Research Council published in 1960, many of the defects and inequities of state and local property taxation were brought forcefully to public attention. A Governor's Advisory Committee to the Louisiana Tax Commission was appointed in October, 1964, and subsequently produced a proposal for property tax equalization. Little reform has actually been accomplished, however, due in part to the opposition of locally elected assessors. Several interested parties, including the state president of the AFL-CIO, Victor Bussie, have suggested court action as a last resort.

It is clear that current assessment practices lead to serious inequities. A major part of the PAR study was an analysis of assessment levels in sixty-three parishes and the seven districts of Orleans. A sampling of sales prices in 1958 was undertaken as a basis of determining property values. Extensive variations in local assessment levels were found. The highest assessment ratio on locally assessed property was the 31.5 percent average in Caddo Parish; the lowest average ratio was 7.1 percent in Lafayette Parish. Ten parishes (or districts) had assessment ratios of 23.1 percent or higher, while ten parishes had ratios of 10.7 percent or lower. The average for the state was 18 percent.

In addition to the variations among parishes, there were wide variations *within* parishes. Different classes of property were assessed at widely different ratios, both within and among parishes. Tax millages varied extensively from parish to parish; in many, but not in all, cases, a high assessment ratio was "offset" by a low millage rate.

While local officials assessed 80 percent of the property in the state in 1958, the remainder was centrally assessed by the three member Louisiana Tax Commission. The PAR study concluded that the Tax Commission's procedure of assessing certain properties throughout the state on a fixed schedule without reference to the local assessment level on other properties had resulted in further inequities because of the wide variation in parish millage rates.[53] Furthermore, it appears that centrally determined assessment ratios on public utility and industrial properties were probably well above those on locally determined residential and agricultural properties.[54]

The differences in assessment levels and tax millages result in a number of other inequities, some obvious and others more subtle. The state government levies a 5.75 mill property tax and the collections from it vary greatly among parishes depending on their assessment practices. Furthermore, the equalization formula used for disbursing state education aid takes into consideration the amount of local support resulting from a 5 mill property tax; as a result of unequal assessments, parishes which provide little local support receive more extensive state aid than do otherwise similar parishes which have higher assessment ratios.

These types of problems clearly call for solutions at the state level. On the other hand, one must not be misled into thinking that Louisiana's property tax problems are unique or the solutions simple. In fact, the majority of states have experienced similar, if not identical, problems in the property tax area.

As James A. Maxwell wrote in his discussion of the property tax, "Is the property tax administered with efficiency? Is it equitable in its incidence? . . . both questions must be answered with qualified neg-

[53] PAR, *Louisiana Property Tax* (3 vols.; Baton Rouge, 1960).

[54] One estimated distribution of property tax burden by use of property (1962) found that Louisiana was below the U.S. average in the percentage of its total property tax revenues attributable to residences and farming, above average with respect to commercial and manufacturing, and well above average with respect to public utilities. McClure, "The Interstate Exporting of State and Local Taxes," 62.

atives. Complaints against the tax on these grounds have been voiced for eighty years . . . Proposals for reform have been advanced for nearly as long . . . The failure to apply remedies . . . must mean that remedies are difficult to implement."[55]

Although the laws of about two-thirds of the states, including Louisiana, require full value assessment, substantial underassessment of locally assessed real property is an almost universal practice as shown by the *1962 Census of Governments*.[56] For the nation as a whole, the assessment ratio of locally assessed taxable real property averaged 29.5 percent, with state ratios ranging from 5.6 percent in South Carolina to 65.5 percent in Rhode Island. Inequities in individual assessments seem related to the problem of general undervaluation if for no other reason than the fact that serious undervaluation obscures the extent of inequality in assessments and prevents the taxpayer from being fully aware that his assessments are out of line. As in Louisiana, other state governments have distributed grant-in-aid money to local governments using assessed values as an indicator, and problems involving centrally assessed versus locally assessed properties have also arisen.[57]

In at least one respect, however, Louisiana has clearly magnified the property tax problems that inevitably seem to confront all states. This is in the area of property tax exemptions, especially those pertaining to homesteads and to new and expanded industries.

In 1961 Louisiana was among a small minority of only six states that allowed exemptions from the local property tax to owner-occupied houses or farms. In Louisiana, homestead exemptions of $2,000 apply to most state and local property taxes with the exception of city taxes (except Orleans) and those of certain special districts.

[55] Maxwell, *Financing State and Local Governments*, 129.

[56] In 1961 roughly 83 percent of locally assessed property in the United States was real; of the remainder, almost all was tangible personal property. Very little revenue is obtained from the taxation of intangible personal property. U.S. Bureau of the Census, *1962 Census of Governments*, II. In effect, intangibles are not taxed in Louisiana, which is in keeping with legal and/or administrative procedures in a large majority of states. Although household personal property was legally taxable in thirty-three states in 1961, and motor vehicles in twenty-two states, both are exempted in Louisiana. As in all but a few states, commercial and industrial tangible personal property is taxed in Louisiana.

[57] See, for example, Advisory Commission on Intergovernmental Relations, *The Role of the States in Strengthening the Property Tax* (2 vols.; Washington, D.C., 1963), and the discussion in Maxwell, *Financing State and Local Governments*, 125–56.

Veterans may receive a $5,000 exemption (about two-thirds of the states grant some kind of property tax exemption to veterans). Being stated in dollar terms, the actual value of these exemptions to the homeowner clearly depends on the extent of underassessment. The greater the underassessment, the greater the value of the exemptions. In a parish with a low average assessment ratio, say under 10 percent, it is clear that a considerable portion of the value of all homesteads would be covered by the exemption, and this would certainly be true in the case of veterans.

In most states with property tax exemptions, the primary impact is an erosion of the local tax base and the introduction of inequities between those covered and those not covered. While inequities exist in Louisiana, the other major problem is somewhat different since the state government reimburses local units (and itself) for the loss of property taxes attributable to homestead exemptions. (This is also done in Mississippi.) The reimbursements are channeled through a property tax relief fund which is financed by revenues from the state income tax on individuals and corporations, the public utilities tax, and the alcoholic beverage tax on liquors and wines. As a result, the local tax base is not narrowed, but the state government is a net "loser" from its involvement in property taxation. That is, property tax collections at the state level are considerably less than the amount of state disbursements through the property tax relief fund. In 1965–66, for example, the state government collected $23 million from the state ad valorem tax and expended $49.8 million on homestead exemption reimbursements.[58] Some observers have suggested that the state government should leave the property tax field entirely, as has been done in many other states, or at least reduce the value of homestead exemptions.

As a result of both unequal assessments and the operation of the property tax relief fund, there is a substantial variation among parishes in the percentage of local property tax revenues accounted for by reimbursements from the state level. According to PAR's study, state reimbursements in 1958 accounted for more than 40 percent of all property tax revenues in two parishes, while in another two parishes the figure was less than 10 percent. As a percentage of taxes due on locally assessed real estate, the overall state figure was 37.8

[58] Division of Administration, *State of Louisiana, Financial Statements, Year Ending June 30, 1966*, pp. 2, 4.

percent; yet in two parishes, the figure exceeded 70 percent and in twelve others, it exceeded 50 percent.[59]

Clearly, a considerable redistribution of the property tax burden takes place in Louisiana. In parishes where homestead exemptions cover a substantial part of the assessments on residential property, a vote by homeowners for higher property taxes may actually cost them very little. Much of the increased tax burden within the parish may fall on commercial and industrial property, while another large portion of the cost will be redistributed throughout the state according to the share of income, alcoholic beverage, and public utilities taxes paid in different areas.

In addition to its homestead exemptions, Louisiana is one of a small number of states to offer an inducement to new or expanded industries in the form of a property tax exemption for a specified period. In Louisiana, the exemption is for a period of ten years. The aim of the program, of course, is to induce industry to locate in the state; whether or not it has been even moderately successful is far from clear. The exempt property does, however, reduce the property tax base and thus shifts the burden to other taxpayers. It is also interesting to note that once the exemption has expired, the industry is likely to be assigned an assessment ratio somewhat in excess of the state average for locally assessed real estate.

DEDICATED TAX REVENUES

One cannot discuss Louisiana's tax structure without some consideration of dedicated or earmarked revenues since the state shares with Alabama the dubious distinction of earmarking the largest percentage of state tax collections in the country. As shown by a Tax Foundation study, Louisiana earmarked 87 percent of state tax revenues in 1963 as compared with the U.S. average of 41 percent.[60] Despite strong criticisms within the state, the extent of dedications has not been reduced in recent years; in fact, the percentage of dedicated tax revenues has risen slightly from the 85 percent figure in 1954, while for the nation as a whole the average has declined by 10 percentage points over the same period.

[59] PAR, *Louisiana Property Tax*, III, 20–23.
[60] Tax Foundation, *Earmarked State Taxes* (New York, 1965). All figures on earmarking in this section are taken from the Tax Foundation study.

The system of dedications in Louisiana is extraordinarily complex. Some taxes, e.g., the sales tax, are dedicated to special funds by statute, and thus theoretically could be undedicated by simple legislative action. Others, e.g., the severance tax, are dedicated by the state's unusually lengthy and antiquated Constitution; repealing the dedication of these taxes would require a constitutional amendment and thus voter approval. Many taxes are subject to multiple and detailed dedications. Only a few taxes of any real significance have escaped dedication entirely, although surpluses from the special funds are often transferred to the general fund.

While the terms of specific dedications are much too complex to describe in detail here, a few generalizations can be noted. The Tax Foundation's method of classification is generally used.[61] In 1963, 94 percent of severance tax collections went to education, with the bulk of the remainder being returned to the parishes. Sixty-three percent of general sales tax collections went to public welfare, with 36 percent going to education. The bulk of the various highway-user taxes were earmarked for highways, with minor amounts of specific levies going to ports and the police pension fund. The complete dedication of severance, general sales, and highway-user taxes virtually dictated an impoverished general fund.

Revenues from the individual and corporate income tax and the alcoholic beverage tax went into the property tax relief fund while beer tax receipts flowed into a veterans' bonus fund; in all cases, surpluses from these special funds were subsequently redistributed in part to the general fund. The tobacco excise was the most significant tax which directly produced revenue for the general fund. After the application of an earmarking formula which resulted in 36 percent of the tobacco tax receipts going to municipalities and parishes and 3 percent to higher education (LSU), the remaining 61 percent went into the general fund. A sizeable portion of the excise license insurance tax (86 percent) and the corporation franchise tax (85 percent) also went to the general fund, as did 100 percent of the receipts from such lesser revenue producers as death and gift, occupational licenses, soft drinks, and power use taxes.

Not only does Louisiana dedicate an inordinately high proportion

---

[61] In cases where revenues are dedicated initially to the bond security redemption fund, only the subsequent transfers are noted since this is essentially a "feeder" fund. For figures on Louisiana, see *ibid.*, 48.

of its total tax collections, but in certain cases the specific dedications are somewhat unusual. Louisiana is the only state to dedicate individual and corporate income taxes to homestead exemptions; it is one of two states to dedicate a portion of property tax receipts to a Confederate veterans fund; it is one of only two states to earmark revenues from either distilled spirits or beer for veterans' bonuses. Other examples could be cited. Perhaps the most significant case, however, is the state's partial dedication of the general sales tax to public welfare. Of the twenty-one states wholly or partially earmarking their general sales or gross receipts tax in 1963, only five dedicated any portion to public welfare (defined here to include state hospitals and institutions). In two of these five states, the percentage dedicated was 3 percent or less. Only in Louisiana (63 percent), Colorado (60 percent), and Oklahoma (95 percent) was a significant percentage of sales tax receipts earmarked for this purpose.

One might suppose that any such relationship between sales tax collections and public welfare expenditures would be particularly inefficient. Other things being equal, when business conditions are especially good and sales tax collections expand rapidly, the need for welfare spending should be less than usual. On the other hand, when declining business activity hurts sales tax collections, this may be precisely the time that welfare needs are the greatest.

Only fifteen states earmarked any taxes for welfare purposes in 1963. Earmarking was much more common in education—thirty-one states—and the generally accepted practice in highways, with forty-six states dedicating large percentages (or all) of their highway-user taxes for this purpose. Earmarking for education came from many diverse tax sources. In addition to its severance and sales taxes, Louisiana dedicated portions of its property tax, corporation franchise tax, excise license insurance tax, and tobacco tax to education (including higher education).

To what extent are dedicated revenues justified? While surprisingly little has been written about a practice which is so widespread, the consensus of writers who have discussed earmarking seems to be that, on balance, it is undesirable.[62] It is often argued that earmark-

---

[62] James Buchanan, however, has attempted to demonstrate that under certain conditions earmarking can lead to a more efficient disposition of tax collections and a smaller total outlay. James M. Buchanan, "The Economics of Earmarked Taxes," *Journal of Political Economy*, LXXI (October, 1963), 457–69. See also the discussion by Deran, "Earmarking and Expenditures," 354–61.

ing hampers effective budgetary control; leads to a misallocation of funds, giving excess revenues to some functions while others are undersupported; makes for an inflexibility of the revenue structure; tends to remain in force after any specific need has passed; and infringes on the policy-making powers of the executive and legislative branches by removing governmental activities from periodic review and control.

While certain justifications for earmarking can also be cited, the practice has been strongly attacked by many observers in Louisiana, including PAR and Ross-Sliger.[63] The latter writers have urged undedication of tax revenues, except perhaps in the case of highway-user taxes earmarked exclusively for highways where the "benefit" relation is said to be strong. They contend that state politics was one of the major reasons for the development of excessive dedications in Louisiana with one administration wishing to tie the hands of the next. It is also probable that distrust of the legislature has led special interest groups to press for earmarking in order to assure the continuance of their programs once instituted—or to raise the funds to support the programs in the first place.

SUMMARY AND CONCLUSIONS

The picture that has emerged from this analysis of Louisiana's fiscal affairs may be summed up as follows. As in all states, general revenues and expenditures have risen at a dramatic pace over the last two decades. In 1964–65 combined state and local expenditures were nearly $1.4 billion. Almost one-fourth of all revenues originated from federal grants, and this figure seems destined to grow even larger in the future.[64] At the other end of the spectrum, slightly over one-fifth of combined state and local revenues were raised at the

---

[63] For a brief summary of arguments for and against earmarking, see Tax Foundation, *Earmarked State Taxes*, 24–28. See also PAR, *Legislative Control over State Expenditures* (Baton Rouge, 1960), and William D. Ross and B. F. Sliger, "Dedication of State Revenues in Louisiana," *Louisiana Business Review*, XIII (April, 1958), 20–23.

[64] In 1957 the ratio of state and local own funds to federal payments in Louisiana was 5.8; in 1962, the ratio had fallen to 4.1. Mushkin and Adams (State and Local Finances Project of The George Washington University) project a figure of 2.8 in 1970. This ratio in Louisiana has consistently remained below the U.S. average. In 1962 the U.S. average was 6.4, and the projected ratio for 1970 is 4. Selma J. Mushkin and Robert F. Adams, "Emerging Patterns of Federalism," *National Tax Journal*, XIX (September, 1966), 236–40.

local level, a figure attributable largely to the relative unproductiveness of property taxation. Taken together, these and other figures indicate that Louisiana received above-average amounts of federal grants and displayed a high degree of fiscal centralization within the state. Only two states raised a larger percentage of their own state-local revenues (excluding federal grants) at the state level. As a result, state government in Louisiana finances many services that in other states are left to local government to a far greater extent.

The three major functions (in order) of state and local government in the U.S. are education, highways, and public welfare. This is also the case in Louisiana. However, the relative weights attached to the education and welfare functions are striking. In comparison with other states, support of the first is below average, while support of the second is relatively generous. Most public welfare expenditures in Louisiana are financed by federal grants rather than from the state's own resources. Education spending, on the other hand, is characterized by an extensive distribution of state funds to local school districts via a state-administered equalization formula.

Louisiana has traditionally been known as a "high tax, high spending" state. In part, this reputation is due to an earlier tendency to compare governmental finances at the state level only. Fairer comparisons are obtained of combined state and local expenditures and revenues. On a per capita basis, Louisiana is seen as providing for its residents an overall level of public services which is about average by U.S. standards. But even this level appears to require a considerable revenue effort because of the state's relatively low per capita personal income.

Perhaps a partial explanation for Louisiana's surprisingly high overall level of expenditures lies in the manner in which these expenditures are financed. In addition to receiving above-average amounts of federal grants—a fact which is attributable largely to the public welfare function—Louisiana appears to enjoy significant revenue sources that represent little burden to the average voter-taxpayer. In particular, the state collects significant nontax revenues from royalties and bonuses on public lands, and the severance tax is the major single tax source at the state level. On the other hand, taxes on income and property are very low by comparison with most other states, while those on general and selective sales and licenses are moderate.

A frequent criticism of the state's fiscal structure focuses on the extensive dedications of state tax revenues. Most major taxes are dedicated wholly or partially to specific purposes, thus severely limiting general fund revenues and introducing a certain inflexibility into the state budget.[65]

One of the most pressing problems facing all state and local governments is their ability to finance education,highways, and other public services in the next decade. Many prognosticators have forecast an alarming divergence between growth in public demand for these services and the ability of most state and local governments to provide them.

According to James A. Maxwell (1965): "Projected expansion of state and local tax revenues, based on present rates and bases, do not match the growth in spending because the yields of the major taxes— sales and property—are not very elastic. As a result, the rates and bases of state-local taxes will have to be increased."[66]

Reasons for the pessimistic forecasts can be found on both sides of the budget. Some population projections indicate above-average growth rates in school-age population and that portion over sixty-five years of age. Both the old and the young are heavy consumers of state and local government services. So are urban dwellers, and as the population continues to move to the cities and suburbs, additional spending will be necessary for water and sewer systems, police and fire protection, parks, roads, schools, urban renewal, metropolitan transportation, etc. On the revenue side it is clear that tax receipts will rise as GNP expands, but the important question is whether the yields from existing taxes at existing rates and bases are sufficiently responsive to economic growth to meet the rising demand

[65] Little has been said in this essay about debt management at the state level. Within the last decade many observers have called for reforms in this area. It has been suggested that the governmental structures designed to manage debt functions are inadequate, partly because the authority to borrow rests with several state agencies rather than being concentrated in a single agency. The creation of special agencies to issue bonds is costly because such debt is not backed by the full faith and credit of the state. For discussions of debt management at the state level, see, for example, "Louisiana State Debt," *PAR Analysis,* April, 1960, and "A Sound Debt Program for Louisiana," *PAR Analysis,* September, 1963; and William D. Ross and Joseph M. Bonin, "A Proposed New System of Non-Highway Bond Financing For Louisiana," *National Tax Journal,* XIII (December, 1960), 364–68.

[66] Maxwell, *Financing State and Local Governments,* 23. See also the discussion in Chap. 10 of this work. For a very brief description of some of the projections that have been made, see Maxwell *Tax Credits and Intergovernmental Fiscal Relations,* 8–10.

for public goods. A pessimistic answer has been based on the lower income elasticity of taxes at the state-local level as compared with the federal level, and this in turn has led many to push for expanded federal assistance to state and local government.

Projections, of course, are not only hazardous but controversial. A recent study by the Tax Foundation, for example, has come to conclusions in sharp contrast to the more widely expressed views. This study finds no need for increased tax rates in the decade ahead.[67] Another study, focusing on 1970, presents a fairly optimistic portrayal of state-local finances, but this projection depends crucially on greatly expanded amounts of federal aid.[68]

How will Louisiana fare vis-à-vis other states? The situation is far from clear. Uncertainties attached to forecasting bonus and royalty income, severance tax collections, and the terms of the eventual tidelands settlement make any projections unusually risky. Two factors are virtually certain, however. First, federal grants will become increasingly important. Second, one of the most pressing problems facing the state will be in the area of higher education. Projected enrollment increases in state colleges and universities are staggering and academic salaries have been rising, and may continue to rise, at around 5 or 6 percent per year. Yet tuitions and fees are relatively low, extensive dedications to other public services have resulted in some budget inflexibility, and on balance, the state's tax structure seems relatively income inelastic.

In recent years economists have attempted to estimate the income elasticity of various types of state taxes. Frequently cited figures for the United States are 1.7 for personal income and death and gift taxes, 1.1 for state corporate income taxes, 1.0 for general sales taxes, and a much lower 0.5 for a composite of selective sales taxes. By the rough but useful procedure of weighting the elasticities assumed for selective sales (0.5), personal income and death and gift (1.7), and "all other" taxes (1.0) by figures indicating their relative importance in each state, Carovano arrived at a figure of .89 for the income elasticity of Louisiana's state tax system in 1964. Eleven states recorded figures in excess of 1, largely because of their above-average reliance on personal income taxation. At the other extreme, eleven

[67] The findings are summarized in Tax Foundation, *Fiscal Outlook for State and Local Government to 1975–*, Government Finance Brief No. 7 (New York, 1966).

[68] Mushkin and Adams, "Emerging Patterns of Federalism," 237–38.

state governments employed tax systems with an overall elasticity of less than .85, and this was generally a result of relatively heavy reliance on selective sales taxes.[69]

It seems likely that Louisiana will be forced to raise its rates on some existing taxes in the next few years. With the exception of the gas severance tax, there has not been a really significant tax increase at the state level in the last decade. Most other state governments, however, have enacted several rate hikes and/or found new sources of revenue. This fact is partly reflected by the following figures. From 1956–57 to 1964–65, its own revenue as a percent of personal income in Louisiana rose from 14.6 to 14.9—a rise of only 0.3 percentage points. This was the *smallest* percentage point increase of any state in the nation! As a result, Louisiana's own revenue as a percent of personal income fell from 145 to 121 percent of the U.S. average.[70] While Louisiana is still well above average in this respect, one must keep in mind its relatively low level of personal income.

If the state government chooses to enact any tax change(s), the best choice may be the personal income tax, and the best means a lowering of personal exemptions and a narrowing of the tax brackets. While in existence for many years, the state has not fully utilized this highly income-elastic tax. Low motor vehicle license fees and modest tuition charges in state colleges and universities could also be raised. Finally, there is little chance of substantially strengthening local government in Louisiana without making the property tax a more productive revenue producer.

[69] Given projected enrollment increases from 1959–60 to 1969–70, Carovano estimated the rate at which state government income would have to increase to accomodate the rising enrollments in the latter year. His findings were generally pessimistic and implied the necessity for additional taxes and/or higher rates on those existing in fiscal 1964. Given the anticipated enrollment expansion, the situation in Louisiana was viewed as difficult because of the inelastic tax revenue system and the existence of an above average tax effort. J. Martin Carovano, "Financing Public Higher Education, 1969–70," *National Tax Journal,* XIX (June, 1966), 125–37.

[70] Selma J. Mushkin, "The Outlook for Federal Support in a State and Local Programming System," *Proceedings of the Fifty-Ninth Annual Conference of the National Tax Association, 1966,* p. 116. Personal income totals used are averages of the two calendar years within which the fiscal year falls.

CONTRIBUTORS

Thomas R. Beard is a native Baton Rougean who received his B.S. and M.A. at Louisiana State University. He took his Ph.D at Duke University and returned to the LSU faculty in 1961, becoming head of the Department of Economics in 1966. He served as economist for the Board of Governors of the Federal Reserve System in 1964–65 and is on leave from LSU to serve as the Fourth National Bank Distinguished Professor of Banking at Wichita State University, Wichita, Kansas, 1968–69.

Roger L. Burford, professor of business statistics at LSU since 1963, received his B.B.A. and M.A. at the University of Mississippi and took his Ph.D. at Indiana University. He has been on the faculties of Georgia State College and Indiana University. The author of three books, he has recently returned from serving as Visiting Fulbright Professor of Economics at National Taiwan University.

Robert A. Flammang was born in Orleans, Nebraska, and received his B.A. from the University of Nebraska. He took his M.A. and Ph.D at the University of Iowa and has been a member of the LSU economics faculty since 1962. Dr. Flammang has written numerous essays for publication in his field of foreign trade.

Stephen L. McDonald is a graduate of Louisiana Polytechnic Institute and took his M.A. and Ph.D at the University of Texas. A former member of the faculty of the College of Business Administration at LSU, he is presently professor of economics at the University of Texas. He is the author of several books and numerous articles in the fields of monetary economics, taxation, and regional development.

Lee J. Melton, Jr., has been a professor of economics at LSU for the past twenty years specializing in economic development and public control. He is a native of Winnfield and Monroe and graduated from Louisiana Polytechnic Institute. He took both his M.A. and Ph.D. at LSU.

231

James P. Payne, Jr., has taught at LSU since 1951 and is now the Alumni Professor of Economics. He took his B.A. at William Jewell College in Missouri, his M.A. at Oklahoma State University, and his Ph.D. at the University of Illinois. He specializes in the fields of transportation and public utilities with particular regard to regulatory enterprises.

Edward B. Selby, Jr., now a professor of finance at the University of Georgia, received his B.S. from Clemson University, his M.B.A. at the University of South Carolina, and his Ph.D. at LSU. He has been an instructor at LSU and professor at Northeast Louisiana State College and has written numerous articles for various professional publications.

Fred H. Wiegmann, a native of St. Mary Parish, received his B.S. at Southwestern Louisiana Institute, his M.S. at LSU, and his Ph.D. at Iowa State University. He joined the faculty of the Department of Agricultural Economics at LSU in 1953 and became head of the department in 1960. Specializing in farm management and agricultural policy, he has written numerous research publications in these areas.